CREATING AND ASSURING QUALITY

CREATING AND ASSURING QUALITY

RICHARD BARRETT CLEMENTS

ASQC Quality Press
Milwaukee

Creating and Assuring Quality

Richard Barrett Clements

Library of Congress Cataloging-in-Publication Data

Clements, Richard Barrett.
   Creating and assuring quality / by Richard Barrett Clements.
    p. cm.
   Includes bibliographical references and index.
   1. Quality assurance — Case studies. I. Title.
TS156.6.C54 1990
658.5'62 — dc20   90-859
                                                                       CIP

10 9 8 7 6 5 4 3 2 1

ISBN 0-87389-087-6

Acquisitions Editor: Jeanine L. Lau
Production Editor: Tammy Griffin
Set in Janson/Dutch Oldstyle by DanTon Typographers. Cover design by
Wayne Dober. Printed and bound by Edwards Brothers.

ASQC Quality Press
310 West Wisconsin Avenue
Milwaukee, Wisconsin 53203

Printed in the United States of America

Finally.
To my parents.

Contents

Preface

Since the late 1970s, quality assurance has become a minor revolution in manufacturing. Today, workers, supervisors, and managers must be familiar with the methods of quality assurance to stay competitive in world markets.

An excellent example of this trend is the wide-scale use of statistical process control. Many major customers, from the U.S. government to automotive makers, require supply companies to use statistical process control.

The revolution in quality assurance has come from two sources. The first is the growing complexity of products. This forces producers to use greater levels of quality and reliability testing. Second, the economics of the marketplace make high-quality products competitive.

These issues and their origins are reviewed in this book. By examining the issues, conflicts, and technologies related to quality assurance, readers gain a greater understanding of how quality affects their lives, their jobs, and their future.

Who Should Read This Book?

This book was written for anyone interested in learning about the fundamental functions of a quality assurance department. Although the story that follows is based on a manufacturing company, many of the issues presented also apply to service-based companies.

Regardless of educational or occupational background, this book is highly readable. Instead of presenting complex theories and sterile mathematical formulas, a series of stories and analogies are used.

This book is intended for business employees, students, or other interested readers who want to add quality assurance knowledge to their collection of personal skills. Unlike other introductory books about quality assurance, readers are not expected to become quality technicians.

Those readers who are already familiar with the basic concepts of quality assurance will want to read this book for a different reason. The stories presented are drawn from actual events and real problems. Thus, this book also serves as a guide to the "real-world" implementation of a new quality system.

Introduction

The following story is fictitious. However, the characters' personalities, the companies involved, and the conflicts encountered are based on real occurrences.

The story's main theme is the conflict of a company encountering the modern revolution in quality assurance. Just ten years ago a company would have been content to relegate quality problems to the quality control department. Today, every employee within a company must take some responsibility for the quality of the products, services, and the work environment.

David Garvin (1987) of the Harvard Business School best described the changes occurring in the quality assurance field.[1] In the past, the definition of quality centered around terms such as *fit for use* and *zero defects*. In other words, the ultimate goal of the quality department was to find and prevent problems.

Today, the definitions of quality look at the competitive potentials of high quality in a world marketplace. Terms such as *satisfying the customers* and *minimizing the loss to society* are common. The highest goal for a modern quality department is to be an active participant in the strategic positioning of a company and its products.

The automobile industry serves as an excellent example of these changes. In the past, a quality department was responsible for the inspection of incoming materials, the production processes, and the quality of the car before shipment. Their main purpose was to find and correct defects.

Today, those same quality people are interviewing customers about their preferences in features, actively seeking the customer's feelings on quality, and inspecting the car's qualities years after it has been sold. In addition, the quality department is an active participant in the design process and the strategic plans of the company.

In short, quality assurance is changing from a form of inspection to a tool of competition. At the same time, the marketplace has also changed. Customers now demand and seek high quality at a fair price.

---

[1]Garvin, David A. "Competing on the Eight Dimensions of Quality." *Harvard Business Review* (November-December 1987): 101-109.

The Function of Quality Assurance

The modern quality assurance department is a technical support group for all the other departments in a company. They participate in the planning and administration of the company. An excellent example of this is the operating philosophies and policies of major companies. These now focus on the assurance of world-class quality in products, people, and services.

A quality assurance department also participates in the control and change of designs. This can be seen in a new technique called Quality Function Deployment. Product development is conducted by a team from engineering, quality, production, marketing, and other concerned departments. This team carefully discusses what customers expect and demand in a product. From this list of customer needs, the team designs a competitive product.

Another function of the quality department involves customer contact. Through user surveys, field service, warranty reports, and other methods, the quality department can evaluate how well the company's product is performing under actual usage.

Some of the traditional roles of a quality department are still in place. For example, the quality department is still expected to help purchasing departments audit vendors and inspect their goods. During production, quality people provide product dimension and attribute inspection. The modern trend, however, is to encourage the machine operators to monitor the critical characteristics of the parts as they are being made.

Finally, the quality department is becoming more of an active agent in providing training and motivation to employees on the importance of quality. Statistical process control is an example of this function. The employees of the company are taught to apply corrective action to problems they detect. Each is taught that understanding the important qualities of a product and controlling them directly are critical job skills. Finding and correcting defects is no longer just a job for the quality department.

What Is Quality?

Before examining the changing dynamics in the nature of quality departments, it is important to pause and consider just what the word *quality* means. Again, David Garvin has provided an excellent definition by pointing out that a single product can have many types of qualities. Each of these he calls the "dimensions of quality."[1]

These eight dimensions of quality are:

1. **Performance** — That is, how well the product works. A car with fast acceleration or good gas mileage is said to be a strong performer.

2. **Features** — Those nice little extras beyond the product's primary function. Cruise control and power windows can be considered features on a car.

3. **Reliability** — How long the product will last. Cars that are noted for their long, trouble-free lives are actively sought by consumers.

4. **Conformance** — Accomplished through meeting customers' standards. Minivans meet the need to comfortably carry groups of up to nine people.

5. **Durability** — The useful life of a product.

6. **Serviceability** — The ease of repair. Some car engines make an oil change a pleasant experience while others make it nearly impossible.

7. **Aesthetics** — The look, feel, taste, sound, and other sensual properties of a product. Leather seats provide a perceived addition to quality for some car buyers.

8. **Perceived Quality** — In other words, the reputation of a product. A Rolls-Royce is widely believed to be a high-quality product.

---

[1]Garvin, David A. "Competing on the Eight Dimensions of Quality." *Harvard Business Review* (November-December 1987): 101-109.

The critical aspect of these eight dimensions is that each product's market will place different levels of importance on each type of quality. For example, car buyers may be willing to sacrifice aesthetics for higher reliability. The buyer of a wristwatch may think perceived quality is most important and ignore price and serviceability.

Thus, those concerned with quality are presented with a world where customers are more sophisticated and knowledgeable, and where manufacturers are using new quality techniques to cut operating costs and still satisfy customer demands. Large manufacturing and service companies are passing the requirements for new quality techniques to their suppliers.

The result is that a smaller company, which has enjoyed years of a small but steady group of customers, suddenly finds itself swamped with new quality requirements. Such a company, one that has faced no real competitive challenges for decades, must play a dangerous game of catch-up with the world marketplace. This is where the story begins.

Prologue

It was five degrees below zero and a southwest wind was blowing at eight miles per hour. The wind pushed newly fallen snow through the cracks of the garage door of a modest home ten miles southeast of Grand Rapids. A lone figure in a heavy winter coat stood facing the wind. The tall thin man crushed out a cigarette as the GMC pickup pulled into his front yard.

Gary VerVoit jumped out of the truck and grunted a hello and a few coarse comments about the weather. The sun would not be up for another two hours and the two men had 120 miles of driving ahead of them.

In a few minutes they had thrown a load of books and papers onto the truck's jump seats. An overhead projector was braced between the two bucket seats. Gary glanced over at his companion. The man's face was gently illuminated by the glow from a laptop computer.

Gary decided that his question could wait. He put the truck into low gear and rammed his way through the drift at the end of the driveway. An hour and a half later the passenger finally folded up the computer and set it on the floor.

"Can I ask you a question?" Gary began.

"Sure," came the reply.

"I've been driving you around for three months now. Why do all of these companies need you to talk to them so bad?"

"Does that surprise you?"

"Well, you're just telling them about quality, right?"

The passenger turned to look at the road ahead. He looked tired. "Yep. I only talk about quality. I tell them that it's profitable and competitive to have an effective quality program. I tell them how to do it, and they pay me a hundred dollars an hour."

"What?" barked Gary. "A hundred bucks just to tell them that quality is important? Don't they know that already?"

The man smiled. "Sure they do. It's like life. We both know that it's important to have close relationships with people, but here we are alone on a highway."

The man lit another cigarette and continued.

"Companies know that quality is real important. It's just that most of them have other demands they must confront. They usually leave quality to the quality control manager and they never think about it much again."

"That's stupid," Gary blurted out. "How can they sell anything if they don't have good quality?"

"An excellent observation, my friend. I only wish the owner of the company we are visiting today could hear you now."

Gary cursed out his confusion. The passenger merely sighed and watched the first rays of a cold winter sun light the eastern sky. How much longer can I keep doing this? he silently asked himself.

CHAPTER 1

Using Quality to
Stay in Business

Robert L. Mead, president of ROB, Incorporated, had just dismissed his Friday afternoon meeting of the company management. Like every Friday the group discussed the problems of the week. The list was long.

The two people from the catering service were picking up the last of the food scraps from their working lunch and the later coffee break. Outside rain was beginning to streak Mead's window. Within a few moments he was alone in the office and deep in thought.

From the center drawer of his rosewood desk he drew out three letters and placed them rank and file upon the desk blotter. After a moment's consideration he drew the middle letter out first. It was a message from his former wife. Although he had read it several times, he studied the message again.

She wanted more alimony, and she wanted him to stay away from the children. The children, he thought. They are all grown now. What difference does it make if I see the children or not?

There was an underlying message in this letter. All of his experiences of dealing with her for the past thirty years had taught him this. But what was she really saying this time? He would have to ponder that question during his free time. The main problem now was the business.

Quickly he picked up another letter and scanned it again. This one was from his largest customer. It had been written by the vice president of purchasing. That fact alone raised a red flag in Mead's mind even though the letter was very similar to the others that had come before it. The

1

customer was demanding an improvement in the quality of the parts ROB, Incorporated produced.

"We strongly recommend that your company adopt a policy of continuous improvement that is supported by statistical methods to assure the quality of production. We would like you to submit a strategic plan that reflects these methods. Otherwise, alternative methods can be discussed."

Alternative methods, Mead thought. Was this a threat? It seemed clear enough that this was not a compliment. In addition, the fact that the head of their purchasing department had sent it meant that the customer was documenting ROB's poor quality record. That could only mean one thing: The business was in danger of losing its largest customer.

The summary of the most recent financial statements the day before flashed through Mead's head. He was well aware that the loss of a major customer could spell the end of the company's solvency. That would mean that he would not be able to buy a new Cadillac every year or spend the three months of winter in his Florida condominium.

Reaching into the top right-hand drawer of the desk, Mead drew out a small tape recorder he often used to dictate messages. Although his secretary, Sally McCord, could take dictation, Mead preferred to work out correspondence alone until he had it perfect.

Placing the recorder and the first two letters into his briefcase to take home, he opened the last letter. This one was written on a coarse paper and was more to the point. Signed by several people, it was a letter of complaint from the union that represented the majority of his workers. He had heard the complaint from the union many times before, but now they were making it an official grievance.

They felt the piece rate established by the company was too strict and unfair. Workers complained that they had to rush jobs to meet the schedule. They were worried about production quality. It was obvious that their morale was not high.

Mead was angry about this letter. The other two were merely obstacles to overcome. But this one struck a nerve. Two years before he had hired Leon Marsden as personnel director, specifically to keep the union in check. Obviously, Marsden had not been doing his job. Mead made a mental note to make Marsden aware of his failings. He decided that after the Monday morning staff meeting would be the appropriate time. Let him sweat all weekend, Mead thought.

Then Mead rocked back in his leather chair and began to sort out these three major problems. The customer had the highest priority since it directly threatened the business. The union problem would also have to be resolved fairly quickly. His former wife could wait.

Next, Mead went through his usual mental checklist of how to handle each of these problems. Should they be delegated to others? No. Could he wait until Monday? Yes. Was there a common thread among the problems? Pause. A common thread? Something buzzed in his head. He drew out all three letters and laid them side by side.

After a few moments, he saw it. Quality. The word appeared in all three letters. His customer wanted higher quality parts. His workers wanted quality in the work place. His wife wanted quality of life for the children. This coincidence was interesting. Mead decided that this common element in the three problems required further investigation.

Without thinking, he banded the three letters together and threw them into his briefcase. Next he drew out his Rolodex®, switched on a small device attached to the phone to detect other people listening, and began dialing.

The first number was that of a young college student who lived next door to Mead's country home. The student's mother answered, exchanged pleasantries, and called for her son. Slightly out of breath, Keith Walker answered.

"Mr. Mead, what can I do for you?"

"Want to earn a fast hundred bucks this weekend?"

"Sounds good. What do you need?" responded Keith, well aware that a hundred dollars would help him finish the payments on his computer.

"I need every recent story published on the topic of quality."

"How do you mean? Quality of products, performance, life, what?"

"I need mostly stories related to industry and business. Can you have something for me by tomorrow afternoon?"

"Sure can," replied Keith, even though he wasn't sure where he would start.

Mead made arrangements for Keith to drop off the material at his home the next day and hung up. Next, Mead called a friend of his, Ronald Headly of Urn Corporation. Headly was president of this small manufacturer of funeral-related goods.

"Ron? It's Bob. How are you?"

"I'm fine Bob. What's on your mind?"

"I need to learn more about quality assurance and meeting my customers' quality requirements. I was wondering if I could tour your plant next week with your quality manager?"

"No problem."

The second phone call was quickly over. Neither man was fond of small talk.

Mead rang his secretary and told her to take the rest of the day off, she was probably going to get extra work on Monday. He then rang the quality manager of his factory, Brenda Patterson, and asked her to bring up a copy of the company's quality manual.

Mead made a few notes on his legal pad and sat back to consider if there was anything he was forgetting. Suddenly, a random thought crossed his mind. That man he had met months ago, the one who had poked him in the chest and said that ROB would soon have serious quality problems.

Mead drew out his wallet from his back pants pocket and dug around behind the row of tens and twenties. There it was, the business card this odd man had slipped into his hands. Mead looked at the wrinkled card for a long time. Finally, he picked up the phone and dialed the number.

After a single ring a scratchy voice answered at the other end. Mead introduced himself and explained his situation. It was the only full sentence Mead completed with the person at the other end. He quickly pulled out his note pad and began to take notes. Ten minutes later the call was over.

Saturday morning, Mead awoke alone at his large country home. He wandered downstairs to make the first of many cups of coffee. Then he settled into the den and drew out several of his favorite books on business. In each one he thumbed through the index looking for the word *quality*.

After three or four books the picture was not getting any clearer. Each author expressed what seemed to be a totally different opinion of how to create and assure quality. Some used quality as a marketing tool, while others talked about customer satisfaction or fitness for use. One Japanese author talked about quality as being a measure of the loss society suffers from poor quality.

Mead was no closer to his answer about quality, let alone a decision on how to handle his three major problems. It was then that he drew out the list of notes he had taken during that last phone call on Friday. The first item was a note to read the classic business books and note the different opinions of the definition of quality.

"Each is looking at a small portion of a larger body. Only you can see the whole." This is what Mead had written.

Mead puzzled over the exact meaning of this note. Soon he became frustrated and put the quality question away for awhile. Instead, he drew out a piece of correspondence stationery and began writing a reply to his former wife. This also frustrated him and he soon quit.

Looking at his watch, he decided that he should get dressed and drive into the nearby small town for breakfast. At the same time he could stop at a bank and get the money for Keith. With luck, he could be back in time for Keith's appointment.

Later that afternoon, Keith Walker rang Mead's door bell several times. No one answered. Instead of walking the quarter mile back to his own house, Keith decided to wait. He knew that Mead's lifestyle meant that he was often late. He made himself comfortable on the swing on the porch and watched the first snowflakes of the year begin to fall. A few minutes later Mead pulled into the driveway.

"How are you Keith? Did you have to wait long?" Mead called out.

"Only a few minutes. I brought over some articles for you to read."

"Well come on inside and tell me about them," said Mead as he threw an arm around the young boy.

The two went inside to the den and pulled their chairs up to a table near the window. "How's your mother, Keith?"

"She's okay I guess. She wants to know if you are going to come over and have dinner with us again."

"Tell her that I would love to. Now, what did you find out about quality?"

Keith cracked open an old leather notebook and drew out a stack of photocopies that was much too thick for the notebook. Mead wondered why the old notebook did not burst the way Keith was always stuffing it beyond capacity.

"Basically," began Keith, "there are three different types of stories I found relating quality to business. One group talks about companies that had to improve their quality because they would otherwise go out of business."

That remark impressed Mead as Keith laid the first pile of articles on the desk. He drew out a second pile.

"The second group deals with companies that discovered that quality might make good business sense. In this last pile, which isn't much, are companies that use quality assurance because it fits their normal method of operating the business."

Keith had done an excellent job of locating over thirty articles. Mead never understood how Keith could find so much in so little time. Mead also didn't know that Keith's computer could dial into a large library database in California to search thousands of publications. He also didn't know that the mysterious girl Keith dated was the local librarian. She was a master at locating obscure journals.

"What one article in each group would best describe the group?" Mead asked.

Keith drew three more articles from his notebook. "These three."

Mead realized that Keith was beginning to learn the way his mind worked. When he graduated, Mead wanted to talk to Keith about working for ROB, Incorporated.

The three articles were written within the last ten years. Each discussed a company that had to deal with the quality issue in a different manner. The three companies were the Ford Motor Company, Harley-Davidson, and Hewlett-Packard.

Mead thanked Keith and paid him the hundred dollars, plus ten extra dollars for doing an excellent job. He walked Keith to the door and then returned to the den for further reading. Mead mixed a perfect Manhattan straight up with a twist. He laid down on the leather couch and selected the Harley-Davidson article.

Mead learned that Harley-Davidson was the last surviving American company in the motorcycle market. Japanese competition had wiped out the other American manufacturers and some of their British counterparts. The management at Harley decided that strong committed actions were required to save the company.

They began by touring the Japanese manufacturing plants. What they saw shocked them. Most of the bikes being produced rolled right off of the assembly line and started on the first try. At their own plant, most of the bikes rolled off of the assembly line straight to a repair station before they could be started.

It became quickly obvious to the management at Harley that product quality had two distinct advantages for the Japanese. First, quality during production saved them hundreds of thousands of dollars in production costs. Second, the higher quality of the bike won and retained loyal customers.

Harley-Davidson implemented a widespread program of quality. They improved production methods, work methods, and product. Then they aggressively marketed the new Harleys by taking them to competitor's racing events and offering free rides. Within a few years, Harley had won back some of the American market and no longer needed government protection.

Mead set down this first article and finished his drink. He was impressed. He remembered how the Japanese motorcycle invasion had been so successful; just like the automotive, power tool, machinery, steel, and a dozen other industries. High quality at low prices from overseas manufacturers had devastated the American economy.

The second article was longer and covered the history of Ford Motor Company's famous drive for quality. "Quality Is Job One," recalled Mead as he began to read.

Ford's situation had been different than that at Harley-Davidson. For years, the competition was right up the street in Detroit. General Motors was the only company Ford watched. Then in 1980, things began to change. Advisors to Ford began to point out that Toyota was becoming the real threat.

Ford sent out teams of auditors to check the quality of Toyota products against their cars. When checking dealerships' service records for the two companies, the auditors received a surprise. There were no repair records for the Toyotas. The dealers' sold cars and never saw them again. In contrast, the Ford customers regularly came back to have warranty work done.

Eventually, Ford developed a comprehensive program of quality improvements to keep the company competitive through the 1980s and beyond. This program put most of the emphasis on a new relationship with the supply companies. If quality was not required early in the production process, then it could not be expected in the final product. Thus, the Ford suppliers were made to compete for a new policy of single sourcing.

The turning point for the company came when they produced more profits than their much larger rival, General Motors. In addition, the quality program had been expanded to other areas, such as design and marketing. The results were a strong and competitive company. Before, overseas competition was directly threatening its existence.

Mead set this article down. He could now see a pattern emerge. There really was no way to isolate quality from other business characteristics. When you spoke of quality, you were also talking about the economic and strategic position of a company. Quality was different depending on who the viewer was. The customer saw one thing, while a production foreman saw another.

Mead mixed a second drink and picked up the third article. This one was only a page long. It described the quality policy of Hewlett-Packard. Surprisingly, the article was supposed to be about how Hewlett-Packard treated its workers. The company was a leader in the idea that workers should be tapped for their ideas and feedback. Who knows more about what is needed for a job than the people doing it?

One item caught Mead's attention. Each worker followed a set of procedures called "best practices." If a worker found a better way to do something, then this was written down and became a new best practice. In other words, the system could grow and develop freely, always improving as it did so.

The sky was darkening and Mead was feeling hungry again. He made some notes before moving to the kitchen table. In the kitchen he spent some time rummaging through the freezer. He finally settled on a frozen pizza. He unwrapped it, ignored the thawing instructions, and tossed it directly into the oven.

Then he settled down with the three articles to highlight the important points. He also glanced at the other articles Keith had brought and selected a few for reading that evening.

Eleven o'clock that night found Mead propped up in bed writing down notes on the actions he would take on Monday. After a while, he paused and began thinking of a common theme to emphasize. Survival? No. Quality assurance? Not really. The problem was set aside for later consideration. He was tired now. His mind felt more at ease, because now he had some concrete information he could use to attack his immediate problems.

Monday Morning

Sally McCord had been on the phone most of Sunday night locating the key managers of ROB, Incorporated. Mead had called her Sunday morning as she was leaving for church. She was told to call each of the managers and make it clear to them that they must be in his office promptly at eight Monday morning.

It was now Monday morning and Sally anxiously took a roll call in her head to make sure that each manager had arrived. She gave a silent sigh when she realized that everyone was there. The problem now was that it was eight o'clock, and no one had seen Mead. His car was parked in its usual spot near the door, but Mead was not in the office area.

Without warning, Mead strode into the room carrying a drive shaft in one hand and a stack of papers in the other. The grease from the drive shaft was smeared on both his hands and the cuffs of his silk shirt. The production manager, Breton Rhodes, was quick enough to realize that this meant the part was fresh from the assembly area. In other words, Mead had been on the production floor that morning. This meant trouble, because Mead never went onto the shop floor.

Before the others could comprehend this odd display from their president, Mead began, "Ladies and gentlemen, if we do not change the way we run our business immediately, we will be out of business within six months."

Mead paused just long enough for this first remark to make a full impact on the managers. "Miss McCord, please hand out these papers."

Sally moved forward quickly and began organizing the papers into what seemed to be logical piles. Mead was not very talented with a copy machine and he had never learned to collate.

"The first piece of paper we will examine is a letter from our largest client." The assembled staff frantically shifted papers looking for the letter, but Mead wasn't about to wait.

"They indicate that we must improve the quality of our product. I have been researching possible methods for the past few months," lied Mead. "And I have selected three possible approaches. They are outlined in the three articles I have copied for everyone."

By this point, everyone in the room was reaching a point of confusion. Was this a real change in the company? Was this some sort of management game for another purpose? Had Mead flipped?

Sensing their confusion, Mead picked up eleven envelopes from his desk. Each had the name of a particular manager. Anna Fitzhugh, purchasing director was handed the first envelope. Lee Enfield of engineering received the next one. Brenda Patterson, quality manager, was sixth to receive her envelope. Breton Rhodes got the last envelope.

"Each of these envelopes contains your specific assignments. We will meet back here in one week to begin the change. We must change. Our customers demand it, the workers demand it, and the market demands it. If we don't make quality our number one concern, then we will not be able to improve our production, capture more markets, or increase our profits. I am counting on the cooperation of each person in the room. If you need help, contact Sally or myself and we will get the resources you need."

Mead paused. The room was silent. A few nervous glances were exchanged. Then Breton spoke up.

"What are you saying? Is the company changing its course in mid-stream? Who's going to make this change?"

"We are going to work together as a management team to make this change," Mead snapped back.

"But what methods are we going to use?" asked Anna.

"For the first couple of months," replied Mead, "we are going to study what other companies in our position have done. Then we are going to draw up a plan of implementation. Next week we will discuss all of the issues involved. I want every concern answered then. If you cannot buy into this plan as a team, then I want you to reconsider your future at this plant. I need to know your concerns, but I want your cooperation and guidance as well."

This was certainly a different Mr. Mead, thought Lee Enfield. Lee had gotten used to a president who delegated matters to others and generally stayed out of their way. Why had Mr. Mead changed so dramatically and so quickly? Others in the room were less curious and more suspicious.

Mead dismissed the group and closed his door. He drew out the legal pad that had the list of notes from his final call on Friday. He made a check mark near the first numbered item, "management commitment." Mead smiled. Yes, this was going to be a challenge. His staff obviously was displeased with his sudden announcement. Their cooperation was less than guaranteed, but for the first time that year, everyone was reacting to what he was doing, not the other way around.

Anna Fitzhugh came back into the room. "Sally said you wanted to see me." She paused. "If it's about that union letter. . ."

"Yes, it is," interrupted Mead. "I want you to bring the union on board with this new quality program. I want them to buy into this change. I want you to invite their representatives to the next Monday meeting."

"Yes sir," said Anna as she backed towards the door.

"And don't let anyone else know about this."

Brenda Patterson returned to her office in the quality control department. She moved a height gauge someone had left on her desk and took out the envelope Mead had given her. Inside, the message told her to review the quality manual, prepare changes, and research something called statistical process control. At the bottom of the message was a note to meet Mead in his office at nine o'clock tomorrow morning. She was also instructed to tell no one else about this meeting.

Brenda paused to reflect on the morning's events. She reached over and shut the door to her office. This was a signal to her staff not to disturb her. Why was Mead so suddenly interested in quality? She had sent memos and had made pleas to him for years to look at the potentials in quality control being given a larger voice.

Brenda thought about getting to work on her assignments, but she decided to check her in-basket first. It was loaded with over a dozen inspection reports from the weekend that needed signing. There was no point in rejecting any of the reports. By the time they reached her desk the product had usually been shipped.

There was also her notes from the disposition meeting on Friday. Every Friday for the ten years she had been at ROB, marketing, production, and she met to discuss the fate of goods rejected by her department. This meeting was really a bargaining session where marketing pushed to have back ordered items sent no matter what their quality.

Near the top of the pile was a note of rejection from the budget committee for her request for better measuring equipment. Part of the request was for automated equipment that would provide the machine operators and quality control with real-time product quality figures. The words *too expensive* had been written across the request in red pencil. That was the famous death stroke of Frank Graves, director of accounting.

Taken as a whole, this Monday was shaping up to be one of the worst for Brenda. "All my troubles and now Mead has a bug in his ear," Brenda said aloud.

Then suddenly, she didn't feel so bad. Maybe, she thought, this is a chance to make some changes I need.

On the other side of the production area Breton Rhodes was coming to a similar conclusion in his office. Three line supervisors were standing in his office trying to out shout each other with their complaints about the newest production schedule. Breton was not listening to any of their remarks. He was thinking about what Mead had said just minutes ago.

"That's the schedule. You'll just have to live with it until we catch up with the General Motors order," barked Breton.

Slowly, the group's buzzing dropped to a mumble as they wandered out of the room. They didn't look pleased, but Breton wasn't paying them to have a good time.

Any change can be exploited. That's what his mentor Jack Knape had taught him years ago when Jack was the production manager. Breton always remembered that phrase because he had seen it work many times in the past. And now, Mead was obviously in the mood for a major change.

Breton opened the letter he had received at the meeting that morning. His instructions were to make a list of all the production department's improvements that are currently under consideration, to be proposed, or that he thinks would be a good idea. At the bottom of the message was the invitation to join Mr. Mead early the next morning for a meeting. He was to tell no one about this meeting.

That's odd. Why all of the secrecy? Mead was hard enough to find on a normal day, let alone trying to get him to make a decision.

Breton's phone rang. It was one of the preventive maintenance people. The stamping press on line 43B was down again and it looked like nothing was going to bring it back up. He wanted authority to call the manufacturer.

"No way!" shouted Breton. "I'll be there in two minutes. Don't touch or do anything until I get there."

Breton was already putting on his factory jacket when he slammed down the phone. As he put on his safety glasses he thought that it might be a good idea to stop at the library tonight and read up on this quality fad Mead was so hot on. By the time Breton's door shut behind him, he was halfway across the production floor.

Later that night, Breton stopped at a small country library on his way home. It was located on Reeds Lake. The sun had gone down hours ago, but the fishermen had their lanterns lit on the lake. The dozen or so glowing lights were a relaxing sight from inside of the library.

Breton went to a back room filled with business-related magazines. It only took him a minute to find the stack of *Quality Progress*. This was the monthly journal of the American Society for Quality Control. The business librarian had told him that it usually carried stories about companies using quality technologies.

Breton selected a few issues and moved to the old leather chair by the window looking out over the lake. Next he removed the articles Mead had given him. For the next hour Breton studied these articles. He liked the Ford and Harley stories. He disliked the Hewlett-Packard story.

Some of my people can't even read. Like hell I'll let them tell me how to run a production department.

Now he picked up the *Quality Progress* for May of that year and scanned a few articles. Within a few minutes this issue had been discarded. The same fate was waiting for the next issue. However, an article in the third issue caught his attention. It was written by a production manager from one of ROB's competitors.

Breton was lost in this article when the librarian tapped him on the shoulder. "We're closing now."

"Huh. Oh, okay. Say, do you have a copy machine?"

Ten minutes later, Breton was on his way home. He felt better. He knew that his competitor had used a quality improvement plan to improve productivity. Breton was happy because he could see several mistakes his competitor had made. Now he would sound informed on the quality issue when he met with Mead in the morning. He also was forming a plan to make the quality initiative pay off for his own department.

That good feeling stayed with Breton until nine o'clock the next morning. As he strolled confidently into Mead's office for his secret meeting, Brenda Patterson was already there. What was this? Breton thought. Brenda and I are constantly at odds over quality questions. Why is she here?

Mead's greeting interrupted Breton's curiosity. "The three of us are going to be working very closely together for the next several weeks. I have chosen you two specifically because I feel that you are the people that can make this quality drive work."

Breton felt a little better upon hearing this. Still, he deliberately sat on the couch instead of the chair pulled up next to Brenda's. This didn't escape Mead's attention. However, he knew about some things coming up for these two people that might change their feelings toward each other.

Before he continued, Mead made a check mark on the list he had transcribed the previous Friday. "Make sure that your production and quality managers work as a team."

CHAPTER 2

The First Step — Management Commitment

"We are going to take a field trip today," Mead announced. Brenda hated Mead's occasionally patronizing tone. Breton unconsciously shook his head and wondered if the surprises would ever stop.

"We are going to tour the Urn Corporation. Mr. Headly has been kind enough to invite us over to see his operation. I want you two to pay close attention to the layout. Come on, I'll drive."

The twenty-minute drive across Grand Rapids was pleasant enough in Mead's Cadillac. Of course, Breton and Brenda didn't exchange a single word during the trip. The snow was coming down steadily. Probably from the effect of having Lake Michigan so close, thought Breton.

After parking the car the three made their way to Urn's front office. All of them were noting the open spaces and modern buildings of the industrial complex here by the airport. Likewise, all three were beginning to have second thoughts about not bringing boots to work today. The light covering of snow was quickly becoming slush in the parking lot.

After they entered the Urn Corporation, the receptionist rose to take their coats and offer them coffee. "Mr. Headly will see you in a few moments. Please have a seat."

As Breton sat, he scanned the waiting area. Three of the walls were made of glass and looked out onto a now frozen reflecting pool in front of the building. Display cases near the door held over a dozen examples of Urn products. Although the decorative handles and plaques on display were attractive, Breton shuddered when he remembered what they were used for.

Brenda was still standing and reading the various customer awards Urn had won. It seemed strange to think of the funeral industry as giving out awards. However, one frame on the wall held something that looked very different from the awards. It was a letter signed by Headly.

"The chief operating philosophy of Urn Corporation is to pursue never-ending improvement in all areas of its operations." Brenda wanted to read more of this interesting document, but Headly walked into the waiting area.

"Good morning, I hope you all had a nice trip across town today."

"The snow didn't slow us down much. How are you doing Ron?" Mead responded. "Let me introduce my production manager and quality manager, Breton Rhodes and Brenda Patterson."

"Glad to meet each of you," said Headly as he shook their hands. "Shall we go to my office where we will be more comfortable?"

The trio followed Headly to his office on the second floor of the building. Brenda and Breton were already noting the differences between their company and this one. For one thing, the office people had open office furniture and partitions, instead of the desks crammed into a single room as at ROB. They were ushered into Headly's office and took comfortable seats that didn't reek of cigarette smoke.

"So, I hear you want to learn about our quality assurance methods."

"That's right, Ron. I wanted my people to hear firsthand what it takes to get to where you are today."

"Well," began Headly. "I'd better start with a quick review of where we are today."

He opened a dry erase board from the wall and began writing some dates. "It all started back in 1982. I had read an article that quality assurance was the hot new item in industry. That fall, I went to a seminar about it sponsored by the local community college. At that time we were doing alright, but we didn't have any real growth in markets since 1973."

"Isn't little growth normal for the funeral industry?" asked Brenda, a little embarrassed for speaking up. She glanced at her companions and continued, "I mean, isn't the death rate fairly consistent?"

"Well, I know what you're trying to say, Brenda. It's true that you normally don't get into this business anticipating growing markets. However, we were looking for a way to expand in a limited market. We are like a lot of the companies that supply to the funeral business. We started as a family-owned business and up to that point, we stayed small.

"When I took this seminar in 1982, I kept thinking that quality was always maintained in this industry because this type of a company always takes pride in its craftsmanship. Without a quality product, no one will buy your wares. Morbid as it may sound, customer satisfaction is paramount in this industry."

Breton was feeling very uneasy about this entire conversation.

"Something happened just before the seminar was over. The speaker pointed out that one aspect of quality was to make a product right the first time during production. He then asked each of us to estimate our internal scrap rates. I quickly noted that ours hovered around 10 percent of the materials we purchased.

"Well, if we made everything right the first time, then we would not throw away 10 percent of our raw materials. In fact, we would not have sorting, rework, or overscheduling of machinery to remake the products we scrapped. Thus, we would save a lot of money in the production area by improving quality."

Headly paused to let this point set in the minds of his audience. Brenda was impressed, Mead was taking notes, and Breton was doubtful of this claim.

"How did you get your program started?" Mead inquired.

"The first step was to do my homework. I went to our strategic plan and looked at it again with an eye toward quality. I quickly saw that quality was never specifically mentioned in the plan. Therefore, I reviewed what several companies similar to our own had done to change their strategy to quality assurance and customer satisfaction.

"Once that information was collected, I called together the top managers of the company and reviewed my intentions to change our strategic thinking. We went away for four days to Gull Lake to debate the issues. For two days we heard nothing but objections to change. By the third day, however, people had finished venting, and we began to put forth some really solid ideas.

"After that retreat, I drew up a new strategic plan that gave each manager specific goals to be fulfilled based on their own suggestions. For example, the production manager here wanted to cut scrap rates in half within a year. So, I gave him that task.

"If there is any one piece of critical advice I can give you, it is the importance of management commitment in any quality initiative. Without the support of the top managers, any quality program will die a slow death."

Headly turned back to the board and continued to write. "By 1984 we had several good ideas implemented. The machine operators had requested training in SPC, statistical process control. We gave it to them, and they ran with it. First they set up control charts to monitor the processes, then they began detecting small problems and correcting them before they got large. That saved a lot of downtime.

"By 1985 our scrap and rework rates were down so far that we could cut the price of our products. We pushed the low-cost, high-quality angle in our advertising. We invited a lot of our customers to our plant to see how we could do it. They were so impressed that they bought more of our goods.

"Nineteen eighty-six saw us spread these ideas to our suppliers. We wanted them to look at their processes through statistical methods and to have formal quality assurance programs. Last year, we stopped inspecting our incoming goods. We now trust our suppliers so well, that we know their stuff is going to be good."

Breton couldn't believe this last remark; neither could Brenda. Most of Brenda's time was spent arguing with suppliers about the poor quality of the material they sent. She had a full-time engineer assigned to touring the supply plants just to keep them in line. Breton's top peeve was having the wrong parts shipped to the production lines. Just keeping the suppliers on schedule was a nightmare in itself.

"Let's go back to your point about management commitment, Ron," Mead piped in. "Can you give us some solid examples of management commitment?"

"Sure. The easiest is what happens when you don't have management commitment. One of the first projects we tried to undertake was the forming of problem-solving work teams. We wanted to let existing shop floor work teams meet once a week to discuss common problems and possible solutions. The idea sounded great until it came to the reality of when we would allow the teams to meet. Production was booked full, and no one was interested in hanging around after their shift if they weren't going to be paid for it.

"Within a week of suggesting the idea, the production and personnel managers were not speaking to each other. Worse yet, we had announced the forming of the groups to the workers. They wanted to see what this was all about, but we couldn't schedule time."

"How did you solve that problem?" Breton asked.

"Simple: management commitment. I called the managers involved into my office and read them the riot act. Then we discussed possible solutions and came up with the idea of having the groups meet during a lunch hour with the company providing the food. The managers were happy, and the workers liked the idea.

"You see, if I had been less committed, I wouldn't have allowed the free food or the group meetings during working hours. Instead, I supported the idea with money and time. Those are the marks of management commitment."

"What's an example of management commitment outside of conflicts?" Mead asked.

"Well, money was tight when we first started the program. The issue of training the workers was high on our project list. We wanted to teach them how to solve problems, measure quality, and cooperate with supervision. We knew that the local colleges had instructors who could come to our plant to teach such classes. Some consultants were also available. Unfortunately, they all wanted around $100 an hour.

"The top managers met as a group to discuss alternatives and possible solutions. Luckily, our chief engineer had once worked with the state. He recalled some sort of program that could help fund such training. We made some calls and discovered that the state would pay for half of the expenses."

"What's the bottom line?" Mead asked.

"You see," replied Headly, "it's not that we make pretty speeches or write plans that we support quality. Instead, our support is measured by the time, people, and money we dedicate to the task."

"Speaking of writing plans, what was that document I saw on your wall downstairs?" Brenda asked.

"Oh, you mean one of these," responded Headly as he drew out three pamphlets from his desk. "You can keep these. This is the advertisement for our products we send to potential customers. On the cover is a copy of the document you are so curious about. It's our policy of continuous improvement."

"Continuous improvement?" Brenda queried.

"Yes. After years of working with a quality strategy, it slowly dawned on us that what we were really doing was encouraging everyone in this company to continuously improve the way they did their jobs. This document was our initial statement that the company's new policy was the never-ending improvement of our business.

"This is another critical step toward management commitment. You just can't say that you are committed to quality. You have to write it down and sign your name to it. I give a $100 reward to any employee who finds a manager giving instructions contrary to this philosophy.

"It cost me a few thousand the first year, but I haven't had to pay a dime since. We used to talk about quality at every employee meeting, but the workers kept pointing out, that while we talked, the marketing and sales people were tearing rejection slips off of parts so that they could be shipped on time. Needless to say, we put an end to that practice.

"Listen, I could talk all day. I want you people to see what has happened here firsthand. Let me call up my production and quality managers and they can give Breton and Brenda personal tours of the plant."

Headly made two quick phone calls and within a few minutes both managers were in the room. Breton took note of this, because at ROB it took up to three hours some days to find Brenda.

The Urn Corporation production manager was Carla Fulton. She introduced herself to Breton and invited him to join her on her morning rounds of the production area. Breton smiled and accepted, but at the same time he was studying her eyes. Where were the dark circles from too little sleep and the yellow tint of the eyelids that gave away the endless smoking?

Brenda was introduced to her counterpart, Bob Barley. She too smiled and accepted Bob's invitation to tour the quality assurance area. The two left with Bob rattling off a list of things they could examine. He left no room for Brenda to respond.

Headly turned to Mead when the two were finally alone. "I hear that you called my friend."

"Yes, he gave me the same list he gave you."

"Still working on putting together a management team I see. Good luck. I don't think your production and quality manager get along."

"No problem, Ron. I have something special planned for them next week."

Strolling away from the two presidents, Breton gave his traditional glance over the body and clothing of Carla Fulton. His primary interest was to pick up clues as to the age and social standing of the woman. Other than being obviously married and middle-class no other clues were present. Breton decided to probe more openly.

"So, Carla," said Breton, "were you here when this quality drive was started?"

"I sure was, but I was only the production planner then."

"How easy was it really?"

Carla stopped walking for a moment and glanced back in the direction of Headly's office. "It was a tough ride for the guy I eventually replaced. He fought the program from the start. Headly tried to change his mind for three years."

"What happened?"

Carla was walking again now. "He fired him."

For the next few minutes there was silence between the two as they walked out onto the production floor. They had to cross over two conveyor belts on steel catwalks. As they approached the third catwalk Carla suddenly stopped and pointed to a machine only ten feet away. Carla had to speak up to be heard over the dull roar of the production equipment. "This is where it all started."

In front of Breton was a large grey machine with hydraulic hoses visible in several places. Breton recognized it immediately as a plastic injection molding machine. ROB had similar machines but not as modern as this one. Breton also glanced to the floor beneath the machine and noted that no oil was visible. In fact, no dirt, dust, or scrap pieces of paper were under the machine. These people must clean under these machines every day, he thought to himself.

"This is our main injection machine," continued Carla. "We use it to mold handles and other decorative items. When Mr. Headly wanted us to pick something to work on this was our first choice. Back then, this baby was producing over 30 percent scrap."

Breton let a slow whistle out of his lips.

"We started by measuring the exact amount of scrap being produced on a daily basis. We found that it varied by large amounts. So, we started to track what it was that made the parts go bad."

"How do you mean?" Breton asked.

"Well, we kept a list of which defects were causing us to scrap a particular part. At that time, we would look at, maybe, thirty pieces every half an hour. What we found was that several major defects were occurring at random. You know, things like sinks and short shots."

"So what happened?"

"We had some meetings among ourselves and the operators were quite adamant that the problems came from using too much reground plastic. They were right. I would watch this machine at work and people were literally taking the bad parts while they were still warm, grinding them up, and putting the plastic back into the machine."

Carla paused to wave to a worker on the other side of the machine. "We couldn't change that practice by ourselves, so we asked the managers for permission. The accountants told them that not using regrind would cost the company thousands of dollars every year. We argued that the defective parts were costing us even more.

"Luckily, the managers decided to try no regrind for a month and see what happened. On average, our scrap rate fell by over 10 percent. We were all impressed. Of course, that meant that regrind wasn't the only problem, but at least we had part of the solution."

Just then a low piercing beep interrupted the conversation. Carla reached down and took off a paging device from her belt. "Looks like I have to confirm a change order. Talk to the machine operator, I'll be back in about two minutes."

Breton turned toward the plastic injection machine. Standing near the automated controls was a young man who had long blond hair that looked as if it hadn't been combed in the past two days.

"Good morning," Breton shouted over the noise of the machine.

"How you doing?" replied the young man. "You here on a tour or something?"

"I'm Breton Rhodes from ROB, Incorporated. I'm seeing how you guys improved your quality."

"You should talk to Mr. Headly about that," answered the man. "Without him we wouldn't have gotten anything done."

"What do you mean?" Breton inquired.

"About seven years ago we had a real S.O.B. for a production manager."

This remark made Breton suddenly aware that the young man didn't know that he was also a production manager. Perhaps it would be better if he remained ignorant of that fact. The machine operator continued.

"Back then Mr. Headly starts asking us operators what we could do to improve quality." He interrupted with a swear. "Sure, we knew a lot of things that weren't being done right. The trouble was that if we spoke up our supervisors would get mad at us. We were supposed to tell the top guys how good we were. The production manager would come down and salt some of our scrap products into the outgoing shipments so they wouldn't show up on the scrap report."

"Did the customers get mad when they received scrap?" asked Breton, even though the temptation to do the same trick had occurred in his own plant several times.

"Sure, but the sales people would point out that we had a 1 percent acceptable quality level. They'd tell 'em that they should expect 1 percent of the stuff to be bad."

"So, what changed it?"

"Old man Headly put the screws on the top managers, and they put the pressure on the line supervisors. Within a few months they were all singing the praises of quality. Of course, few of them were actually doing it. They would find some improvement that occurred due to some normal change and then they would take all of the credit for it.

"Eventually, Mr. Headly caught on to that and chewed them out. That's when we hired a quality auditor. He went around and monitored the activities of each work group and confirmed quality improvements. Now, if we make a real improvement and can demonstrate it to the auditor, the whole work team gets a bonus based on 10 percent of the costs saved."

"How much did you make in bonuses last year?"

"Our team took home $3,500."

Breton was just starting to react to this revelation when Carla tapped him on the shoulder. "Are you learning anything here?"

"Too much," replied Breton.

"Come on, I'll show you another success story."

Carla lead Breton through the maze of machinery. His last encounter with the machine operator had left a numbness in his brain, but his power of observation was still active. On the way through the plant he made several more interesting observations. First, the plant itself was relatively cool despite the ongoing operation of several heavy machines. Second, everyone was wearing eye protection and steel-toed shoes. Third, the housekeeping in this plant was possibly the best he had ever seen. And finally, he noticed red lights above each work station. Pulling on Carla's shoulder he asked, "What's with all of the red lights?"

"If a machine operator has the slightest problem with production that he can't fix in five minutes, he switches on the light. Supervisors then know where they are needed. The lights are turned off when the problems are fixed. If the light stays on for more than thirty minutes, it will set off an alarm in my office."

"Clever," remarked Breton.

"Yeah, we got the idea from a Japanese manufacturer south of town."

The two continued on their trek until they reached the incoming shipment area. "Mr. Headly probably gave you the management commitment lecture, right?"

"Yes, he did."

"Well," began Carla, "here's a good example of where it works well. After we watched what was causing our problems in the plant, it soon became obvious that a lot of our supplied materials were not of the high quality we needed. If you start with bad stuff, you're going to make more bad stuff."

Breton nodded in agreement.

"We documented the problem repeatedly to the top managers. We kept that up for about six months so that they would be very aware of the problem. Then we went to them and recommended that they review our purchasing contracts to see if we could assure quality at the supply company. They balked, but finally agreed to let Chuck Wu, our purchasing director, review the idea."

"That must've killed the idea fast," noted Breton. "A purchasing director isn't very likely to admit that his own purchasing system is flawed."

"Yeah, that's what the other managers thought would happen. What they didn't know is that we had been taking Wu out for dinner and drinks every week for months. We slowly convinced him that if we could certify the vendors, we would ship less stuff back and forth and he could claim the cost reduction. When the company management offered him a chance to change the system, he jumped at it."

Carla walked to one of the nearby skids of brass accessory pieces and lifted a red and white tag. "This is the vendor certification tag. They put it on the skid after their own quality assurance people have made sure that only parts of good quality are in this shipment. We keep a score by vendor for how many parts per million shipped we can't use because the quality wasn't high enough."

"Where's the incoming inspection approval tag?" asked Breton.

"There isn't one. We don't inspect incoming materials any more."

"Did you lay off the incoming inspectors? I would think that you could save some money that way."

"Nope," snapped Carla. "They were reassigned to auditing the production lines."

Breton had made up his mind about one thing; this was not an ordinary week for him. Monday, his boss had demanded a complete change in the way the company was run. Today he was looking over a production plant equipped with many of the same machines ROB used, but it was like a different world. When Carla waved to workers, they waved back. Breton didn't even want to think about what his workers would wave back.

On the second floor of the office area was a snack bar for the front office people. Headly and Mead selected a Danish from the rack and poured themselves large cups of coffee. Mead noted that Headly had stopped smoking. Headly noted that Mead looked tired.

"How have you been?" asked Headly as the two drew up chairs in the small windowless room.

"Busy," responded Mead as he took note of the fact that Headly and his workers freely shared the same break area. Then after an awkward pause, "So, Ron, how did you really get started?"

"I'll tell you, Bob. This quality program didn't just happen. It wasn't like I told everyone to change and they did. I had to make real changes to the way we ran the company."

"What was the first step?"

"I started with that written statement about never-ending improvement. Of course, it was a mistake to write it so fast. If I had it to do over again, I would have waited until the top managers had reached a consensus about how we were going to change."

"The management commitment step really is important then?"

"You bet, Bob. How a company achieves that commitment is usually dictated by how they normally get the managers to buy into a new idea. For us we did three things: One, we created a continuous improvement committee; two, we trained the committee members; and three, we rewrote our operations procedures."

Mead fumbled for his pen and note pad. He made some notes about what Headly was saying. "Do you mind if I ask some questions and take some notes?"

"Not at all. What would you like to know?"

"Who was on the committee?"

"The continuous improvement committee," began Headly, "was made up of the key managers. Specifically, production, quality, purchasing, personnel, engineering, sales, and accounting. I made it quite clear to this group that I expected them to meet twice a month."

"What did this committee do?"

"They were assigned the task of first developing, and then driving our quality program. I wasn't going to let the other managers delegate the task to the quality assurance manager. Barley had better things to do.

"Let me give you some examples of what the committee was assigned. Let me start with the creation of the quality program goals. I gave each member of the committee a copy of the company's strategic plan. For most of them, it was the first time they had ever seen it. The accounting manager blew a fuse because he didn't want the managers to know the actual costs and profit margins we were using.

"Needless to say, I had to put out a few fires. I made it clear that this was a new age the company had entered. We were going to put facts on the table and debate each issue logically. No longer would emotions and petty political turf battles rule the day.

"Anyhow, once they had the strategic plan, they had to draw up a list of quality-related projects that could help us achieve our strategic goals."

"But," interrupted Mead, "they aren't strategic planners."

"That's where the training came in. I hired an outside consultant to teach them how to create strategic plans. He also reviewed the quality systems other companies had established. A few of the managers resisted the training and said that they already knew this stuff. More fights and more firefighting for me."

Mead smiled in understanding. Headly continued.

"By the time the training was over, most of them were thanking me for introducing them to a new way of thinking. Within a few weeks, they were at the meetings with dozens of ideas. First we would discuss the merit of an idea, then how we could implement it, and then track its progress."

"Could you give me an example?"

"Sure, you know that on-time shipments are very important in business?"

"Life and death," Mead replied instinctively.

"Well, we discussed the goal of achieving 100 percent on-time deliveries. The problem was we had no idea how many on-time deliveries we were already making. Then, once we started to discuss how to check, we discovered that we didn't even have a definition of on-time.

"Think about it, Bob. What does on-time really mean? It obviously hurts our production schedule to receive critical components a day late. However, it can overtax our inventory system to receive a large shipment a day early.

"We decided that customers would probably be less upset to get something early, but still it could mess up their receiving plans. That's when Carla came up with a plan to measure delivery accuracy by awarding a point for every day late or early a delivery was shipped. That made our strategic goal zero points.

"Of course, once we measured our current situation we discovered that we were racking up a thousand points a month. Clearly, this was going to be a tough nut to crack."

"So," Mead asked, "how did you crack it?"

Headly pulled his chair a little closer. "Just putting the goal into the strategic plan would not make things happen. We pulled the shipping procedures and rewrote them. For example, we made the point system for measuring accuracy the job of the shipping foreman. We also assigned the production manager the task of assembling and training a work team to address the problem.

"Carla organized the shipping dock people into a team. There are only seven people who work the docks so the team was quite manageable. They met once a week to discuss the shipping situation. In between meetings, the foreman was keeping a delivery score and posting it by the docks. The team got mad because they knew that most of the shipping schedule problems occurred because production was not keeping its schedule.

"Carla brought that information back to the continuous improvement committee and recommended that she form a second team consisting of the production planners and the line supervisors. The committee approved the idea. Thus, we had gone through a single cycle of the committee activity. The committee assigned a task, the work team reported to the committee, and then the committee assigned further tasks."

"Sounds simple enough," said Mead.

"Sure, it sounds simple, but it's not. It was too easy in the beginning to over-assign tasks and bog down the whole plant. We spent months finding our pace. In addition, some of the goals lead to dead ends. Take the example of optimizing the stamping presses. After three months of fooling around with those machines, we had to admit that they were already doing the best they could."

"So, where should I start?" asked Mead.

"Once you form and train the continuous improvement committee, you should take the role as chief advocate of the quality drive. You're the top man, and if you don't support the program no one else will be able to. As for changing procedures, I would start with your quality manual."

"Why the quality manual?"

"That's the first thing that your customers are going to examine when they inspect your plant. Besides, it's real easy to write a new quality manual. Just take one of ours and pick one new method at a time to implement. But, be careful to read it thoroughly so that you don't include a technique you will never use.

"After you have most of the quality manual changed, start to branch out into other important areas, like scheduling and sales. We started a program to make our products very traceable for the customers. Now if a customer has a problem with one of our products, we are able to trace it to the people who made the part, the machines used, and the sources of the raw materials."

Mead was impressed. Headly's system seemed complete and well planned.

"So, Ron. When will you be done?"

"Never," replied Headly. "That's the whole point of continuous improvement. You never stop. When I had the managers buy into this program they were doing it for life. A few of them have left since then, and I know that one left because he didn't believe in what we were doing.

"On the other hand, continuous improvement has paid big dividends to the company. We have located and eliminated over a hundred production problems since 1984. We've reduced the cost of running this plant so much that we now underbid all of our competitors."

Mead's coffee was gone and the Danish was still lying in front of him uneaten. He took a larger than normal bite and wondered how his staff people were doing out in the plant.

Breton and Carla had finished their plant tours and were now down in the production offices. Carla was demonstrating the materials requirement planning software the company used to create the master production schedule. She also showed Breton how information on production problems found by the work teams was being used to modify the schedule. To his left, Breton spotted the delivery points chart Carla had mentioned earlier. This month they had scored only fifteen points.

Next to the production offices were the quality assurance laboratories and offices. Bob Barley and Brenda Patterson had quickly finished their tour and had retired to the solitude of Barley's office. They had stopped in the production snack area to brew two cups of herb tea. They were hitting it off.

CHAPTER 3

The Organization
of Quality

Bob Barley, quality manager of Urn Corporation, and Brenda Patterson, quality manager of ROB, were finishing second cups of tea when Bob suggested that they look over the quality department.

"I don't know how you run your shop," began Bob, "so, I'll show you everything we do here. You can tell me what you do different."

"Sounds fine," Brenda responded.

"Good. Well, we had better start right here." Bob pivoted in his chair and snatched up a worn copy of the company's quality manual. Then he swung back to his desk and opened a bottom drawer. Soon he produced another well-worn document and dropped it on the desk. "This is our quality manual from ten years ago."

Brenda quickly noted that this document was very thin. The current manual held in Bob's hands was at least five times as thick. "Looks like you've added a few things."

"We sure have. Back then we were called quality control. I used to have a phrase I'd use a lot back then. I used to say that the person least likely to control quality was the quality control person."

Brenda chuckled at Bob's remark, but underneath she knew the truth in what he was saying.

"Today we are called quality assurance because we do so much more to directly assure the quality of our goods, services, and working conditions."

"Tell me about the past," Brenda said somberly.

"Well, back then we had only five functions: vendor inspection, process inspection, final inspection, lab testing, and helping the rework teams sort out bad products. In reality, we were the test and inspection people. To the guys out on the assembly line we were the cops."

"The cops?"

"Yeah, well, that was the polite term they used for us. The quality manager who had this job before me was a strong believer in quality control as the enforcer in the plant. I remember my job interview with the guy. He said that the role of quality control was to find the people who were slacking off on their jobs and creating quality problems. He thought that every quality problem occurred because people weren't doing their jobs like they were supposed to."

The hair on the back of Brenda's neck was standing straight up now. When she had interviewed for the opening in the quality control department that started her rise to manager, she had heard the same speech. Hoping that Bob wouldn't notice the nerve he had touched, she prompted him to continue.

"We still call those times the hell days, because the attitude at the time by production and management was, who the hell cares what QC thinks?"

Bob paused long enough to shake his head slowly and glanced down at his feet. "Process inspection was a daily study in frustration and personal tension. Each department in the plant had an inspector on every shift. For example, the stamping area had inspectors on all three shifts. After a couple of thousand parts were stamped out, the machine operators would call over an inspector. The inspector would examine the pieces and tell them whether the parts met the quality requirements. You could just imagine the problems that created."

Brenda's mind wandered for a moment and thought about the lot of three thousand door handles she had rejected that very morning.

"If the parts weren't good enough, the shift had to make them over. Not only did that waste a lot of time, but the operators lost their quotas. Naturally, quality would never improve. The adjustments to the process to make the part right was done by the operators, but the information they needed on the quality of the parts wasn't available until after the inspection. By then it was too late."

"I take it you do things differently today," Brenda stated.

"Come on, I'll show you how different it is."

Bob jumped up from his desk and headed for the door. Brenda had to pick up her note pad and pen and scramble to keep up. Bob lead her through the quality assurance lab and up a flight of steps to a catwalk overlooking a large section of the plant. Bob leaned over the railing and swept his arm through a ninety degree arc. "This area down here is the assembly area. How many inspectors do you see down there?"

Brenda reached into her purse and drew out her glasses. She needed them for driving and for answering sudden requests to search a room. Bob was watching her and smiling. This was a challenge, and Brenda wasn't going to flinch in the face of a difficult situation.

Brenda began by scanning the room for the distinctive white coat and clipboard of the typical quality inspector. None could be found. Then Brenda carefully examined each person in the room. Everyone seemed to have an assembly job. Nobody was watching over anyone's shoulder. "There aren't any inspectors down there," she answered.

Bob made a buzzing sound and shouted over the noise. "Wrong. Everybody down there is inspecting. We took away the person called an inspector and made inspection part of everyone's job."

"How did you do that?"

"We introduced SPC."

Brenda knew that SPC stood for statistical process control and she had attended a lecture on it years ago. Unfortunately, she felt that her knowledge of it was so limited that it was best not to discuss it. Instead, she made a covering comment. "Good idea."

Bob was now heading back down the steps they had come up just a moment before. "I'll show you another disaster area we recently cleaned up."

Bob headed through the assembly area toward the shipping docks. Brenda weaved her way through the tubs of parts sitting on the floor. She flinched when she passed a calendar with a picture of a young girl in a bikini holding a large power tool. She laughed a few seconds later when she passed a woman at work who had another calendar featuring a picture of a bare-chested man holding the same tool.

"This is the loading and receiving area," Bob stated. Brenda took note of the openness of the area compared to ROB's crowded loading dock.

"Over here," continued Bob, "used to be our incoming inspection area. We used to have five full-time people checking everything that came in the door. All of them had the familiar red and green tags. If something passed the military standard 105-D inspection plan, it got a green acceptance tag. If it didn't it was rejected and got a red tag."

Brenda felt it was time to speak up about her own quality control department. "We're still doing that at our plant, except we have a yellow sticker for holding a shipment. What it really means is that we should reject the incoming shipment, but production needs the material so badly that they won't let us ship it back to the supplier."

"Well, I wasn't going to say this," Bob said hesitantly, "but we used to do the same thing." Bob continued, "We also had production supervisors coming down here and tearing the red stickers off of skids of materials they needed right away. For awhile, we tried locking the defective goods in a separate area. The guy in charge of the key made a lot of friends quick," he said with a wink.

"What do you do now?"

"About five years ago it finally dawned on us that this was a pretty silly way to run things. Checking the stuff at the door made us everyone's enemy. Suppliers were mad when they found out that the stuff they had sent us was not going to be accepted. The production people and the loading dock crew didn't like the delay, and we didn't like taking all of the heat.

"Finally, we had the receiving inspectors talk to the vendor inspection group. The vendor inspectors were in charge of checking up on the suppliers at their own plants. Well, we had so many suppliers that the vendor inspectors were constantly traveling. When the two groups finally met they decided that they could both save a lot of work if the company would require suppliers to certify their goods to our standards before shipping.

"Luckily, the company implemented that idea and wrote tough new purchasing agreements. Now, we receive a shipment and it goes straight to the production area where it's needed. If a part from the supplier should fail to do its job out on the production line, we charge a substantial penalty. In addition, the supplier is called in to explain the problem. That makes the supplier responsible for tracing down the actual cause of the problem and fixing it."

"Are you kidding?" asked Brenda rhetorically. "You mean to say that you actually expect a supplier to trace one bad part to its actual cause?" Brenda was thinking of the thousands of parts she rejected every week.

"I know it sounds awful, and it took years to achieve, but believe it or not, the suppliers love it. It puts some tough requirements on them, but they know that nothing is going to be shipped back. That saves them plenty in predictable schedules and fixed prices."

Bob turned and began walking to the far end of the loading docks. Brenda thought that he was heading into the shipping offices but he pulled up short.

"These last three bays are where we ship out our finished goods. The shipping people have more office space today because we removed the final inspection staff from this area."

"You're kidding," said Brenda. "Do you mean that you are not checking the quality of incoming material or the stuff going out the door? How do you know the quality of your product?"

Brenda recalled the day ten years ago when the president of another company she worked at was asked about quality. "I know everything is good," he had said. "We check the stuff coming in and our product going out. How could anything ever be wrong?"

Bob seemed taken aback by the outburst and Brenda was a little embarrassed. Bob frowned for a moment and then he continued. "We decided that by the time a product was ready to ship it was too late to change its quality. Therefore, we put all of our resources into assuring that the production processes were operating at their highest quality capabilities."

Just then Brenda spotted a person in a white coat opening a few random boxes of products in the shipping area. The woman would examine a few pieces in each box and make some notes on her clipboard. If that wasn't an inspector, thought Brenda, she would eat her hat.

"Who's that?" asked Brenda indicating the woman.

"She's one of the quality auditors. She's checking the shipment to confirm its predicted quality."

"I thought you didn't have outgoing inspection."

"We don't. She has no power to accept or reject the shipment. Instead, she will collect some information on the number of defects on this shipment, and will compare that to the predicted quality of the shipment, based on the information gathered during production. So, we're not inspecting the shipment, we are confirming that the rest of the quality system is accurate."

Brenda nodded in agreement, but to her this still sounded like outgoing inspection. Bob started to head back to the test lab. Brenda tapped him on the shoulder and asked, "Where's your scrap and rework area?"

"We don't do rework any longer. Once in a great while something will happen to a product where we just have to rework it to make it right. But then we usually have caught it after very few parts have been made. The reworking can usually be done at the site of production. This," said Bob as he waved toward a corner of the shipping area, "is the scrap retention area."

Brenda was clearly surprised by what she saw. On the floor near the corner was a square painted on the floor clearly marked SCRAP. The area couldn't have been more than eight feet on a side. A small plastic chain roped off the area. Inside the chain were two small boxes filled with various parts.

"Is that a typical amount?" she asked.

"Oh, sure. After a week's production we usually have at least a box of scrap parts. We have two in there now because someone didn't disposition last week's scrap parts."

Bob had made this remark almost casually. Brenda was dumbstruck. In her own plant the scrap area took up over five hundred square feet and had to be emptied every day. When she had left ROB that morning there were eleven skids of parts waiting to be scrapped.

She was still trying to comprehend the scrap situation when Bob ushered her back into the test lab. The room was mostly open space. Test and measurement equipment was placed around the outside walls of the room either on or between spotless work benches. In the center of the room was a granite table with a large gantry arm over it. This was the coordinate measuring machine. As they entered, the machine was swinging back and forth over one of the company's famous urns.

"I see you have a CMM," Brenda said.

"Yeah, and isn't it a beauty? We paid $150,000 for it, and it's worth every penny."

As they stepped closer Brenda could see the probe at the end of the gantry arm touching off points on the urn. "What's so critical about the dimensions of an urn that you have to use a CMM?" she asked.

"A couple of things are important on an urn for it to function properly. For one thing the cover has to fit snugly enough to keep out moisture, but not so snug that you can't open it. The tolerance for circularity has to be maintained to within a thousandth of an inch. The CMM helps us confirm that the forming machine that creates the lid is matching the dimensions of the casting machine that makes the body of the urn.

"The test and measurement function," continued Bob, "is one of the old areas that had new life breathed into it because of our quality drive. It quickly became obvious to the company's management that it was very hard to improve the quality of something that you had no measurements of.

"Therefore, they put together a larger budget for test and inspection. However, there was a catch. Instead of testing and measuring just for the things customers requested, we also had to respond to requests from the production people. In a sense, the production department became our largest customer."

"How do you mean that?" Brenda inquired.

Bob reached over to a nearby workbench and picked up a pair of calipers. With a flick of his wrist he turned the calipers over and held them up to Brenda's face. She could see a bright orange sticker on the back of the small measuring instrument.

"That sticker is the calibration expiration date for this set of calipers. This was our first assignment for the test and measurement people. Every gauge in the entire building was registered in this lab and calibrated. Then this sticker is placed on the measuring gauge that tells its user when to bring it in for another calibration."

"Whoa, that sounds like quite a job!" Brenda exclaimed.

"It was. Even worse when we issued the call to bring in measuring devices, we received several surprises. We found that many of the delicate measuring gauges brought in were not owned by the company. The were the personal property of the tool-and-die people. We also discovered that these had never been calibrated in our labs. In many cases they were the wrong measuring system.

"Another nightmare was discovering that the people in the stamping department had been issued steel rulers to measure tolerances to the thousandth of an inch. Needless to say, we quickly convinced management to issue the proper gauges."

"And, how many gauges disappeared from the shop floor?" Brenda inquired.

"At first we lost a good number of them through carelessness or improper use. We soon learned to sign the gauges out each morning to specific people. If they didn't bring the gauge back they would be charged for its replacement. You might have noticed the holsters some of the operators designed and made to carry micrometers. It helps them keep track of the micrometers by keeping them close at hand.

"The important thing is that we wanted the people to bring us the gauges if they were damaged. It used to be that if someone dropped, say a pair of calipers, they didn't think twice about it. Now, if they drop them they report it so that they can get a new gauge. We encourage the reporting, and we don't punish them for the damage. It's cheaper to replace gauges frequently than to collect bad data."

Brenda nodded in agreement. Then tilted her head to indicate to Bob that she wanted to say something a little farther away from the test and measurement people. Bob shuffled sideways a few more feet away from the lab technician testing the pull strength of a coffin handle.

In a low voice Brenda said, "Let me see if I have this straight. You used to do all of the testing and inspecting in this plant. Over the past several years you phased out supplier inspection, incoming inspection, final inspection, and sorting/reworking jobs."

"That's about it in a nutshell," Bob replied.

"What happened to all of the inspectors?"

Bob smiled and pointed toward the offices next to the testing lab. "Come on, I'll show you where those people are today. All but three of them are still here ten years later."

Brenda quickly noted the low turnover rate. She regularly had 20 percent of her staff leave every year. Bob turned and marched into the office area. Modern office cubicles were organized in the center of the room. Near the walls were a few computers, a pen-plotter, a laser printer, and a facsimile machine. It looked as if the room was built for twenty people, but only five or six seemed to be present.

Bob moved immediately to a cubicle where a young man was sorting through stacks of papers. On his desk were several pens and pencils, a hand calculator, and a very large glass of iced tea.

"This is Hal Stanton, our quality planner," beamed Bob.

"Pleased to meet you," said Brenda as she reflexively shook his hand.

"Hal, why don't you tell Brenda what you do for a living?"

"Besides keeping you a very happy person, Bob?" responded Hal as both he and Bob broke out in an honest laugh.

"Seriously," continued Hal, as he motioned for Brenda to have a seat, "I am in charge of planning the activities of the quality assurance department. Officially, I am the representative of the quality assurance department at the strategic management meetings."

"Is that the continuous improvement team Mr. Headly told me about?" asked Brenda.

"Yes," replied Hal, "that's the same group. We meet monthly to discuss the strategic plan. For every goal we have set for the company, we ask how it relates to our quality goals. Usually, we concentrate only on this year's goals and just sketch out a few years into the future."

"Sort of our version of a five-year plan," Bob added.

Hal glanced an acknowledgment. "These reports I'm wading through today are the results of the quality audits for the month. I'm comparing the performance of the company against the goals and objectives we have stated in our strategic plan. Here, let me show you an example.

"Last year we decided that all trim pieces should be free of visual defects. When we stated that goal we measured an average of thirty-seven visual defects per every one hundred parts. That's an average for the 134 different trim pieces we produce. By this month, our goal was to have that average down to less than five visual defects per one hundred parts. These audits from production indicate that we have met the goal, but just barely.

"What I'm doing now is comparing suggestions made by the various work teams on how we can further reduce the number of defects. I will summarize these and their merits for presentation to the committee. If they like some of the ideas, they will pass approval back down to the teams."

"How do you determine the merit of the ideas?" asked Brenda.

Hal replied, "I've been trained to analyze the effectiveness of prevention methods based on historic data of similar situations. When I see a suggestion that is based on documented and successful methods, and when the team has formed the idea based on information they have been collecting, I give the idea high marks."

Brenda was impressed. Imagine, she thought, a person dedicated to planning and analyzing the course of improvement for the company. There was no such job description in her department. She made some notes. Then an unrelated question occurred to her. "What did you do before this job?"

"I was one of the incoming inspectors."

Brenda thanked Hal for his time, and she followed Bob across the room as he intercepted a woman heading out the door. "Ethel," he cried. "There's someone here I want you to meet."

The woman turned and examined Brenda very closely. Then she stuck out a hand and said, "Hi, I'm Ethel Campbell, the statistical analyst. Who might you be?"

"I'm Brenda Patterson. I'm the quality manager at ROB, Incorporated. Bob's giving me a tour of the plant."

"And why are you interested in us?"

Brenda was struck by the amount of caution Ethel was displaying.

Perhaps this was the way she always was, or maybe there was something about herself that put her on the defensive.

"Ethel, if you've got a minute, can you tell Brenda a little bit about your job?" Bob asked.

Ethel set down the blueprints she had been carrying. "I'm the company's statistical consultant. If anybody working here or any of our suppliers has a question concerning the use of a statistical method, I'm the person they call."

Ethel paused to see if Brenda would respond. She didn't, so Ethel continued. "About 60 percent of my time is spent with the work teams in the production area. They are forever asking me to show them a new method or to explain the best way to analyze the data they collect."

She picked up the blueprints she had been carrying a moment ago. "These are the prints for a plaque we produce and plate with gold. The guys in the plating area want to know a good way to sample a piece to measure the average thickness of the gold. If they can plate thinner without creating voids, they can potentially save the company tens of thousands of dollars a year.

"I'm going to recommend that they test a single piece by cross-sectioning it on a jeweler's saw and finding where the gold is normally the thinnest. Then they can make a few quick measurements at those points. You see, it's not the average thickness they should worry about." Ethel moved a few inches closer to Brenda. "It's the thickness of the minimum they should monitor."

"I see," Brenda replied. Ethel doubted that she did.

"Another thing they're going to have to do is invest in an ultrasonic thickness gauge or some other nondestructive method for taking the measurements. Right now they're using a probe that pierces the gold to measure its depth. That's so outdated, it isn't even funny. Somebody should be giving that team the equipment they need."

Ethel was definitely opinionated, Brenda thought.

"I've got to get out to that team. It was nice talking with you, Brenda."

With that Ethel swept out of the room and was gone. Bob shook his head in understanding. Brenda was struck by the abruptness of Ethel's style. It was a good thing that she didn't work for her at ROB.

"Ethel's quite a character," remarked Bob. "She used to be in the government before deregulation forced her out. She started here as a final inspection supervisor. In fact, she was here three years before I found out from personnel that she had a master's degree in statistics."

"You're kidding," Brenda said.

"Nope, she also has a PhD in economics. Terribly bright woman, but wants people to like her for what she is, not what she knows. And she obviously has no time for people who don't know something."

Brenda wasn't sure if she had just been insulted. However, she did feel that twinge of inadequacy that had been her near-constant companion all of her life.

"Stan, can you spare us a moment?" Bob called at the office cubicles.

"I guess," replied a voice from somewhere inside.

Bob turned to Brenda and whispered, "Here's a more interesting person."

From behind one of the cubicles walked a short man in his late fifties. His face was beaming and his stride bright. "Stan's the name, experiment's the game." He shook Brenda's hand briskly.

"Glad to meet you," Brenda replied.

"Stan's our Taguchi man."

"Your what?"

Stan piped up, "I run experiments on our industrial processes based on a method originated by Dr. Taguchi in Japan."

"How interesting," Brenda observed.

"Stan also traces problems with production or quality. And, just to keep him busy, he tracks the quality of vendor goods," Bob added.

"How do you do all of that in a single day?" Brenda asked.

"It's real easy for the vendor goods. I have the receiving people enter what we get and who sent it. If anything goes wrong, it's registered in the computer. Also, any quality audit information is also entered. I have an artificial intelligence program set up to monitor the whole situation and alert me if anything unusual occurs."

Brenda was impressed, but since she shied away from computers as a rule, she didn't ask Stan to see his computer.

"The problem solving," continued Stan, "is also a snap. I meet with the work teams after they have identified the exact problem and its possible causes. A simple test and I can usually pinpoint the problem. Otherwise, a short experiment and we are done."

Bob said, "Stan still has time to watch his afternoon movie, right Stan?"

"Yep," replied Stan proudly.

Before Brenda could ask, Bob explained. "Stan eats his lunch at his desk and watches an hour of some classic film. I think he has seen over four hundred films since he started working for us."

"Nice to meet you Brenda, but I gotta go. Bogart's on in ten minutes," said Stan as he shook her hand again. He turned and scurried back into the cubicles.

"Quite an interesting staff you have here Bob." There was a trace of sarcasm in Brenda's voice.

"Thanks. I like them too," Bob replied.

Bob looked at his watch and then gestured toward the open door. "I'd better be getting you back to Mr. Headly soon. I've got a couple of more people you should meet but we can see them at work in the production area."

With that the two strolled out of the office area and back into the production area. This time Bob headed straight for the small room constructed in the center of the plant. He had avoided it on their brief tour of the plant earlier that morning. This time, however, he walked right up to the small structure and peeked in the door before motioning for Brenda to enter.

When she stepped through the door she was surprised to find about ten people turned around in their chairs looking at her. As soon as Bob closed the door behind them the people in the room turned back to face the woman at the front of the room.

"All right, I think we have just about exhausted our time today. Why don't we put this to a vote? Gary, pass out some blank pieces of paper and everyone write down your choice for which problem you want to attack first."

As a man in a blue work shirt passed out small slips of paper, Brenda took note of the flip chart at the front of the room that listed several topics.

> Plating problems
> Burrs on the parts
> Cracks in the finish
> Missing screws
> Scratches

There were several other items, but these had been crossed out. A slip of paper was filled out by each person. The woman collected these and began to tabulate the results.

"Well, it looks like we really didn't have to discuss this so much. Burrs seem to be the overwhelming choice of the group. Good. Now, make sure that you continue to track how often you see burrs on the parts. When we meet next week, we will use this information to set some targets. Good luck, and good hunting."

Instinctively, the group rose and filed silently out of the room. No one gave as much as a glance at Brenda or Bob. The woman followed the group to the back of the room and smiled at Bob.

"Did you bring me a visitor today?"

"Yes, this is Brenda Patterson. She's the quality manager over at ROB."

Brenda went through the usual rituals of greeting. Then Bob began to explain the women's role in the quality assurance department.

"Lori here is in charge of facilitating the work teams on the floor. She trains new teams in problem-solving methods then shepherds them through their first few problems."

Lori added, "This group is made up of new employees hired to run the automotive door handle production line we just added."

Brenda turned to Bob in surprise. "Automotive? I didn't know you supplied the auto industry."

"We just started. Mr. Headly figured that there was very little difference in making a handle, whether it's for a coffin or a car. So, we went for it." Bob turned toward Lori. "Why don't you tell Brenda about our work team program."

"You see," began Lori, "seven years ago we struck a deal with production. We would remove all floor inspectors from the production area if they agreed to take on the job themselves. In turn, they also had to use quality assurance as auditors and consultants. Thus, the production department took over the job of quality control, and we took on the job of quality assurance."

"What's the difference?" Brenda asked.

"As quality assurance, we monitor the suppliers and the customer needs. We pass this information on to the departments that need it. In the production area, we audit the accuracy of the monitoring system the production people developed. In constrast, the production department monitors the quality of the product as it's being produced. Their monitoring system involves the machine operators inspecting the process and the product. In other words, they have the physical control of the quality of the parts."

"So, you're a service organization, and the production people are pure manufacturing, including the responsibility of quality control?" Brenda asked.

"Exactly," Lori replied.

"We've got to run, Lori. Thanks. I've got to get Brenda back to the front office in the next ten minutes." And with that, Bob pulled on Brenda's arm to lead her back out onto the production floor. "We have to move quickly to catch John while he's still on site."

Bob's stride was much quicker now, and Brenda had to struggle to keep up with him. Soon, Brenda could see that Bob was honing in on an office near the point where they had started. Through the glass window of one office she could see a group of men talking. Bob went straight for that office and entered a door that separated a hallway from the plant.

Once inside of the hallway Bob came to a halt in front of the door marked PERSONNEL. Bob paced nervously in front of the door as he stared at the carpet. "I want to catch John for you, because he is so rarely at the plant."

Brenda settled on leaning against the wall while they waited. They didn't have to wait more than a minute. A tall man came out of the door and looked at Bob. "Waiting for John, Bob?"

"Yeah, will he be out soon?"

"He's right behind me."

Then a young man in his mid-twenties emerged. He glanced at the two people standing in the hall. "Oh, oh," he said.

"Hi, John," said Bob. "If you got a minute I want to introduce you to Brenda Patterson, from ROB, Incorporated.

With that remark John noticeably relaxed. "Oh, good. I was worried that this young lady might be from accounting. I'm about two months behind in my reimbursement reports."

John shook Brenda's hand warmly. "Has Bob told you that I'm in charge of personnel recruiting?"

"No, he hasn't. Don't you work for quality assurance?"

"I do, but what I do for a living is visit high schools and colleges looking for the type of people we want to work at this company. People with some quality skills and a good technical background. I also help interview people from other plants who apply here."

"And, on your days off. . ." prompted Bob.

"I also train all new employees in our quality methods. You know, things like problem-solving skills, SPC, and using measuring gauges."

"I'm impressed. How long have you been doing this?" Brenda asked.

"Two years now."

Bob gestured toward his wristwatch. "It was nice meeting you, but we have to get back to Mr. Headly's office," Brenda said.

"A pleasure to meet you." John again shook Brenda's hand.

Bob and Brenda headed for a set of steps leading to the second floor as John disappeared around a nearby corner. Halfway up the steps Brenda grabbed onto Bob's arm and brought him to a halt.

"Let me see if I have this straight," she began. "You used to have the traditional test and measurement functions. Several years ago you decided that most of these should be handled by production. You then transformed the quality control department into a quality assurance team. They consult, audit, advise, train, monitor, and test the quality of the product."

"Yes," responded Bob. "But they only do this in cooperation with other people in the plant. Let me give you an example. We didn't meet the quality engineer today but he works in engineering. He's not on my payroll or even on my staff roster. Instead, he's one of the engineers the company has trained to constantly check for quality in the designs and manufacturing plans. He plays the devil's advocate for quality concerns.

"He also doesn't work alone. He consults with the product liability and the market research people to stay in touch with the quality issues normally thought to be outside the realm of engineering. He figures that if he can help design a product or process that will prevent problems for these people, then he's only doing his job."

"I've never seen a quality department run like this one," Brenda stated.

"Nor I," smiled Bob. "But, this is all paying off for the company. I've got a team of auditors that traces every improvement and problem to an exact dollar amount it either saves or costs the company. When we take that information up to top management they sit up and listen.

"I told them an important story a long time ago about the difference between quality control and quality assurance. I told them that a quality control department only played police officer and thus was only an additional cost to the company. Then I told them that somebody assuring the quality of a product usually found and fixed chronic production problems. I said that if we reduced the cost of making something by $20,000, we could add the amount to the bottom line, directly.

"Then as a kicker, I asked them to calculate how much more they would have to sell in the field to increase their profits by $20,000. They figured $400,000. I didn't have to justify the change at all after that."

Bob turned and continued up the steps. Brenda paused on the landing for a moment lost in thought. Then she bounded up the steps behind Bob, taking two stairs at a time.

A few minutes later Brenda, Bob, Carla, and Breton were in Headly's office. The visitors from ROB, Incorporated thanked their hosts and exchanged business cards. Smiles and handshakes were also exchanged. The visitors were just beginning to digest the information they had obtained in a single morning.

Later, as they rode back to their own plant in silence, Mead suddenly asked, "Anyone for lunch?"

Brenda and Breton exchanged glances and Breton finally replied, "Sure."

"My treat," Mead said. This was a very different Mead to Breton and Brenda. Neither could remember Mead taking anyone except his sales staff to lunch.

Two hours later, Mead returned to ROB, and parted from his two managers. He climbed the steps to his second floor office. He noticed the way he had to catch his breath at the top of the steps and made a mental note to start exercising again.

Sally wasn't at her desk when he turned the corner, so he strolled right into his office. His ex-wife was sitting in his chair.

"What are you doing here?"

"Robert, I'm getting married."

"What?" shouted Mead, while another voice inside his head said, thank God.

CHAPTER 4

Making Measurements

The following Monday the top managers of ROB, Incorporated were in Mead's office. Brenda Patterson positioned herself next to Lee Enfield. Breton Rhodes was sitting near Anna Fitzhugh. Frank Graves and Leon Marsden sat between the two groups.

Mead quickly called the meeting to order and began to ask each attendee to report on the assignment he or she had been given. Frank Graves began with a comment that he had investigated adding standard quality expenses to the cost accounting system. He estimated that his people should have some estimates available by the end of the month.

Lee Enfield produced a written report for the group on how the engineering department could track and control blueprints better. He also outlined his investigation into the possibility of cooperative visits between his engineers and customers' assembly plants. Lee was obviously excited by this possibility. It would give his engineers a chance to see the exact problems customers were having with their products.

Anna presented a list of training sources the company could contact. She also had some information on state grants that would pay for at least half of any training they scheduled. This included special testing to see which workers were deficient in reading and math. Anna recommended basic training in reading and math skills for these workers. Mead instructed her to begin the screening process and to schedule statistical process control training to follow.

Breton and Brenda both objected but were cut short by Mead. He drew out a letter from his top drawer. "Ford Motor Company has written to me and asked when they can inspect our SPC system. I suggest we develop one as soon as possible."

There was no point in arguing now. Everyone knew that Ford could only be stalled a few months at best. They would have to hurry to get an SPC system into place.

Brenda and Breton delivered their reports in kind. This was followed with a spirited discussion about which project should get priority. Mead sat back and let his managers argue for ten minutes. Then he interrupted.

"That's enough discussion. We have all heard the arguments for and against each project. In truth, all of these projects will have to be implemented within six months. I suggest that we vote on which one to start with."

The room was filled with a confused silence for a moment. Vote? Nobody had ever asked the managers' opinions in public before, why would they be voting now?

Sally passed a slip of paper with the projects listed in alphabetical order to each person. Everyone had to rank the priority of the projects from highest to lowest. A few minutes later, Sally collected the slips and began calculating the highest priority projects.

Meanwhile, Mead said, "While we are waiting for the count I should tell you that I have hired a consultant to come into the plant and teach the managers group problem-solving skills. Specifically, she will be teaching us how to cooperate as managers. Any questions?"

More silence.

"Her name is Lynn Spree. She has taught the managers at many of our customers' companies. I thought it would be a good idea to have a management decision system that closely matches theirs."

Mead paused, and then he lowered his voice. "Besides, it will give us a chance to quiz her on what our customers are planning." Grins broke out around the room. It was one thing to be forced into a seminar; it was quite another to get the chance to play spy.

"I have the results," Sally declared.

"Good," said Mead. "Let's hear them."

"The top vote getter was the screening and training of workers. Second place was a complete examination of our measurement gauges. Third was the tracking of blueprints."

"Excellent," declared Mead. "Breton, you and Anna work together to schedule the testing and training."

"But," interrupted Breton, "what about the production schedule?"

"If necessary," said Mead slowly, "pay the people overtime."

Breton visibly fell back in his chair. For all of the time he had been at ROB, the watchword had been NO OVERTIME. Now, the rules were changing just a little too fast. Breton made a note to schedule an appointment alone with Mead to discuss these changes.

"Brenda," continued Mead. "You and Lee work together on the gauge project. Lee, I believe that you can handle the blueprint tracking project." Lee nodded in agreement as he scribbled notes onto his yellow pad.

Mead looked over at Frank. For a moment he was confused. The accounting department didn't fit in neatly with any of these projects. Finally he said, "Frank, you report back to us in two weeks on the new estimates for quality-related costs. Don't worry if they're not all complete, just tell us what you've found out so far.

"Well, any questions? If not, you all have your assignments. We will meet here briefly next Monday for an update. Brenda and Breton, can you stay for a moment?"

The others shuffled out of the room. Nobody was talking. Instead they were all trying to mentally schedule time to complete their tasks. Brenda and Breton sat uncomfortably across the room from one another.

Mead closed his door and said, "We are all going to class."

The Class

Brenda turned down Lyon Street and then left at Division Avenue. She had missed the turn for the junior college parking ramp for the second time. She swore out loud and hit the steering wheel of her 1974 Maverick. She hated downtown and she couldn't understand why Mead felt she needed to take a class on quality assurance.

"This class is different from anything you have taken before," Mead had explained last Monday. "I want the three of us to be up to date on the latest issues in the quality field."

Brenda accelerated up Fountain Street and made a quick left two blocks later. She had found an entrance to the ramp at last. She quietly hoped that finding the classroom would be much easier.

Breton was already in the classroom a good ten minutes before the hour. He wanted to talk to the instructor if he or she came in early. Little did he know that Mead was downstairs in the instructor's office introducing himself.

Students began drifting into the room. Most carried cups of coffee and had pencils stuck behind their ears. Breton noticed immediately that most of the class was at least as old as he was. In fact, nobody seemed to be what he thought was junior college age. Instead, most of these people seemed to be factory employees.

Brenda came into the room out of breath and plopped down into a chair next to Breton. "I hate parking downtown."

Breton mumbled a reply but he could tell that Brenda wasn't really listening to him.

At exactly seven o'clock, the instructor, Jack King, came into the room. Close behind him was Mead who took a seat on the other side of Breton. Jack King set his briefcase on the table at the front of the classroom, opened it and said, "Welcome to Quality Assurance. If you *parlez vous francais*, you want the room next door."

A brief chuckle came from a few students.

"I'm Jack King, but just call me Jack." Jack pulled a stuffed teddy bear dressed in a three-piece suit from his briefcase. "And, this is Teddy." Jack pulled a string on the bear and it barked out, "You're the best!"

The three ROB students were equally shocked by this display. Jack continued, "Teddy will be playing the part of management in our lectures."

A louder chuckle could now be heard among the students. Both Brenda and Breton were beginning to have serious doubts about this instructor. What kind of an expert on quality assurance travels with a teddy bear?

Before they could answer that question, Jack began writing on the blackboard. "Bust out your pencils and papers, because what I say for the next five minutes is vital to the entire class."

A rustling noise behind her prompted Brenda to pull out her yellow pad and pen. Breton and Mead were already writing.

"Quality assurance," began Jack, "should be a profit center for any company. It should not be a police force or an inspection squad. In fact, in a perfect company there would be no quality department." Jack turned back toward the students. "Now, if you give me sixteen weeks, I'll prove to you why this is so. When we are done you will have enough knowledge to out-compete the majority of American companies. Your company will be profitable, and you will be successful. That was your cue. Repeat after me, I will be successful."

"I will be successful," chanted the class.

"Good."

Brenda, Breton, and Mead all had the same thought: This is going to be an unusual class.

For the next several minutes Jack took attendance and reviewed the outline of the course. There were the usual questions about break times and tests. Finally, Jack launched into his lecture.

"Let's begin with measuring things. Most classes in quality assurance start with theory and management systems. We're going to talk about those last because they are the least important. What's important today is the fundamentals of quality assurance. Measurement is the first and most fundamental activity in the world of quality. There are carvings from ancient Egypt that show people double-checking the quality of another's work.

"The whole point of QA is to quantify the qualities of a product."

Jack turned to the board and wrote, *Measurement = to quantify the qualities of a product.* He then drew a strangely shaped metal object out of his briefcase.

"This is the housing for a water pump on a small car. A traditional job for a quality department would be to measure the dimensions of the part and compare the results to the tolerances on a blueprint. Today, you would also check its weld strength and its resistance to salt spray. All of these activities involve measurements."

Next, he drew a small black chip from his briefcase. "This is the memory chip used on a cruise missile." He glanced outside the door a moment and lowered his voice. "Don't ask me where I got it." More laughter.

"To measure this chip we would pass electrical pulses through it and measure the logic abilities. Again, a measurement function. The idea is to see how close a part conforms to the specifications it has been given." He turned back to the board and added, *Metrology = the science of measurement.*

"Metrology is a science because it uses internationally recognized standards with which to make measurements. The problem is that these standards are usually kept in a central location within the country. In America, the standards are maintained by NIST. Therefore, we cannot get direct access to these standards. How do you suppose we can get access?"

There was a short but silent pause. Jack said, "This is the part where you say, I don't know."

"I don't know," chimed in a few students.

"Thank you. Well, I'll tell you how. Certified measurements labs around the country send their measuring standards to NIST to have them certified. You as a company then hire these labs to calibrate your measuring equipment. If you are a supplier to the government or the automotive industry, then you are required to show that a certified lab calibrates all of your measuring gauges."

Brenda was now taking notes. She knew that only the gauges used in the quality lab were certified by a local measurement lab. The gauges used in the production area were another matter.

Jack was adding a third note to the board, *Traceability = the documentation of calibration that leads back to the National Institute of Standards and Technologies (NIST).*

"Now, let's talk about individual types of measurement gauges and their proper use." Jack reached into his briefcase again and jerked out a dial caliper. The caliper seemed to slip out of his hands and fly across the room, ricochetting off of two walls before crashing on the floor.

"Whoops!" said Jack. The gasps from the class were audible. "Don't worry," he quickly added. "That's a broken pair from last year. I just want to emphasize how not to treat a measurement device." Several students muttered statements of relief.

He then drew out a wooden box and carefully placed it on his desk. After opening the top, he withdrew a shining new dial caliper. He handled it as if it were a fine watch, delicate yet important. "This," he said, "is the respect you must give a measuring instrument."

From his briefcase he took out a small bag of steel parts and scattered them on the desk. He picked up the first and measured its length by closing the jaws of the caliper on the part.

"This is 0.503 inches long," he declared. "I would guess that the intent of the manufacturer was to make this part a half an inch long.

"Before we are done tonight, we are going down to the measurement lab on the first floor and try measuring some things with several different instruments. But first I want to talk about gauge performance. Is the measurement I took just now accurate?"

"I don't know," Breton spoke up. Brenda shot him a quick glance.

"Very good," replied the instructor. Breton was already trying to score points in class. "Not only don't you know, but neither do I. In fact, if we look at what defines gauge performance, we may never really know the exact size of this part."

Jack turned back toward the blackboard and erased his previous notes. He listed four topics.

> 1. Resolution
> 2. Accuracy
> 3. Repeatability
> 4. Reproducibility

"These are the traditional methods for describing how well a measurement gauge performs," he said. "Resolution is the limit of where a measuring tool can detect a change in the size of the part. In other words, if I began to change the length of this part, how much must it change before the caliper detects the difference? With this caliper I have run tests that show it will detect as little as a five ten thousandths of an inch of change. Therefore, we say that it has a resolution of 0.0005 inches.

"Accuracy is the agreement between what the gauge reads and the actual size of a known standard. Let me show you how that works."

Jack reached into his coat pockets and drew out a pair of cotton gloves. He slipped these on and reached into his pants pocket for his keys. With a small brass key he opened the top drawer of his desk and drew out a large flat walnut box. He set the box onto the desk gently and opened the lid. He then turned the box toward the class.

Inside were eighty-one silvery bars of metal. Each bar was of equal height and length, but of different widths. "These are eighty-one steel alloy gauge blocks, grade two. Some of the smaller blocks cost more to buy than a comparable piece of solid gold."

A low whistle came from somewhere in the back of the room. Brenda was impressed. Her department had a set of gauge blocks, but that set had only nine blocks and they didn't look as impressive as these.

Jack reached into the box with a gloved hand and drew out the one-inch standard. "This is the one-inch block. It is certified and traceable back to the national standards. At room temperature, this block is within a ten thousandth of an inch of one inch."

Jack lifted the calipers in his other hand and gently clamped the jaws of the gauge around the block. "If I repeatedly measure this standard, what should my average reading be?"

"One inch," Brenda stated.

"Very good. The accuracy of this caliper is determined by how closely it measures a known standard, on average."

Jack placed the calipers on the desk. He then drew out a bottle of alcohol from a bottom drawer. He dabbed a cotton cloth with the liquid and gently rubbed the block before putting it back in the case.

"Why are you being so careful with those blocks?" asked a student seated behind Mead.

"A fingerprint is thick enough to be detected by some measuring instruments. In fact, for precison grinding shops that work in millionths of an inch, a fingerprint can be thicker than the tolerance range of the parts they make. Also, if I should drop that block even a small distance onto a hard surface, it will mushroom the shape of the block enough to require its replacement.

"How many of you work at companies that have a surface plate? You know, that large marble table in the measurement lab where you can measure from a flat surface." Several hands went up.

"You don't know the number of times I have visited a plant and found that plate covered with dust and dirt. When that happens, you can't be sure of its flatness, and the accuracy suffers."

Brenda shuddered as she remembered leaving the plant to go to class that night. As she said her good-byes to the second shift inspectors, they were having their lunch on the surface plate. She made another note on her pad.

"Does everyone understand resolution and accuracy? That's what is meant by calibrating a measuring gauge. We determine its power of resolution, and we check its accuracy.

"That's all well and fine, but in industry today there are two more checks that have to be made on all measuring devices. The first is called repeatability." Jack pointed to the words already written on the board.

"Remember how I measured this steel part before, and found it was 0.503 inches long?" Several heads nodded in agreement. "Who wants to bet me now that if I remeasure this same part for length that I will get the exact same reading?"

The room remained silent. "What's the matter? Doesn't anyone trust the accuracy of the gauge? I'll tell you what, I'll bet one hundred dollars."

More silence.

"It seems that you know about repeatability already. Repeatability is the ability of the gauge to successfully obtain identical readings measuring the same part. We find it by measuring this part over and over. Then we look at the range of readings we got for the same dimension."

Jack proceeded to measure the small part and then called out, "0.501 inches." He measured again. "0.502 inches," he declared.

"Can you see what's happening?" he asked. "It's the same part, dimension, and gauge, but the readings are a little different each time. We have a discrepancy of 0.002 inches after only three readings. That's the repeatability of the gauge.

"Later in the course we will learn how to do a formal repeatability study. When that happens, we will learn to compare the range of differences against the tolerance for the dimension we are checking. This will end up being a percentage repeatability.

"Our final measure of gauge performance is reproducibility. I have been measuring this part over and over. Who wants to bet me that if I give the gauge to Mr. Mead here, that he will get the same readings I got?"

A few cries of "no way" came from the class as several people shifted in their chairs and shook their heads.

"Cowards," cried Jack, as he handed the part and the calipers to Mead. "Go ahead, show them that they have to trust the operators of the gauge."

Mead took the part and locked the jaws of the caliper across its length. He fumbled a little with the part, revealing that he wasn't used to doing manual labor. Brenda leaned over to help him read off the measurement. "0.499 inches," she stated.

Laughter broke out in the class.

"All right, all right," said Jack. "Let's calm down and look at what we have learned. This caliper has been calibrated to measure accurately. I have tested it to find that it has a pretty good resolution. However, when we tried to measure real parts with it, the readings were different. Using a different operator only made things worse.

"You see, calibration is a laboratory procedure. It only tells you whether the gauge is working properly. Repeatability and reproducibility, on the other hand, show us how well the gauge works in the real world. Therefore, we need to know the performance of a measuring gauge in all of these dimensions to know whether the data we collect are good.

"Speaking of data, that's what we will discuss after our first break. Now the rules for the break are simple. Everybody jumps up, runs out of the room, smokes cigarettes like mad, downs several cups of coffee, and then gets back here by ten after. Any questions?"

"Are those really the rules?" Breton asked.

"No. We had a regular set of rules, but everyone does this anyway so we might as well make the chaos part of the rule. Class dismissed."

Suddenly several students jumped up at the same time and headed for the door. By the time the three ROB students reached the break room down the hall, many of the students were puffing on cigarettes as they dumped lose change into the coffee machine.

Breton turned to Brenda as they entered the break room. "This is one bizarre class," he said.

"But," she added, "you're learning, aren't you?"

Score one for Brenda. Several minutes later the class was settling back into seats waiting for the second half to begin. They didn't have to wait long.

"Questions?" barked out Jack. Several students wanted clarification on the definitions of gauge performance. One person in the back of the room asked about repeatability and reproducibility studies. Jack answered them politely.

Finally, Jack asked his own question. "Isn't anyone going to ask how we prevent some of the sources of error we have been discussing?"

The room was silent. "I'll wait," said Jack.

After a few more moments of silence Breton said, "Okay. How do we prevent some of these problems?"

"I'm glad you asked," replied Jack. He then turned toward the board and began writing and talking at the same time.

"The most important preventive measure you can take as a company is to create and maintain a thorough gauge calibration program." This statement obviously cued Mead, for he began rapidly writing in his leather-bound notebook. Jack continued without pausing.

"Such a program would track the location and use of every gauge. It would assign gauges to specific jobs in the plant so that the same gauge is measuring the same parts every day. On each gauge would be a sticker indicating when it was time for calibration of the instrument." Brenda recalled seeing such stickers on the measurement gauges at the Urn Corporation.

"At least once a year, all measurement gauges would be calibrated by a lab that was certified by NIST. Myself, I recommend at least twice a year. In fact, when you buy measuring equipment, ask the supplier to provide regular calibration as part of the contract.

"In daily use, keep your gauge blocks and other standards handy so that each gauge can be checked for accuracy before it is assigned to a job.

This is the way that you will detect broken gauges or gauges that have experienced other problems."

Jack wrote a large number two on the board and continued. "The next preventive action is to train your operators in the proper use of measurement gauges. Don't just teach them how to read the gauge. Teach them about care and maintenance of these tools. I will show you some of the common mistakes people make with measurement equipment in the lab a little later tonight.

"The third preventive measure is to have written procedures for how a measurement is to be taken. Here John, think fast," Jack called out as he tossed one of the parts on his desk to a student behind Breton.

"How would you measure the diameter of that part? High point to high point? Low point to low point? Its circularity?"

"Well," began John, "actually any of those are possible procedures. You could also take the average diameter after taking two readings at right angles."

"Very good, John," Jack beamed. He then looked at the rest of the class. "Without a written procedure specifying the exact way to measure that part, every operator in your plant will probably come up with his or her own method. The result is a jumble of data.

"Don't just write and distribute the procedures, either. Make sure that they become part of your gauge-use training. And every year, go around and audit the procedures. Make sure that they are being followed and that they really get the measurements you need.

"Another good thing to do is to audit the measurement gauges themselves once a year. You have to assure that the right gauge has been assigned to the jobs currently in production. A lot of times you will assign a micrometer with a resolution of a ten thousandth of an inch to a job, but a few months later the gauge is lost and the guys are using steel rulers.

"Gauge repeatability and reproducibility studies are other ways of knowing if you have the right gauge for the right job. Some people call these R&R studies for short. Like I explained before, they measure the error of the gauge in the real world. We'll learn how to do these studies later.

"Of course, if you really want to get serious about measurement gauges, you can keep control charts for the gauges. These will monitor the variation in measurements a gauge records over time. If the variation starts to drift or increase, you will be able to detect it before you lose valuable data from gauge inaccuracy."

Jack paused when he noticed everyone's head bent over their note pads as their hands scribbled like mad. He waited until everyone looked up in anticipation of what he was going to say next.

"Here's one important rule about measurement equipment I want to see everyone write down. Always use a ten to one ratio of gauge resolution to tolerance units." He paused so that everyone could record his statement.

"What that means is that if your part blueprint states tolerance in hundredths of an inch, use a gauge that measures in thousandths of an inch. If the tolerance is in thousandths of an inch, use a gauge that measures in ten thousandths of an inch.

"I rememember going to a plant on the northwest end of town that was cutting metal bars. The blueprint said these bars had to be twelve inches long, plus or minus two hundredths of an inch. These guys were measuring the bars with tape measures."

"Sheesh!" explained a lone student near the front of the room.

"Now at most, a tape rule can distinguish differences of a sixteenth of an inch. In addition, when you go home tonight, take out your tape ruler and grab that little metal hook at the end of it and pull. It probably moves back and forth a little, right? Well, that motion is probably farther than the tolerance range on most blueprints. Needless to say, this company was not doing well at getting accurate measurements."

A brief outburst of laughter followed. Then a student near the door asked, "Which type of gauge would you recommend for measuring bars like those?"

"You have a couple of choices. There are calipers that can open to over a foot wide. There is also the possibility of building a fixture that can hold the part. At one end would be a dial gauge that would instantly read off how many thousandths of an inch you are off target from twelve inches."

The inquiring student looked a little confused.

"I'll show you such a gauge downstairs. If we don't have other questions, let's head down to the second basement. Go to the elevator, press SUB 2, and look for Room 8. I'll meet you there in five minutes."

The room had five rows of black lab tables. In one corner of the room was a large piece of marble on a steel frame. Brenda recognized it as a surface plate. Jack was in an opposite corner digging through an unlocked metal cabinet.

Breton made a point of sitting next to Brenda. He knew very little about proper gauge usage and he wanted to be near the more experienced Brenda. Jack started by passing out to each table a small pile of plastic and metal parts. Next, he gave each group of two students a pair of six-inch calipers.

Brenda picked up a pair and slowly opened the jaws of the gauge while watching the dial's needle swinging around wildly. Where the movable jaw stopped would indicate the measurement in inches and tenths of an inch. The needle on the dial would read off the hundredths of an inch.

Jack demonstrated to the class how to read the caliper and how to measure parts properly. He emphasized the need to stay parallel and perpendicular to the part when measuring. To reinforce his point, he deliberately tilted the caliper against the part. His new measurement reading was many hundredths of an inch off of the first reading. Several students made some notes.

As Breton and Brenda began to work through the first exercise of checking several dimensions and recording them, Brenda noticed that Breton was unsure of how the gauge worked. She suspected that Breton was staying close by to learn as much as he could about measurement procedures. She made a mental note to watch her step around Breton.

For the next exercise, each student received a six-inch steel ruler. With it they learned how to take simple measurements in fractional units. Many students felt bogged down in this exercise as they tried to count out the number of sixteenths on the scale. Jack looked amused at their frustration.

As the final part of this exercise, he had the students try to measure with their rulers, the diameters of the steel parts he had been using. This demonstration of the wrong measurement gauge for the job was quickly realized. The students had great difficulties determining where to start and stop measuring. Jack laughed.

The third exercise involved the use of one-inch micrometers. These were more difficult to learn than the calipers. The short probe could be easily screwed down onto a part and a slip clutch prevented over-tightening. After that, though, there was the job of trying to read the correct measurement by first looking at the markings on the stem of the gauge and then adding the results of the markings on the handle.

Jack told the class to practice using the micrometers until break time. He asked if any student had used them before. Several hands went up. Jack encouraged the other students to work with the more experienced members of the class. Brenda's hand had gone up but not Breton's.

It took Brenda three tries to get Breton to understand how to read the markings on the handle of the micrometer. When he did learn how he quickly measured several pieces successfully. Brenda was impressed.

Break time came and students rushed out of the room in search of rest rooms, cigarettes, and coffee. A few stayed behind to experiment with the gauges they had already learned. Ten minutes later, with only half of the class back, Jack began the next exercise.

"Aren't you going to wait for the others?" asked a student in the front row of tables.

"Nope. This is how they will learn to come back from a break on time."

Over the next few minutes the rest of the class came sauntering back into the classroom. As each student saw the others working with a new gauge, they quickly assumed their chairs and began measuring again.

The new gauge was a depth micrometer. This particular device could measure up to two inches in depth. A large perpendicular steel flat was laid across a hole on a part, and the depth probe was slowly screwed into place. Again, the readings had to be taken from the shaft and handle.

Students' progress was slow.

After about fifteen minutes of work, Jack reached into the cabinet and drew out six wooden boxes. He placed one on his table and one at the end of each row of tables.

"Here, I'll make your day with this one box. Open it." The students at the end of each row opened a box and drew out a micrometer with a large bulge on its side. In the center of the bulge was a small gray window with three blue buttons below.

"Press the first blue button on the right." Each student did and almost immediately their heads moved back in surprise.

"Twist the handle." As each student did, numbers began to flicker in the screen.

"Digital micrometers," announced Jack. "They automatically read out the exact measurement using either English or metric units." A round of applause erupted from the classroom.

"Wherever possible," continued Jack, "automate your measuring instruments. You'll find that accuracy improves because it is so much easier to take a reading with a digital gauge. In addition, if you'll look on the side of your gauge, there is a small plastic plug.

"That is an RS-232 port. You can plug a cable between this gauge and your computer. With the right software, you can have each measurement recorded by the computer. If you're too lazy for that, the gauge also has the ability to calculate several statistics based on the most recent readings you've made."

Smiles broke out around the room. Mead was still taking notes at another table. He would be on the phone tomorrow morning asking Anna to line up three possible gauge vendors.

For the remainder of the class, Jack briefly reviewed the use of some other measurement gauges. He showed how a height gauge worked on the surface plate. He also showed how he could stack gauge blocks under the height gauge to enable it to take accuracy measurements for parts taller than the gauge.

For a few minutes, each student did an exercise involving the use of a protractor. Several angles were measured. This was followed by a demonstration of a color analyzer. Jack called on a woman in the back of the room who was wearing a brightly colored dress. He asked her what color it was. "Sort of a dark red," she replied.

Jack picked up the probe of the color analyzer and held it against the sleeve of the dress. He pulled a trigger and a brief flash of light was seen. Instantly, a set of numbers appeared on the readout.

"That's the tint, hue, and reflectivity of your dress," Jack stated. Then he spoke louder so that the entire class could hear him. "If I put several of you in separate rooms and told you to select a dark red color, I would get several different answers. But, with this machine, I can define the color precisely. All of you could re-create the color exactly.

"This is the lesson of measuring. Everything we will talk about for the next fifteen weeks will require that we can quantify the meaning of quality in a part. Now that you know how to measure, we can proceed. If you want to stay and play with the gauges some more, please feel free. Otherwise, class dismissed."

No one left the room right away. Several strudents gathered around Jack asking questions. Mead was in the thick of that group. Brenda and Breton separated and floated around the room examining the different gauges. Brenda was interested in the color analyzer. Breton was more interested in the digital gauges.

Breton finally stacked his textbook on top of his note pad, put his pen in his pocket, and looked around the room. Both Brenda and Mead were gone. He picked up his stack and went out the door. He passed up the elevator in favor of the stairs. The main level of the building was only two flights up.

As he emerged into the main level hallway, Brenda was coming down the hall toward him. She looked frustrated. "Breton, where is the parking ramp in this place?"

Breton pointed to a door farther down the hall. Brenda turned and stomped down the hall in disgust. Breton laughed to himself. He hadn't expected a thank you from Brenda. Instead, he fell in behind her and followed her to the ramp. He made sure that she found her car and then went up to the blue level and his car.

"Such a strange woman," Breton said to himself as he climbed into the chilled seat of his car. "Pride before the fall," he muttered as he inserted his keys into the ignition. Ten tries later it was obvious to Breton that his battery was dead. He pushed on his light switch and noticed that it was already on. He had left the lights on for over four hours. Breton muttered an expletive series of words and headed back to the junior college.

CHAPTER 5

Inspections

Within a few weeks the character of the Monday morning meetings had changed dramatically. The managers had gone through their teamwork seminar, and the skills they had learned were beginning to show.

Anna reported that the person from community education was coming in that week to begin testing the reading and math skills of the employees.

Mead nodded and turned toward a new participant in these meetings, Harris Harrison. Harris was the union representative for the shop floor people. His blue work uniform was a sharp contrast to the suits in the room. Breton sat near him so that he could "keep an eye on him."

"Harris, I take it that the union approves of the screening," Mead said.

"Yes, we do. We interviewed the screeners and talked to several of the companies where they have done work before. As long as no disciplinary action is taken against those that test weak, we have no objections."

Breton cringed whenever Harris spoke. He usually had no problem working with the union, but Harris as a person was annoying to Breton.

"Frank," said Mead, turning toward the accountant. "Where's that cost accounting report?"

Frank drew out a stack of computer sheets and waved them in the air. "Right here. Sally has made copies of the report for each manager."

"What's the story on the cost of scrap?" Mead asked.

"It seems," began Frank, "that for every dollar in material we throw away, it's costing the company seven dollars."

"How's that again?" Breton asked.

"Well," replied Frank, "when we have to throw away a dollar of material because it does not meet specifications, we have to schedule more machine time, personnel time, extra material, and other related expenses to make a good piece to replace the bad one. In addition, we are paying people to sort out the bad material and to fill out a lot of paperwork related to scrap."

Mead stated, "I think that the bottom line of what Frank is saying is that if we focus our efforts on reducing scrap rates, we can see a substantial reduction in the cost of running this company."

The meeting went on for another half hour discussing the status of each person's tasks. Where one person was having difficulties, other members of the management team were assigned to help out. Finally, the meeting broke up and Mead asked Brenda to stay behind.

"I got a letter from our largest customer today," said Mead. "They want me to write back on how we are changing our inspection systems to meet their requirements."

Brenda drew up a chair. She could tell that this was going to take some time.

"I need to know how we currently inspect our goods and how we could change that system to meet these requirements," Mead said as he tapped a finger on a thick folder sitting on his desk.

"If you want," replied Brenda, "I can explain how it works."

"No," said Mead. "I want one of the inspectors to explain it to me. I want to know how they feel about the current system. I want to go out on the floor and be trained to be an inspector. I want to know the system inside and out."

Mead paused long enough to realize that Brenda might take this request as a slap in the face. "Your time is too valuable to follow me around teaching me about inspecting, Brenda."

The expression on Brenda's face perked up. "I have just the person to help you," she replied. Brenda was thinking about Harold Thomas. Not only was Harold their best inspector, but he was a certified quality technician. He knew the theory of inspection inside and out.

"By the way," said Mead as Brenda got up to leave, "I'm interested in learning why a company with an excellent inspection program like ours still has such high scrap rates."

"So am I," replied Brenda. "So am I."

Harold Thomas' shift began at seven o'clock every morning. Harold liked to read his *Detroit Free Press* and have breakfast before he began work. Therefore it was six o'clock when Harold arrived for work. The third shift crew would walk by the break area and rib him about being so early for work. "Can't get enough of this place, hey Harold?" they would call out to him.

Usually a well-aimed piece of his morning donut chased them off. However, this morning Harold had something that would chase everyone off for days. When he came in at six o'clock, the president of the company was already in the break area waiting for him. Mead was having a cup of coffee and was reading the *New York Times*.

"Good morning, Harold," Mead said as Harold pulled up a chair.

"Good morning, Mr. Mead. I hear that you're my student for the next few days." Harold noticed that Mead was wearing the white lab jacket of an inspector. Embroidered above his pocket where most jackets said something like BOB or AL, was MR. MEAD. Harold knew that he couldn't get too casual with this student.

After they finished their papers and breakfasts, the two men headed for the receiving area. "This is the best place to start an explanation of how an incoming inspection is done," Harold stated.

He glanced toward Mead as they walked to see if the president had any comments. Mead gestured for Harold to continue speaking.

"The idea behind an inspection is to determine whether a group of parts meets requirements. In most cases, the stuff we make or receive is grouped into units called lots. We usually look at each lot." Harold pointed at a stamping press that was rhythmically turning out parts. "Take for example that press. One shift of production from that press will receive a single lot designation.

"Now, sometimes we can look at every part made in a lot to determine if there are any bad parts, you know, parts that don't meet the requirements. But, that takes time and money. So, in most cases we sample a lot and estimate whether there are too many bad pieces. That's what's called attribute sampling."

"Attribute sampling," repeated Mead.

"Yeah," said Harold. "Come here, I'll show you how that works."

Harold made a sudden turn just before the receiving area and headed for the quality control offices. Mead followed. Harold went straight for a bookshelf over the first desk they saw as they entered the office. He thumbed through some manuals and finally drew out a thin one with a clear plastic cover. This he threw down on the desk.

"Military standard 105E," he stated.

Mead could see the emblem of the Department of Defense and the title *MIL-STD-105E* on the first page of the manual. "Of course," continued Harold, "it's called ANSI Z1.4-1981 today, but it will always be 105E to anyone who has inspected for over ten years."

Harold flipped open the manual and passed the first several pages. He finally settled on a page that had a simple-looking chart. "The big question," he began, "is how many pieces to sample from a lot. And there is also the question of how many bad pieces you can find before you say that the whole lot has to be rejected."

"So," chimed in Mead, "we're not sorting out bad pieces. Instead, we check and either accept or reject an entire lot."

"That's right. Let me give you a concrete example of how we do that." Harold reached across the desk and began going through a stack of shipping bills. He drew out one of the green sheets and laid it next to 105E.

"Here's the shipping orders for five thousand bolts we received from one of our suppliers. The entire shipment has only one lot number." Harold's finger circled the middle of the form once and then jabbed it into the paper. "Right here. ADC-1483-B3."

Next, Harold moved his finger from the shipping bill to the page he had opened in the sampling manual. "This chart tells me how many pieces to sample from a shipment of five thousand pieces. We would have to draw a sample of two hundred bolts. That sample size is coded with the letter L," he reported.

Harold turned the page and looked down another list of letters and numbers. He stopped his finger on a line beginning with the letter L. "What are we looking at here?" Mead inquired.

"This second table is the sampling plan for normal inspections. We have another table for tightened inspections. We use that one with either critical components or troublesome vendors. It requires the same sample size, but it will reject the lot much quicker than the normal plan.

"We also have a reduced inspection plan for unimportant components or vendors with excellent records. It takes a smaller sample size."

"I follow you so far," Mead replied. "What comes next?"

"On this master table we follow the L sampling plan over to the AQL for the material."

"Hold it," interrupted Mead. "What's the AQL?"

"It stands for acceptable quality level. That represents the percentage of defectives we can tolerate in our sampling strategy. For this type of part we have an AQL of 1 percent."

Mead asked, "Does that mean that the supplier is supposed to ship us no more than 1 percent defective bolts?"

"Not really," said Harold. "An AQL is really just a statistical reference point. Just because we have an AQL of 1 percent, it doesn't mean that this sampling plan will reject any shipment with more than 1 percent defective. Instead, it means over the long term the plan would accept shipments with less than 1 percent defective, 95 percent of the time."

"What about shipments with 2 or 3 percent defectives?" Mead asked.

"Well, most likely they would be rejected, but there is still a substantial chance that we would accept some of those shipments. Because we sample, there is always the chance we would be wrong."

"Okay" Mead replied. "Now you've lost me. Are you saying that we

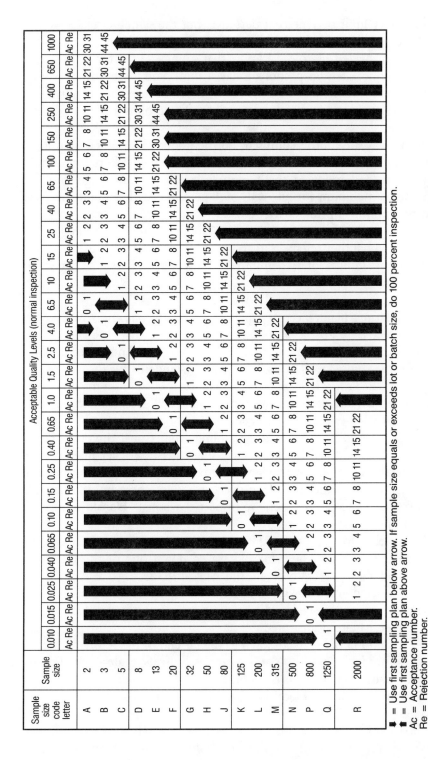

Figure 5.1 Single sampling plans for normal inspection (master table)

➡ = Use first sampling plan below arrow. If sample size equals or exceeds lot or batch size, do 100 percent inspection.
➡ = Use first sampling plan above arrow.
Ac = Acceptance number.
Re = Rejection number.

set a quality limit of 1 percent defective, but the sampling plans we use could let shipments below this quality through the door?"

"Yes," answered Harold. "I know that sounds a little funny but once we have done a few inspections today, I think you'll see how it works. For right now, remember that the AQL is for our internal use only. The suppliers should not have any interest in it. Their job is to ship us defect-free material."

Mead was still a little confused, but he nodded and urged Harold to continue. Harold went back to the master sampling chart for normal inspections and followed the L sample size across the page until he intercepted a column for an AQL of 1 percent. At that point the page had two numbers printed, five and six.

Harold looked up from the page. "These are the accept and reject numbers. What they tell me is to accept the lot if I find up to five defective bolts in my sample of two hundred. However, if I find six or more defects, I will reject this lot."

"That seems easy enough," Mead said.

Harold tore a blank piece of paper off of a nearby pad and wrote down, $N = 5,000, n = 200, c = 5.$

He pointed at the note and explained, "This is how I note the sampling plan for the shipment of bolts. The large N standards for the size of the shipment. The little n represents the sample size to draw from the shipment. The c is how many defectives we can find and still accept the shipment."

"That's a lot easier to understand," Mead remarked.

Harold moved from the desk to a filing cabinet near the door. From the third drawer down he drew out a single plastic packet filled with a few sheets of paper. On one edge of the packet was the part number for the bolts. "This is the inspection instructions for these bolts. This will tell us what to look for when we inspect the bolts." Harold motioned toward the door. "Shall we?"

Mead fell into step behind Harold as they headed for the receiving area. When they got there Harold waved down one of the lift truck drivers and shouted, "Where are the ADC-1483's?"

The driver pointed toward a stack of boxes near the far end of the receiving area, then asked, "Who's the new guy with you, Harold?"

"Trainee," Harold answered.

Mead and Harold walked down to the far end of the receiving docks. Harold's head began to bob and weave as he walked along the line of boxes. Finally, he placed his hand on a stack of five relatively small boxes stacked in a column. "Here they are," he announced.

Mead walked over to the stack and noted that the part numbers on the boxes matched those they were seeking. "What now?" he asked.

"We have to randomly sample 200 bolts from this shipment. We've got five boxes, so we will have to take forty bolts from each box." Harold grabbed the top box and began to carry it over to an open spot on the floor when he paused and looked back at Mead. "Feel free to grab a box."

Mead hesitated for a moment and then lifted the next box. The strain of the weight of the bolts went straight to his back. He could feel his face turning red. Still, he had to show that he could carry his weight around the plant. He lugged three of the boxes, one at a time, over to the open area. Harold promptly sat down on the concrete floor. Mead followed.

Harold placed the plastic packet on top of one of the boxes and began to read. "It says here that the bolts should be silver in color, free of burrs, and have visible threads. Possible defects include missing threads, burrs, cracks, delamination, and missing heads. If we find any with a missing head we reject the shipment."

"I thought we could reject only if we found more than five of these bolts defective?" Mead asked.

"Oh, you see that's for regular defects, what we call major defects. A missing head is considered a critical defect, so we reject any shipment where we find a single critical defect."

"More rule changes?" Mead asked.

"I should have given you the full lecture on sampling. This is how it works. To be defective, a part has to have one or more defects. Defects are grouped into three categories. Critical defects will endanger the production people or the customer. Take these missing heads for example. If we assembled something with such a bolt, it could fall apart and hurt someone.

"A major defect means that the part is not usable for our purposes. In other words, it doesn't conform to our requirements. The cracks and missing threads would be such defects. These are the defects we count for the sampling plan.

"A minor defect is just something annoying, like the delamination of the bolts. We count these just to note them on our report."

"How do you know which defects are major and which are minor?" Mead inquired.

"This inspection instruction form has a listing of defects by category. Now, if I can't figure out the defects by this written description," Harold turned the packet over, "on the back side of these forms are drawings of the defects.

"Take a look at these drawings. The first shows a really small burr. If I find one this size or smaller, I call it a minor defect. If it's bigger, I'm going to count it as a major defect. Taken together, we call this information the defect checklist. It takes the guesswork out of determining the type of defects you are looking for." Mead was impressed.

Harold continued, "Now, keep your eyes open for bolts with the defects listed on this sheet. If you think you found some, set them aside and I'll take a look at them."

Harold drew out a knife and cut open the first box. He grabbed a handful of bolts from one corner of the box. He counted out ten bolts and put the rest back. He then drew ten bolts from another corner of the box. The third set of ten came from the center of the box, but this time he dug down a little ways. Then he tilted the box and drew ten bolts from even further down.

"Is that random sampling?" Mead asked.

"Not really, but this is as close to it as we can come without emptying the box on the floor and carefully choosing what to inspect."

Mead shook his head and began to grab bolts from his own box. On the first grab pain shot through his hand. He turned his hand over to see it scratched in several places and bleeding from two other locations.

"Oh, yeah," called out Harold without looking back at Mead. "You might want to go easy on grabbing bolts. They can be plenty sharp along the edges."

Mead drew out bolts one at a time from two of the boxes. He stacked them into two neat piles of forty bolts each. Then he began to pick up each bolt for examination. The ones where he could see no problem he threw back into its original box. If he questioned the appearance of a bolt, he placed it into a pile.

As Mead finished the first pile of bolts, he was unaware that Harold was watching him. Harold was already done with his three piles of bolts. He had four bolts sitting on the floor. Harold watched the painful slowness Mead exhibited as he inspected each bolt.

Finally, Mead finished and called Harold over to check his work. Harold saw seven bolts laying on the floor by the president. He picked up each one and examined them. Four of the bolts he threw back into the box. "Minor defects," he declared.

The other three bolts he lifted and stated, "Major defects. Good work." Mead smiled at his accomplishment.

Harold continued, "Along with the four bolts I found defective, that makes seven. I'd dare say that this is too many for the sampling plan. This lot will be rejected."

"What does that involve?" Mead asked.

"This means that I have to put a red REJECTED BY QC sticker on these boxes. The lift truck people will move the material to the retention area. I'll fill out the usual reports for purchasing, and they will call the supplier to tell them to come back here and get their defective goods. Unless production decides they need them badly enough. Then a USE-AS-IS sticker is applied, and the bolts go to production."

It suddenly dawned on Harold that perhaps he shouldn't have said anything about the production department's habit of using defective goods when they were behind schedule. It was too late now; he could see that Mead had taken note of this procedure.

To Harold's surprise, Mead did not react in anger. Instead, he said, "I'm ready for another inspection."

"All right, I'll let you select the shipment and sample size this time."

The two men walked back to the quality control office. Mead drew the first shipping bill from the stack. It was for a shipment of gearbox covers. A total of fifteen thousand had been received under three different lot numbers. The first lot had two thousand covers. Mead went to the sample size chart and determined that a coded sample size called *K* should be used.

He then turned the page and looked up the sampling information from the normal inspection sampling plan. It called for a sample of 125 with the lot being rejected if it had four or more defective parts.

His next step was to look up the part number and the corresponding inspection instructions. He and Harold studied these before they headed back out to the receiving area. Harold let Mead cut open five randomly selected boxes from the twenty used for this part of the shipment. From each box Mead checked five covers. Harold double-checked.

When they were done, they had found only one defective cover. "Your decision?" Harold asked.

"Accept the lot," declared Mead. Harold agreed and began placing the green ACCEPTED BY QC stickers on the boxes.

When they had finished it was break time. Harold was notorious for eating at least four meals a day. His metabolism was so fast that he stayed thin despite his constant eating. He also wanted to talk to Mead to see if he was understanding how an attribute sampling plan worked.

"Don't tell me everything we buy is 1 percent AQL," began Mead as they sat down at a snack room table.

"No it isn't," Harold replied. "The more critical items have a lower AQL and the stuff that is not critical at all has an AQL of 4 percent."

Mead sensed some nervousness in Harold. "So, talk to me, Harold. What's the advantage of using the sampling plans?"

Harold began, "Well, if you compare a sampling plan against the idea of checking every piece of every shipment, there are several advantages. For one thing, even if we looked at everything that came through the door we'd probably miss some of the bad pieces."

"Why is that?"

"Remember when you checked that first shipment this morning? Think of how long and boring it would have been to check the entire shipment. Your attention would drift, and some bad pieces would get through your inspection. Therefore, a sampling plan saves time and money while actually improving the effectiveness of the inspection. Because we are taking samples, there's less handling of the materials and less chance for damage. Plus, we can make decisions about entire lots, instead of having to sort out just the bad pieces."

"That," added Mead, "makes it easier to train people because we're using a standard other companies use."

Harold paused. "That's right."

"So," Mead asked, "what are the problems with sampling plans?"

"You've probably seen the obvious problem. We found some defective goods in the one shipment, but we still accepted it for use. In addition, there is always the chance that we will accept a lot with more defectives than the 1 percent AQL.

"Another problem is that we don't learn much about the actual quality of the shipments we look at. We usually reject as soon as the maximum number of defectives is reached. The problem is that we don't finish the sample and estimate the actual quality of the parts."

"So," Mead observed, "you'd prefer a sampling system that gave us some hard data about the material we buy?"

Harold felt that he was being cornered. "It would be nice information for the production people. As an inspector, I can work with any system."

"Don't worry, Harold. I'm not asking these questions to punish anyone. As a company, we have to grow into new modes of operation. I only want to know what path to follow."

Harold smiled and pointed to his watch. "Time," he said. With that, the two men rose and headed back toward the receiving area. Harold diverted to the quality offices again on the way and brought back another sampling plan. It looked a little like the first one Mead had seen, but this one had *MIL-STD-414* written on the cover.

Harold slapped the manual down on a box of bolts destined for the assembly area. "This is another type of acceptance sampling. It's called ANSI Z1.9-1980. We used to call it military standard 414. Instead of checking for attributes, it works with dimensions and other measurements." Harold tore open the box of bolts and pulled out a handful. "These are the type of parts we check with 414."

Harold held one of the bolts lengthwise between his thumb and forefinger and said, "Do you see the length of this bolt? It's supposed to be three inches long. We're going to check the length of five of these bolts and decide whether the length is close enough to three inches."

Mead was now struggling to understand Harold. He could understand that the bolts had to be three inches long. He knew that they went into the assembly for a lawn tractor blade shield. If the bolts were too long the ends would stick out and catch grass and other debris. If the bolts were too short, they might work themselves free and cause a failure of the shield. But how was Harold going to know the length of all of the bolts after looking at only five?

"Our first step is to get some calipers and measure five randomly selected bolts," stated Harold.

Mead smiled and went to the QC lab. He returned only a moment later with a pair of six-inch calipers. Harold was impressed that the president of the company even knew what calipers looked like. Mead further impressed Harold by quickly taking five readings. The class at the college was beginning to pay off.

Harold wrote down the five measurements. Then he drew out a pocket calculator and began entering the numbers. He pressed two buttons and wrote down a number.

"The average length of these bolts is 3.02 inches." Harold pressed another set of keys and announced, "The standard deviation is 0.20 inches." He wrote these figures down on his clipboard.

Mead continued to smile, but he could feel a flash of warmth. He had no idea what a standard deviation was or what importance it possessed. He would try to bluff his way through this explanation.

Harold continued, "This is how 414 works. We compare the average and standard deviation against the specifications for the bolt. Let me show you." Harold drew out the inspection plan for the bolts from his pile of plans.

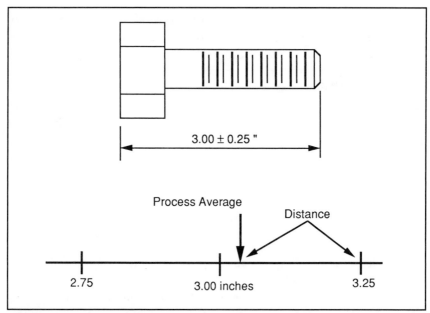

Figure 5.2   Measuring the distance from a sample average to the tolerance limit.

"The plan says that the bolts have to be within a quarter of an inch of three inches. That means that the average bolt size cannot get too close to the specification limits. In our case the average is a little high, so we will look at how far it is from the upper specification of 3.25 inches."

Harold drew a straight line on the paper and marked off each end. He put 2.75 inches at one end of the line and 3.25 inches at the other end. In the middle he made a check mark and wrote *3.00 inches.*

"This is the tolerance for the bolts," he stated. "The upper specification is 3.25 inches. Our average is at 3.02 inches." Mead moved closer to see Harold make a small mark just to the right of the center of the line. Then Harold drew an arc from the average to the upper specification point.

"What we have to do is calculate how far the average is from the upper specification. However, we use standard deviations as our unit of measurement. Here's the formula." Harold wrote:

$$QL = \frac{\bar{x} - upper\ spec}{s}$$

where, $\bar{x}$ = the average
s = the standard deviation

He pointed at the equations. "That's the formula for the lower quality index. We will convert this number, using a table in the manual, to an estimate of how many parts are above the upper specification. This is what we will compare to a number we look up on the 414 table."

Mead was making mental notes to find out more about standard deviations.

Harold replaced the symbols in the formula with the values they already knew.

$$QL = \frac{3.02 - 3.25}{0.20} = -1.15$$

"We drop the negative sign and look up this value on the B-5 table."

"How's that?" Mead asked.

"Here, look." Harold said as he turned to a page in the inspection plan. "This table takes the value we just calculated and tells us how many pieces will be above the specification. See we just look up our value and cross-reference it to the sample size we drew, five."

Figure 5.3 Table for estimating the lot percent defective (p_L or p_U) using standard deviation method (values in percent) (Table B-5 of MIL-STD-414*)

Q_U or Q_L	Sample Size							
	5	10	20	30	40	50	100	200
0	50.00	50.00	50.00	50.00	50.00	50.00	50.00	50.00
0.10	46.44	46.16	46.08	46.05	46.04	46.04	46.03	46.02
0.20	42.90	42.35	42.19	42.15	42.13	42.11	42.09	42.08
0.30	39.37	38.60	38.37	38.31	38.28	38.27	38.24	38.22
0.40	35.88	34.93	34.65	34.58	34.54	34.53	34.49	34.47
0.50	32.44	31.37	31.06	30.98	30.95	30.93	30.89	30.87
0.60	29.05	27.94	27.63	27.55	27.52	27.50	27.46	27.44
0.70	25.74	24.67	24.38	24.31	24.28	24.26	24.23	24.21
0.80	22.51	21.57	21.33	21.27	21.25	21.23	21.21	21.20
0.90	19.38	18.67	18.50	18.46	18.44	18.43	18.42	18.41
1.00	16.36	15.97	15.89	15.88	15.87	15.87	15.87	15.87
1.10	13.48	13.50	13.52	13.53	13.54	13.54	13.55	13.56
1.15	12.10	12.34	12.42	12.45	12.46	12.47	12.49	12.30
1.20	10.76	11.24	11.38	11.42	11.44	11.46	11.48	11.49
1.30	8.21	9.22	9.48	9.55	9.58	9.60	9.64	9.66
1.40	5.88	7.44	7.80	7.90	7.94	7.97	8.02	8.05
1.50	3.80	5.87	6.34	6.46	6.52	6.55	6.62	6.65
1.60	2.03	4.54	5.09	5.23	5.30	5.33	5.41	5.44
1.70	0.66	3.41	4.02	4.18	4.25	4.30	4.38	4.42
1.80	0.00	2.49	3.13	3.30	3.38	3.43	3.51	3.55
1.90	0.00	1.75	2.40	2.57	2.65	2.70	2.79	2.83
2.00	0.00	1.17	1.81	1.98	2.06	2.10	2.19	2.23
2.10	0.00	0.74	1.34	1.50	1.58	1.62	1.71	1.75
2.20	0.00	0.437	0.968	1.120	1.192	1.233	1.314	1.352
2.30	0.00	0.233	0.685	0.823	0.888	0.927	1.001	1.037
2.40	0.00	0.109	0.473	0.594	0.653	0.687	0.755	0.787
2.50	0.00	0.041	0.317	0.421	0.473	0.503	0.563	0.592
2.60	0.00	0.011	0.207	0.293	0.337	0.363	0.415	0.441
2.70	0.00	0.001	0.130	0.200	0.236	0.258	0.302	0.325
2.80	0.00	0.000	0.079	0.133	0.162	0.181	0.218	0.237
2.90	0.00	0.000	0.046	0.087	0.110	0.125	0.155	0.171
3.00	0.00	0.000	0.025	0.055	0.073	0.084	0.109	0.122

*The actual Table B-5 of MIL-STD-414 contains more sample sizes and about 10 times as many values for Q_U or Q_L.

Harold traced the corresponding values on the table. "See," he said. "We get a value of well above ten."

Harold turned to a new page and cross-referenced the sampling size against the AQL of 1 percent. "Now, the plan tells us to take a sample of thirty-five. I'm using these five as an example. The maximum value we should have gotten was 2.68. Our value of ten is much too high, so we would reject this box of bolts."

"Let me see if I have this straight," Mead stated. "With this sampling procedure, we find an average and a standard deviation. We then calculate something called the lower quality index. We take the lower quality index and look up what percentage of the shipment will be out of specification. We compare that percentage to a number on the sampling plan and either accept or reject the lot."

"In a nutshell," replied Harold, "you are pretty much correct. The one point to remember is that we are only interested in the specification limit closest to the average. In other words, we estimate how many parts are beyond that limit."

"I see," said Mead, even though he didn't.

"Let's try this one for real," Harold said. "We need to take thirty-five bolts and measure them for length. You seem to know how to handle a pair of calipers, why don't you take the measurements and I'll pump them into the calculator?"

Mead carefully drew out thirty-five new bolts from various locations in the box. As he drew each one out he measured their length and called out his results. Harold wrote these down and then would enter each one into his calculator. After a few minutes they had the thirty-five measurements and both men were hovering around the calculator.

"Based on thirty-five readings," Harold began, "the average is 3.01 inches with a standard deviation of 0.15 inches."

Harold wrote these numbers down and then proceeded to calculate the lower quality level. He got an answer of −1.60. By looking on the B-5 table, he estimated that about 5.27 percent of the bolts were above specifications. Double-checking with the sample plan showed that they had to reject the bolts if more than 2.68 percent were estimated.

"It's still a rejection," Harold stated. He shook his head and reached for the red stickers he kept in the left-hand pocket of his lab coat.

"At least we know a little more about the quality of this shipment," Mead replied.

At three-thirty that afternoon the two men had finished their work. Mead would be back again every day for two weeks. But, today he could feel the strain in his back and neck. He had seen a lot. He knew that there was much more he would have to learn.

Mead went back to his office that first day to answer the usual phone calls that had come in while he had been on the factory floor. As he sorted through the various messages, one grabbed his attention. The purchasing agent from his largest customer had called. Mead dialed this number first.

"Anderson," barked a voice at the other end of the line.

"Don, it's Bob Mead from ROB calling you back."

Anderson paused and Mead could hear him shifting papers on his desk looking for the note about ROB, Incorporated. "Oh, yeah," Anderson finally responded. "I haven't seen any SPC data coming in with your shipments yet. How's the implementation coming?"

"Just fine," Mead lied. "We should have something for you shortly. I've been out on the factory floor all day making sure that the system is being used."

"Good. We like to see the CEO get involved with SPC. I'll make sure our supplier representative stops by in six weeks to help you out. Good-bye."

An abrupt click stopped the phone call before Mead could respond. Great! Mead thought to himself. I got six weeks to have what looks like SPC in the plant, and I don't even know what a standard deviation is.

Mead picked up his briefcase from the corner of the room. He shuffled through the papers inside and finally drew out the course outline for his class. This week the class was addressing the use of statistics and other auditing tools.

Perfect thought Mead. He read on and discovered that SPC techniques would be covered during the following three weeks. It didn't leave enough time to get the system going in the plant. Mead knew that he needed an idea. He also knew he wasn't going to get the idea while totally exhausted.

An hour later Mead was finishing a perfect Manhattan. He sat alone in a small dark room in a rundown bar just a few blocks from the factory.

CHAPTER 6

Audits

Brenda and Breton met on the elevator at the junior college. They exchanged nervous greetings and speculated on the upcoming lecture. When they got off the elevator, Mead was just coming in a door that lead to the parking ramp skyway. Brenda noted that Mead looked a little more relaxed than normal.

The three ROB employees went down the wide hallway and into a new extension of the college. Room 402 was the meeting place for tonight's class on quality assurance. The class outline stated:

Class #3 — Audits. How to use capability studies and basic statistics to evaluate the effectiveness of a production process.

Once inside they noted that a large table had been placed at the front of the room. Two student assistants were removing a ceiling panel to gain access to the steel beams above. To one of these beams they attached a rope and let it hang down to the top of the table. Breton knew that this meant King was planning another wild demonstration. Brenda was noting that this room had padded auditorium seats, which was a welcome relief in comparison to the metal chairs they sat on in the gauge laboratory.

At exactly seven o'clock, King entered. Following him were the two student assistants carrying milk cartons filled with various items. On top of the second carton was Teddy the bear. "Good evening," King said to the class.

"Good evening," replied the majority of students.

"Tonight, we are going to learn about process capability studies, auditing techniques, and other measures of production processes. But, first I have to teach you statistics."

King looked at his watch and said, "I'll need . . .oh . . . say, five minutes to teach you a complete course of statistics. Does that sound all right?"

There was no immediate reply from the class.

"Say yes," commanded King.

"Yes," responded the class in unison.

"Good." King opened his now familiar briefcase and drew out a small box of steel parts. They were small pistons. He explained to the class that these were the lifter pistons found in most car engines. He then lifted the box of parts into the air and asked, "What is the quality of these parts?"

After an embarrassing pause, a lone student in the back of the room ventured, "I don't know."

"Correct," responded King. "You don't know. How would you find out?"

Breton shot his arm into the air. Brenda hated how he always attempted to make his intelligence obvious. King pointed to Breton.

"Well," started Breton, "I would need to know which specific qualities are important to either the customer or myself. Then I would measure those qualities."

"A good start," King answered. "How would we then summarize what we measured?" No one ventured a guess.

"We summarize with statistics," King stated. "Let me show you how. There are three things we report about a particular quality on a part. They are the average, the variation, and the distribution."

King turned toward the board and wrote *average, variation,* and *distribution*. He then put down the black marker and picked up a red marker. Next to the three words he wrote *center, scatter,* and *shape*.

"The average," he explained, "is the center of the data set we collect. The variation is how scattered the actual data are from the average. The distribution of the data forms a shape. That shape is critical to auditing."

King looked back at some confused students. "I have a set of demonstrations that will show you how all of this works."

He then pulled out a pair of six-inch calipers and a single piston from the box. "These pistons are supposed to be exactly one inch in overall length. Does anyone believe that the fifty pistons I have in this box are all exactly one inch in length?"

Many students shook their heads and a few softly said "no."

"Good," responded King. "You were paying attention during the first class." With that he also drew a yardstick out of the first milk carton. On one side was the standard thirty-six-inch marks, but on the other side was a scale drawn on paper and taped to the stick. In the middle of the scale was *1.000 inches*. In equal units on both sides of the center were markings in thousandths of an inch.

King measured the first piston and announced, "This piston is 1.003 inches long." He then set the ruler down on the desk and the piston above the 1.003 marking. He then measured the next part as being 0.999 inches long. He set that piston at the corresponding 0.999 marking on the ruler.

"Watch and learn," King said as he measured another piston and placed it on the proper spot along the scale. The students in the class looked on as King measured each piston and placed it in its proper position. Soon, King had two pistons of the same length. He merely stacked these on top of each other along the scale. While he worked he told a joke about quality assurance.

A few minutes later all fifty parts were stacked along the scale. They made a bump-shaped hill of parts. "Now," said King, "let's see if you knew about statistics all along. Ms. Patterson, where is the average size of these pistons?"

Brenda was caught by surprise by King's questions. She stammered a second and said, "Right about in the middle of that pile. I'd say, close to 1.002 inches." At the same time she pointed to the reading on the scale that corresponded to the peak of the piston pile.

"Very good. Mr. Navarro, how much scatter do you see?"

"From 0.997 to 1.008 inches. From the smallest part to the largest."

"Excellent. Now, would anyone say that this pile of pistons has somewhat of a bell shape to it?" Several students nodded in agreement.

King explained further. "You see, an average is really the center of a set of data readings. Each of these pistons is physically representing its own length measurement. If we want to know how many parts were exactly one inch in length, we just count the number of pistons in the one-inch pile. When we do this same counting-by-size exercise on paper, we will call it a histogram.

"The average is the center of the pile and the variation is the distance from the smallest piece to the largest pieces. Now, that's fine for telling me about the quality of these fifty parts, but can I also estimate the quality of parts I don't look at?"

King paused for emphasis. "Yes, we can. The shape of this pile is all important for making summary statistics very powerful."

King reached into the second milk carton and pulled out a large plastic sack filled with sand. He walked over to the rope dangling from the ceiling beam. It was only a few feet to the left of the pile of pistons. He tied the bag to the rope about three feet above the surface of the table. Then he paused long enough to step back and smile at his own handiwork.

With one quick and sudden move King drew a large kitchen knife from his briefcase and slashed the bottom of the bag. It happened so fast that

Brenda and two other students gasped. The sand slowly spilled out onto the table. King continued to smile and watch the demonstration. Then he tossed the knife back into his briefcase.

"Take a look at the pile of sand," commanded King. "What shape does it have?"

"A big bump?" queried one of the students in the front row.

"That's right. Would you also say that the basic shape is very similar to the pile of pistons?"

The eyes of the students darted from one pile to the other. King could see that a few light bulbs in their minds were beginning to light up.

"What caused the sand to make a shape like this?" asked King as he waved a hand over the pile of sand.

"Gravity," ventured one student.

"Particle size," said another.

Someone else said, "Friction."

"All correct answers," King said. "Would you also call these factors natural?"

A few more light bulbs went on.

Without waiting for an answer, King continued, "You see, this classic bump shape occurs when natural, random forces are at work. When I look at the way that my pistons distributed themselves I can see a similar shape. That means that natural forces created this distribution. In statistics this is called the normal distribution. It is called normal because when left to nature, this is the shape that is created."

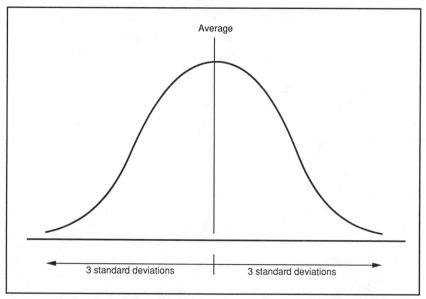

Figure 6.1 The normal distribution.

Again, King paused for emphasis. "When this shape appears, nature is at work. Any other shape tells me that someone has interfered. Let me show you."

King reached into the first milk carton again and pulled out a small, powerful fan. He plugged this into the wall and pointed the blades toward the pile of sand. The sand particles began to blow down the length of the table.

"The custodians really hate it when I do this demonstration." Most of the students laughed.

In a few seconds the pile of sand was taking on the shape of a sand dune. The leading edge of the pile was becoming steep, while the trailing edge was stretching out. King then switched off the fan.

"See? If a human-made fan is blowing on the pile it takes a different shape. The error it introduces is consistent, not random. The same thing would happen to my distribution pistons if someone interfered consistently with the production process."

"Can you give us an example?" Mead asked.

"Sure can. Suppose that these pistons are made by an automatic screw machine. Also assume that the operator checks the length of the part after every cutoff. If the pieces that are too long are thrown into a rework pile, the final distribution of the data will change."

King moved to the pile of pistons and placed his hand like a karate chop down the far right side of the distribution. "These pieces out here would be removed. The operator's action would chop off this tail of the distribution."

"So?" asked Mead reflexively.

"Because these parts are taken out of the distribution, you don't know how much total scatter the screw machine creates before rework. It may be just the data you need to correct the process and eliminate rework. I'll show you how in a few minutes."

King then looked around the room for further questions. Then he said, "I need a few volunteers."

No hands went up. It seemed logical to King. Not many people volunteer after a demonstration involving a large knife. Nonetheless, he selected a few students and gave them a second box of parts. Nervously, each student used a caliper to measure these new parts and place them on the other side of the scale on the desk.

Within two minutes a second pile of pistons had been built in front of King's pile. This time the pile looked more like the sand dune King had created with his fan.

"This is called skewness in statistics," said King. "I'll refer to it as skewed data. That means that a normal distribution is not present. A production process that is fully capable will produce the normal distribution. If I find another shape, I know that there is still room for improvement in the process." Mead was making lengthy notes on this point. "Furthermore, when I have a normal distribution, I can estimate the quality of the entire production run from which these parts were sampled. To do that we need to use some math."

Amongst a few moans, King walked to the board. He wrote:

$$\overline{x} = \frac{\Sigma x}{n}$$

where, Σx = the sum of the measurements
         n = the number of measurements
         $\overline{x}$ = the average

"Now a lot of you have seen this crooked E in equations before. It represents sigma in the Greek alphabet. What it really says is add everything up. In other words, add together whatever is next in the equation. In this case, an x appears. An x is used to signify individual measurements. Therefore, we add up all of our measurements. The n in the equation represents the sample size." Mead remembered Harold telling him the same thing only a few days ago.

"Thus," King continued, "this equation is the statistical shorthand for an average. To be formal, we call this the mean. The use of a bar over a symbol represents an average. Therefore, x-bar means average measurement, or mean."

King wrote five numbers down on the board and totaled them. He then divided the total by five, the size of the sample. When he finished he turned to the class and said, "You see, the average of these five numbers is three."

No problem so far, thought Brenda to herself. She was worried that these calculations would get worse. They did.

For a few minutes the class calculated a series of averages for data sets King wrote on the board. Then he introduced them to the standard deviation. Mead was paying close attention now. He had looked up the meaning of a standard deviation in several books. Despite lengthy descriptions of how to calculate one, none of the books told him what the standard deviation was.

King wrote down a much more complex formula on the board. Under one large square root sign were a mixture of sigma, x's, and x-squares.

"Don't panic," reassured King. He proceeded to explain how the formula could be calculated in a simple form. He wrote down the same five numbers he had originally used in the average calculation. Then he started a second column of numbers. These were the squares of each number.

King paused to show the students how to square a number on a simple four-function calculator by entering the number and then pressing the multiplication key followed by the equal key.

He then totaled both columns. The total of the first column was the sigma for the measurements. The second total was the sigma for the square of each reading. He then took those totals and placed them into the formula where they belonged. In a few more seconds he had calculated the standard deviation.

"Difficult?" he inquired. Several students nodded in agreement. "Let me show you a short-cut."

King drew out his ten-dollar statistical calculator and entered five numbers. He then pressed a key for standard deviation and the same answer appeared.

"Make it easy on yourselves," said King. "Spend the ten dollars and get one of these calculators. Besides, the actual value of the standard deviation is what's important. It doesn't matter what you had to do to calculate it.

"The standard deviation," he continued, "is the key to estimating the quality of a production run with only a small sample. The key word in its name is standard. That means that this is a universal measurement of variation for all forms of data."

King walked back to the piles of pistons. "If I have a normal distribution, the amount of variation will be six times the standard deviation. In other words, if I take the average and add three standard deviations, that will be my estimate of the largest piece made during production."

King moved his hand from the center of the pile to the outside right edge of the pile. "And, if I subtract three standard deviations from the average, this will be my estimate of the smallest piece made during production."

King paused to see if this was making sense to any of the students. "Let's try it," he said.

King wrote down the average and the standard deviation for the five numbers. He multiplied the standard deviation by three and wrote this value down on the board. He subtracted the value from the average, then added the value to the average. The resulting two numbers were written in larger characters on the board.

"These should be the largest and smallest pieces in the production run. It may seem a little unclear now, but I have a demonstration of how it works that we can try after our first break. Right now, I'm going to show you some capability studies done on production processes and how to read them."

King's assistants began to pass out papers. At the same time King went to a nearby corner of the room and wheeled out an overhead projector. He pulled down the screen on the wall and turned on the projector. He laid an overhead of the first handout on the projector and adjusted the focus.

King announced, "Handout number one is a capability study conducted on the closing effort of a car door. Whenever you see a capability study, the first thing you should do is look for what is being tested and what the specifications are for that characteristic.

"In this case, they were testing the force it takes to close the door on a car. The car is a two-door coupe in this example. The engineers want a door that takes between seven and twelve pounds of force to close. If the force is too high, then customers have a hard time closing the door so that it will lock properly. If the force is too low, a wind will slam the door shut, usually while the customer is still getting out. So, you can see the importance of getting this right."

A few chuckles could be heard. "The next step is to look for the three statistics I listed at the beginning of class, the average, variation, and distribution."

King placed a finger on the report near a histogram of the readings taken. "These are the actual readings organized into a histogram. See how the normal distribution is evident? That's the second thing I look for on a capability study. It tells me that there is no human-made interference occurring. If the data looked skewed, then the estimates of variation and other statistics would be erroneous.

"The next thing to look for is the average and standard deviation." He moved a finger to a box of numbers on the right-hand side of the report. "We can see that the average closing strength is ten pounds. This is well within the specifications for the door. However, if we look at the standard deviation we can see that it is almost three foot-pounds. Multiplying this by three means that the variation of effort spread out nine foot-pounds in each direction from the average."

King moved his finger farther down the list of data. "Look here. These items marked above spec and below spec confirm this. They say that closing strength for all of the doors will land between one and nineteen foot-pounds of force. That's well outside of the specifications. How do you feel about the capacity of this process?" King asked.

Many students shook their heads while others mumbled various expressions of dissatisfaction.

"I see you're beginning to see how this all fits together. With a sample of parts we can estimate the quality of a production run. We then compare this to the specifications and see if our process is capable. Specifically, whether it is capable of achieving the quality we demand. Any questions?"

There were none, so King had the class turn to the second capability study. Several students were called on to tell the class what various aspects of the study told them about the quality of the production parts.

Brenda followed along with these exercises but her mind was really focused on the mountains of raw data her quality control department had collected over the years. No one had attempted a complete summary such as these. The order of the day was to follow the sampling plan and that's all.

Breton asked King whether the same capability study didn't also tell us about the quality of the production machinery. King answered that it did indeed.

Mead made several more notes, but he was attempting to piece together an alternative to the sampling plans he and Harold had been using all week. He couldn't see the answer yet, but an inner voice kept telling him that this might be the right path.

At eight o'clock King dismissed the class for their first break. As the students filed out to the break area, the student assistants and King got brooms out of a nearby closet. They had a few demonstrations to clean up. A custodian down the hall spotted them carrying his brooms and exclaimed, "Damn, King's at it again!"

By ten after eight the students were back in their seats. King's trick of always starting on time was beginning to have its desired effect.

The room was now cleaned of the piles of pistons and sand. The milk cartons were pushed against the wall and the board was clean. King began: "I want to shift gears for a moment and talk about auditing a quality system.

"A lot of people are confused about what an audit really is. They use terms like seagulls and grasshoppers to describe auditors. You know, they fly in, eat a lot, and crap all over everything." Laughter and applause filled the lecture room. King smiled. So did Mead.

King continued, "In reality an audit is the confirmation of the terms of a contract. In medieval times one person would read the accounts aloud while another person checked their accuracy. We got the word audit from the root for audible.

"In modern companies you have two types of contracts an auditor is checking." King walked to the board and drew out a green marker. He wrote two words, *implied* and *written*. He underlined each word.

"A written contract is exactly that, an agreement stated in writing. The classic example is your customers' purchasing agreements. They specify what they want, how many they want, and what quality should exist. A good example is the U.S. government. If you try to sell them something they will probably start by sending you books of requirements to meet. For a sensitive contract, say for the Department of Defense, an auditor will show up from time to time to make sure that you are following the guidelines."

Mead's thoughts drifted for a moment to the time that ROB tried to get defense contracts a few years back. He shuddered as he remembered the endless list of specifications and management requirements.

King continued: "An implied contract is a little bit more interesting. Take the example of your quality control system. What authority do you have to check its performance?" King paused and glanced around the room before answering his own question.

"You have an implied contract with the quality control people. They were hired to monitor the quality of production. You probably have a quality manual that spells out how the production is to be monitored. Therefore, you, as management, have the right to audit the quality control department to make sure that your written procedures are being followed."

Brenda didn't like the way Mead was taking notes at this point in the lecture. King paused again to make a few notes of his own on the board.

"Now, here's the rub. The bad name that auditors get comes from the fact that some managers instruct the auditors to stray beyond their authority. The worse offense is when a manager does the auditing. You see, managers have power. If they find a mistake, their instinct will be to punish those involved on the spot. That's not the job of an auditor."

King turned back toward the board and wrote *continuous improvement*. "The idea of auditing is to seek continuous improvement. The auditors check the quality system to ensure that it will survive the scrutiny of a customer and to seek opportunities for improvement."

Mead's hand went into the air. "Can you give us an example of finding an opportunity?"

"Sure can," King responded. "Suppose I was auditing your quality people and I discovered that they took a long time to confirm that a blueprint on the factory floor was the most current version. I could write in my report that there is cause to appoint someone, or design a computerized system, to track blueprint revisions. Then when QC wants to confirm a blueprint as being current, they know where to go to get the information. That saves time, and prevents confusion and mistakes."

"And that saves money," Mead added.

"Ah," replied King. "Mr. Mead has a firm grasp on why we do all of this quality assurance stuff." Mead reddened noticeably at the remark.

King continued with his brief lecture on what an audit was and the proper ways to conduct an audit. He began by noting that there should always be an audit committee made up of managers. That committee appoints the actual auditors and gives them a detailed list of what they checked. The auditor takes the assignment and creates audit checklists. Some of these checklists are just a list of documents to review and things to examine. Other lists are series of questions to ask the people in the department being checked.

King spent a longer period of time cautioning the class to audit with polite patience. He suggested that each person who will be audited be provided in advance with a list of the things that will be checked. He had two different books on etiquette that he suggested the students read, so that they are welcomed assistants and not the dreaded auditors of the company.

King explained when the audit is completed, the auditor must write a report that is submitted to the audit committee. The committee reviews the report and recommends changes and additions. Only then is the final report printed and distributed.

King spent ten minutes describing the most important step of an audit, taking action. Using the report as information, the managers on the audit committee drew up a list of changes needed and opportunities that should be exploited. This list is divided up into tasks that specific managers are assigned. In turn, each manager must report back on his or her progress in implementing the tasks. King called this last step a form of project management. An audit won't create improvements unless the managers get tough and thorough.

By this time it was nearing the second break. King entertained a few questions. Then he asked the class to vote for either an early break now or the chance to get out ten minutes early with no break. The vote was close but too many people wanted to rest now to absorb what King had said.

As he filed out of the room with the other students, Mead saw Brenda flip a quarter to Breton. Breton then vanished down the hallway. Mead didn't know why this sight alerted his attention. He decided to file it away for later consideration.

As Mead sat down in the break area with his cup of coffee, a young woman sat down across from him. She seemed anxious to hear his reaction to King's talk on auditing. After a few defensive questions, Mead learned that this was Doreen Johnson, a manager from a small plastic injection molding company on the southwest end of town.

"One of the students told me that you're president of ROB," Doreen said.

"Yes, I am."

Doreen smiled and cocked her head to one side. "Have you ever mentored anyone?"

"Mentored?" Mead asked.

"Sure, you know, guide, instruct, and develop a younger person in the lessons you have learned as an executive."

Mead spotted a copy of a popular woman's magazine in the pile of books Doreen was carrying. Gee whiz, he thought, here's one of those power women. "No, I haven't," Mead stated coldly.

"I would like to talk to you about it sometime," Doreen said as she pressed a business card into Mead's hand. "Call me sometime and I'll buy lunch."

Mead was still sitting a moment later looking at the card. His first instinct was to throw it away. For some reason he put it in his shirt pocket instead of his business card holder. Then he noticed that everyone else had gone back to class. He grabbed his notebook and noticed that he still hadn't drank his coffee.

Back in the classroom King was pulling out the second milk carton and preparing for the next demonstration. "Sorry," whispered Mead as he took his chair. A nervous glance toward the back of the room revealed Doreen sitting only a few rows back. She smiled at him as he swung around to sit down.

King began, "Now that we are all here, I have an excellent exercise for you. I'm sure that several of you doubt that a few pieces sampled from a production lot will have much accuracy in describing all of the other pieces. Therefore, I think we should try it and see what happens."

King pushed the milk carton along with his foot. "Inside of here are over one thousand plastic parts." He lifted out a single part. "This is part of the locking mechanism on a General Motors car. It has to be 0.020 inches wide to work properly in the mechanism. The tolerance is plus or minus 0.005 inches."

King wrote this information on the board. Then he continued, "What I want you to do is measure every piece in this box and find the smallest and the largest piece. Don't panic. If we let everyone in the class check about fifty pieces we should finish in no time at all."

The class was beginning to look uncomfortable. King asked, "Who doubts that a small sample could tell us the same thing?" A few scattered hands rose. "Good, you've just volunteered for this exercise. Come forward and take a random sample of thirty parts."

The four volunteers straggled up to the front of the class. King handed the first two people a pair of calipers. The last two people to arrive were handed a table of random numbers. King dumped the box of parts onto the table and scooped out ten separate piles of parts. Each pile was roughly equal in size. He then told the class that each pile had roughly one hundred parts. The people with the random numbers were the samplers. They would select parts and organize them on the table. The people with the calipers were the inspectors.

The samplers choose three random numbers for each pile of parts. The last two digits told the samplers which pieces to select. For the first pile, the numbers thirteen, eighty-nine, and forty-two were selected by the sampler who dropped a pencil onto the list of random numbers. She then counted out pieces from the pile. The thirteen, forty-second, and eighty-ninth pieces were pulled off to one side. An inspector measured these pieces and wrote the measurements on the board.

The other inspector and sampler were soon into the act using the other piles of parts. Within ten minutes, the thirty pieces had been found and the measurements recorded on the board.

"Let's break out those fancy calculators," King said. The room was soon filled with the sound of clicking keys. King wrote down his answer for the average and standard deviation. He waited until a couple of students got the same answer as confirmation.

"Now for the magic," said King. "I take three times the standard deviation. I first add it to, and later subtract it from the average." His hand rapidly wrote down the calculations. "The two results are the prediction of the largest and smallest pieces in all of these parts."

Next, he drew two large red rectangles on the board. Into the first, he wrote *Largest*; in the second, he wrote *Smallest*. "The largest piece will be 0.029 and the smallest piece will be 0.011 inches."

King paused for dramatic effect. "Let's find out what they really are. I want each person left in the room to come up and grab half of one of these piles. Measure the pieces and write down their sizes. When you have finished, look for the smallest and largest part on your list. We'll have a little contest and see which are the smallest and largest pieces in the room."

As students filed forward to collect their respective piles of parts, King and his assistants handed calipers to each person. Some students took their parts back to their seats while the rest crowded around the table. The actual measuring and writing took over fifteen minutes. At the end, each student discarded the measured parts back into the milk carton.

Breton, Brenda, and Mead returned to their seats and began comparing their results. Each had selected a largest and smallest piece in their pile of parts. They exchanged the lists of measurements to confirm each others' findings.

King directed everyone in the class to take their seats again. "The smallest piece I predicted was 0.011 inches. Who had a piece that small?"

"I did," shouted a student from the back of the room.

"And who got a lower reading?" King asked. There was silence in the room as everyone looked at each other. No volunteers. The prediction was correct.

"How many people had a piece at the largest prediction, 0.029 inches?" King asked. Again, silence. "Oh, I see that we're a little off in our prediction of the largest piece. Do I hear a bid for 0.028 inches?"

"Here," shouted two students at once. Eyes in the room widened noticeably.

"Not bad," King stated. "We took a sample of thirty pieces and missed the actual variation in one thousand pieces by a thousandth of an inch."

King then had the students total the numbers on their measurements. He showed how the data could be coded for easier calculation. One at a time, each person called out a total. King wrote these on the board along with the number of readings taken. When he had collected all the totals, he calculated an average for all one thousand parts.

"The average was 0.021 inches," announced King. "If we go back to the average the volunteers calculated with only thirty pieces you will see that it is also 0.021 inches."

King turned back toward the class smiling. "Any doubters left in the room now?" More silence. "Thank you," he said. "I think we have all learned something. Now, let's finish our discussion of how these types of statistics are useful for an audit.

"If I know the quality of a production run with a small sample, I can use this information to make production and quality control decisions. Let me show you a few examples.

"To begin with, let's look at the case of the process that is off target. I want to be specific." King glanced at his class list. "Ms. Letts, what kind of production does your company do?"

A startled Ms. Letts replied, "Ah, metal stamping."

"And what is your favorite metal stamping?" King asked.

"You mean my favorite part that we make?" King nodded. "Well, gee, I guess our gearbox cover."

"Please, Ms. Letts, pick a dimension that is critical to the performance of the cover."

"That's easy. The inside width has to be fifty centimeters or it won't fit on the box."

"And what is the tolerance for that dimension?"

"Plus or minus three millimeters."

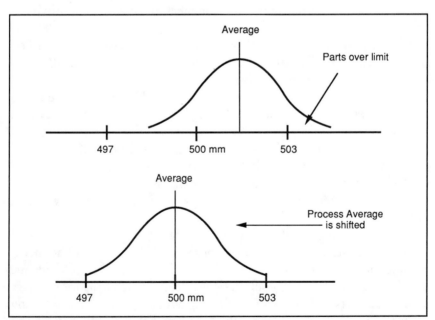

Figure 6.2   The positive effect of shifting a process average to an optimal.

King wrote this information on the board. Then he continued, "Now let's suppose that I do a capability study on this machine by drawing thirty covers at random. If I get an average of 51.1 centimeters, then the process is slightly off target. However, I must know something about the variations involved to see if this is a problem.

"If I find that the variation goes three millimeters in both directions from the average, then being off target will push part of the distribution out of specification." King drew a bracket representing the tolerance range. Above this he drew a normal distribution with the right tail above the upper specification.

"Now if I tell the machine operator to shim the press so that the average falls back to the required fifty centimeters, then all of the parts will be inside the tolerance range." King drew a second picture on the board. The same distribution shifted to place the average over fifty centimeters pulled the right tail back into tolerance.

"Is this easy or what?" asked King.

"Yes," replied the class reflectively.

"Okay, let's try another one. This time we'll pick on Mr. Jones in the corner."

Jones had nodded off during this part of the lecture. The student next to him jabbed him sharply with an elbow. A startled Jones flashed an angry glance at his companion until he noticed the entire class looking at him. The companion pointed toward King.

"What was the question, again?" Jones asked.

King smiled. "What do you produce at your company?"

"Foam inserts," replied a confused Jones.

"And which foam insert is your favorite?"

"How's that again?" The class erupted in laughter.

"Pick a part that you produce. What is it?"

"Oh, I don't know. Maybe, the footpads we make for personal computers."

"What is the critical characteristic of this footpad?"

"It has to be a quarter of an inch thick when fully compressed," Jones stated.

King returned to the board and drew the familiar bracket for tolerance. "Suppose," he said, "that this is the tolerance range for the compressed footpad. If I had a skewed distribution, the extended tail would go right over the tolerance limit."

King drew a second bracket on the board. "Now, we have learned that skewness is a sign that some consistent error is being made during production. I will assume that I can find and eliminate that source of error. When I do so, the distribution curve becomes normal."

King drew a new distribution curve above the second bracket. "Because the curve is normal, its variation is less than the skewed distribution. Therefore, it now fits within specifications. Questions?" There were none.

"Well, then let's look at a third example. Suppose that I sample a production run and find that the average is right on target, but the variation I can expect will exceed tolerances. I can't move the average to improve this situation. I also can't seek a normal distribution to reduce variation because the curve is already normal.

"What I can do is search out the sources of variation. Perhaps this is a plastic molded part and I'm using various amounts of reground plastic or several plastic resin suppliers. Maybe I don't use a setup sheet for the machine so that every operator sets the machine differently. Maybe people keep opening a door near the machine in the winter, and this cools the molds rapidly.

"The point is, I don't know what is causing the problem until I investigate the situation thoroughly. I can't do that investigation until I am sure that the normal procedures are being followed. That's what an audit is intended to do. It finds out if the day-to-day procedures are in effect and whether the information reported is accurate.

"You see, I cannot discover if I have improved a process until I know what the normal behavior of that process is."

King paused again for emphasis. "Any questions?" There were none.

"Next week we start talking about statistical process control. That's how we constantly monitor the production processes after auditing has established capabilities. See you all in a week. Good luck and good hunting."

Most of the students were anxious to leave. The parking ramp would soon be full of people trying to get out. However, Mead stayed behind for a moment. Doreen came over and sat next to him.

"You're not a manager at any company are you?" Mead began.

"No, I'm not," she replied. "We have a mutual friend. He sent the information you wanted on your competitors."

"Where is it?"

Doreen pointed at her head. "I know a quiet place around the corner where we can talk." She got up and walked toward the door. Mead watched her for a moment. Then he got up and followed her.

CHAPTER 7

What Is
Statistical Process Control?

Breton Rhodes liked the Holiday Inn North. It sat on the river, and the bar had an excellent view. The drinks were cheap and the food free before six o'clock. Breton finished his drink at six and left a tip on the bar. He put his suit coat back on and headed down the hallway to the meeting rooms.

Pictures of sailing ships dotted the walls as he searched out the meeting room for the local section of the American Society for Quality Control. A friend had recommended that Breton attend a couple of their meetings and pump the members for information. Tonight was an especially good night to do just that, because the meeting topic was statistical process control (SPC).

After paying his fifteen dollars to get in, Breton eyed the small knots of people that had already formed in the room. He selected one that didn't seemed wrapped up in an important conversation. He introduced himself as a visitor and was immediately greeted with questions about his operation.

Eventually, Breton found himself talking to two people in particular. The first man, he learned, was David McCabe, a quality engineer with a local chemical company. The second was Tom Cox, a quality manager. The two explained the importance SPC played in their organization.

"We're going to have a videotape of a successful SPC program before dinner tonight," Tom said.

"Yes," David responded. "I've seen it before. It has a good explanation of SPC in the beginning. I think you'd enjoy it, Breton."

Both men directed Breton to a side room where a video machine and television were set up. Breton joined the dozen or so people already in the room. He cursed himself for not bringing a drink.

After a few minutes, the tape was introduced. The television set showed only static for the first two minutes. Eventually, the static cleared and the logo of a large manufacturer appeared. The voice of an unseen narrator began.

"SPC helps the machine operators participate in actively solving manufacturing problems. It also helps the company compete by showing how well the manufacturing processes work. The best way to understand SPC is to look at some examples of controlling quality as a product is being made."

The scene changed from the logo to a shot of people working in a large industrial company. This screen was titled *The Problem with Inspection*.

The narrator's voice droned on. "Mr. Barrett owns a metal fabrication shop in the Midwest. One of his hottest selling products is a small drive shaft used in electric motors. Being aware of the need for higher quality in today's products, Mr. Barrett is constantly worried about the quality of the shafts.

"One day Mr. Barrett calls together his shop floor managers to tell them that several inspectors have been hired to monitor the quality of the shafts during production. The idea is to find and sort out the shafts that don't meet specifications before they are shipped. Combined with final inspections, Mr. Barrett assumes that his company will now ship very few shafts that don't meet customer requirements."

Breton twisted uncomfortably in his chair. The detached voice from the VCR continued.

"A few months later, Mr. Barrett discovers that customers are still sending back some of the shafts because they do not meet requirements. Also, the expense of the extra inspectors has forced up the price of the products. What has gone wrong?

"It is possible to inspect goods as they are being made. However, looking at every piece produced by a machine will not find all of the defective parts. We also know that a sample of parts from the manufacturing process will give us a good estimate of the quality of all of the parts being produced. Unfortunately, by the time an inspector finds a bad part, it is too late to make a correction. Instead, the part has to be scrapped and that wastes time and money.

"Mr. Barrett's company is still shipping bad shafts because the inspectors' sampling plans do not prompt sorting for bad shafts until about 1 percent of the production lot is found defective. Therefore, when only a few bad shafts are made, they tend to slip through the inspection process. Thus, they are discovered by the customers."

Breton shifted in his chair just as the words *Continuous Improvement* covered the screen.

"A better alternative would be to prevent the bad part from being made. Instead of using inspectors during production, the machine operators could monitor how well their machines are doing. When a problem with the machine begins to occur, the operator could make an adjustment before bad parts are produced.

"This alternative is called statistical process control, or SPC. It is based on the idea of continuous improvement. Continuous improvement occurs when the management of a company encourages workers to actively solve common production problems. Each day workers seek new ways to do their jobs a little better. The primary tool of continuous improvement is statistical process control.

"Mr. Barrett calls his shop managers back for another meeting to discuss the quality problem. He asks if anyone has an alternative to the current method of inspection."

Breton smiled as the scene switched to obvious actors trying to play the part of managers.

"Yes, I do," the quality assurance manager, Bob Winston, said.

"What is it, Bob?"

"We could switch to SPC. That's where we would monitor how well each step of the manufacturing process is working. If we detect a process starting to have a problem, we can correct the situation before bad shafts are made."

"But Bob, how can we predict a problem is beginning to occur?" Mr. Barrett asked.

"We can use control charts."

Now the screen was bright blue with the words *Control Charts* spelled out in white letters. The narrator's voice returned.

"A control chart works by monitoring the amount of variation in a process. To see how it does that, we have to talk about a couple of related concepts."

Underneath the words *Control Charts* appeared *Variations in a Process.*

"Let's take a moment to discuss variations that occur in a process. The electric motor shafts have several dimensions specified on a customer's blueprint. We will look at a single dimension, the shaft length. The blueprint says that it must be six inches long. It would seem to be a simple process to set a machine to cut rods into six-inch lengths. However, several factors present in the production area can create variations in the length of the cut.

"First, material. The steel rod expands and contracts a little due to temperature and handling. This can change the length of a shaft.

"Second, the machine. The precision of the cutting saw can be affected by the tightness of the blade, temperature, vibrations, the quality of the steel, and several other factors.

"Third, the operator. The setting for the cut can be off by very small amounts due to how the stock is loaded and how the saw is operated.

"And fourth, measurement. The caliper used to set the cut may read six inches, but it could be out of adjustment and give a false reading.

"The combined results of these sources of variation is that each rod is cut to slightly different lengths. Thus, the average cut could be six inches, but individual cuts will vary around this average. This amount of variation around the average is called the process variation. You can think of it as the data noise the cutting saw produces in the lengths." Now the words *Data Noise* appeared on the blue background.

"The amount of data noise, or process variation, is usually consistent for each step of the production process. Let's assume that our example of the cutting of steel rods produces variations of up to 0.002 inches. This would be the normal data noise of the process. What a control chart does is measure the size of this normal noise. When a problem begins to occur in the process, the noise will increase and the control chart will detect it.

"For example, if the cutting saw began to come loose from its mounting, the variation in cuts would rise. The operator would be sampling a few parts at regular intervals. If a significant increase in variation is detected, the process can be adjusted. In this case, the saw blade mounts would be tightened."

Suddenly, a close-up of a machine operator's face appeared on the screen. He asked, "What is a critical characteristic?"

The now soothing voice of the narrator explained, "The machine operator's time is precious. Therefore, he will not have the time to check every dimension of a part. Instead, the managers will select a critical characteristic, the one dimension that is most important at a specific step in the process. For example, when the steel rods are being cut, it is critical that a six-inch length be maintained. In this example, the length is the critical characteristic."

The scene switched to the actors. "We must identify each critical characteristic at each stage of making the shaft," Mr. Barrett said.

"We can do that by reviewing customer requirements and our own operations," Bob Winston answered.

"How will we set control limits?" asked a senior engineer.

On a green background, the words *What is a Control Limit?* were printed in bright white letters.

"To understand a control limit we have to look at a control chart. If the rod-cutting process is trying to achieve six-inch lengths, then the control chart will have a solid line drawn at six inches. The machine operator will pick a few bars every hour to measure. The average of these measurements are then plotted against the six-inch line.

"Most of the averages will be close to the six-inch standard. However, a few will appear farther away. Some of this drift will occur from the random sample drawing. Perhaps the operator picked all short pieces. The question then becomes, how far from the six-inch standard can an average fall merely by chance?"

A partially completed control chart appeared on the screen.

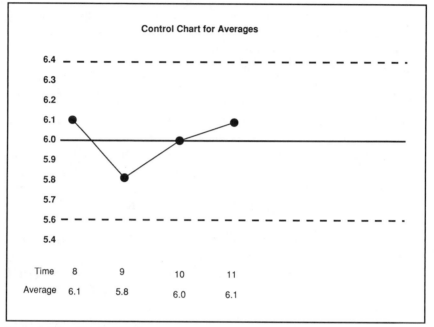

Figure 7.1 Control limits.

"The control limits on a control chart mark the limits of chance." Bold, black arrows magically appeared on the chart to highlight the control limits. "This limit is found by multiplying the process variation or noise into predetermined statistical factors."

"We can use a capability study to set the control limits," Bob Winston said. "In a capability study, we take several samples of the parts over time to determine the normal behavior of the process. This is the first step in finding out if a process is in statistical control."

Bob continued, "The control limit on a chart is really a prediction. Take our rod-cutting operation. Our concern is the length of the rods. If a control limit is set for the average length, it is predicting how far the averages will fall from six inches.

"After the control limits have been set, the operator begins to measure rods and to plot the averages. After many hours and samples, the management checks the chart to see if all of the averages fall within the control limits. If they did, the chart made a successful prediction. The technical term is that the process is under statistical control. This means that statistical methods have successfully predicted how much the averages would vary."

The narrator's voice returned. "Control limits can be set for averages, ranges, percentages, ratios, and counts. Therefore, control charts are possible for a wide range of industrial applications.

"By using control charts a company can control problems as they occur in production. You prevent problems, instead of merely detecting them with inspection. This gives you an edge on the competition."

Breton winced as corny "triumph music" he would normally hear in a B-grade movie ended the tape. The lights were switched on and Breton blinked instinctively from the brightness. He stumbled out of the room back into the meeting area. He overheard someone asking, "How is a chart used?" He headed toward that group. In it was Tom Cox.

"How will these control charts help us?" asked a shop floor supervisor.

"Well, let's look at the rod-cutting process as an example." Tom responded. "If we set control limits on the average length of a cut, we will know when the cutting machine starts to act up."

"I don't quite follow you."

"Let's say that an operator is using the chart and making entries every hour. If at the end of one of those hours he finds an average that is too high, he knows he has a problem. Because that average exceeds a control limit, we know that he has lost statistical control." Tom waved his hands as he talked.

"What does out of statistical control mean?" asked a student attending the meeting.

Tom eyed the youth's face and open shirt before responding in an annoyed tone, "When an average, range, or other measure crosses over a control limit, we know that chance is no longer the reason for the deviation. Instead, it is very likely that the process itself has changed a little bit."

He waited for a reaction from the student's face. When none came, he continued. "The machine operator can now stop the process and check the parts a little closer. Perhaps a floor inspector is notified to inspect the parts using larger samples. Either way, the parts produced for the past hour are now isolated. The inspector will determine whether the quality of the parts is still good enough for use. If not, it is easy to eliminate these defective parts, since they have already been isolated from the rest of the production lot."

An engineer from a competing company joined Tom's group and interrupted. "Meanwhile, the operator has a strong clue as to what has changed in the process. He already knows that the average lengths of the rods have increased. This has to be caused by something that moved the cutting blade away from the guide. A quick check of the machine may find that the blade has warped, or that the guide has loosened."

Tom broke back into his conversation. "Once the problem is located, it is corrected and noted. The process begins again and a sample of parts is taken. If the average from this sample returns to within the control limits, the operator is fairly sure that the problem has been corrected. In most cases, the problem is found and corrected long before the quality of the parts is affected. Control charts are remarkably sensitive."

The group began to break up as the dinner bell rang. Breton was now very curious about what Tom had said. He followed Tom to a table and selected the chair to his right. As they both sat down, Breton leaned over and asked, "How is it that these control charts can detect such small changes using so little data?"

"Well, if you have a moment, I can explain."

Breton nodded. Tom drew out a napkin and pen and began to doodle.

"The first important link in creating a control chart is the capability study. By taking samples at regular intervals for days we are seeing the natural variation of the process."

"In other words, you take samples during normal changes, such as using new materials, changing operators, and after routine machine adjustments," Breton responded.

"Yes, that's mostly true. However, we do try to keep changes in machine settings to a minimum. We want to know what the everyday good performance of the process is. We want to see the capabilities of the machine, the people, and the other parts of a process."

"I'll assume that this leads to a better prediction of future performance."

"That's right, Breton. Once we have the data from a capability study, we can estimate control limits. However, these first calculations are only estimates. It is best to try these test control limits for thirty days of production before we know that they really work."

"And if they don't?"

"Then we run a more extensive capability study."

A man sitting on the other side of Tom added, "Tell him about reaction plans. You don't have SPC if you don't have reaction plans."

Tom continued to talk and draw. "A control chart by itself is only a picture. It is a snapshot of the process. To make a control chart an effective problem-solving tool of continuous improvement, a reaction plan is needed.

"A reaction plan is the steps an operator should take as soon as a process is found to be out of statistical control. The reaction plan details the actions to be taken and the records to be kept. Our steel rod-cutting process example can illustrate how a reaction plan works."

Tom continued to draw on the napkin as he spoke. "On Tuesday at 3:05 P.M., Denise, the cutting operator, takes a sample of five rods and measures them for length. After two minutes, she has recorded the measurements and found an average length of 5.950 inches. Plotting this on the control chart reveals that the average is beyond a control limit. Denise has lost statistical control of the process.

"Underneath the control chart on the clipboard is a reaction plan. Denise turns quickly to this and follows its instructions. First, she circles the point out of statistical control on the chart. This will indicate to others that she detected a problem at this time. Later, a supervisor will initial this point to confirm that supervision was aware of the deviation.

"Second, Denise stops the cutting machine. This prevents the production of any more questionable parts and should alert the plant supervisor to a possible problem in the cutting area. It will also give Denise time to check the machine and to make necessary notes.

"Third, Denise moves the parts produced during the last hour away from the other part bins and tags the parts as IN-PROCESS HOLD. This alerts the inspectors to examine these parts before they are either put back into the production process or rejected as scrap.

"Denise now turns over the control chart and begins to make notes on the situation. She records the time and date of the loss of statistical control. As she checks the machine for possible causes for the problem, she will note these on the back of the control chart. Once a solution is found, she will note this too.

"Finally, the reaction plan informs Denise that if the solution is discovered, she should restart the machine and continue production. However, if after a set number of minutes, no solution is found, then a supervisor should be notified and support people called to the scene."

"Sounds like a lot of paperwork," Breton stated. "What kind of benefits can I expect?"

Tom responded slowly, "A reaction plan accomplishes two major tasks. First, it forces the recording of actions taken and the eventual solutions. This helps the company build up a database of information on solutions to common problems. Then, a mistake won't be repeated and each correction will occur a little faster.

"A reaction plan also gives a structure to the correction of production problems. By having the instructions printed on a separate sheet of paper, even a new operator of a process will know what to do and in what order. This helps save time and supervision."

Breton's conversation was interrupted when dinner was served. As the salads were being passed out, a familiar person took the chair across from Breton. It was Bob Barley, the quality manager from Urn Corporation. Bob and Breton exchanged greetings.

Another man joined Bob. He took a forkful of salad and said, "Bob, I have to talk to you about these control charts and SPC stuff."

"No problem. How can I help you?"

"I'm having problems convincing my people that the control limits are more important than the tolerances given for the part. Take a look at this chart for the motor shaft."

Bob turned toward Breton and said, "Breton, this is Leon DePaul, one of our new line supervisors." The two men exchanged nods.

Leon quickly produced several blueprints. He shifted a few of the pages and folded over one that was covered with coffee and grease stains.

"The print," said Leon, "specifies a shaft length of six inches and gives us a tolerance of plus or minus a tenth of an inch. Your SPC chart has control limits set at about five hundreths of an inch on either side of the six-inch average. That's only half of the tolerance!"

"I see your problem," Bob responded. "Let me finish dinner, and I'll explain how control limits and tolerance limits can live in harmony."

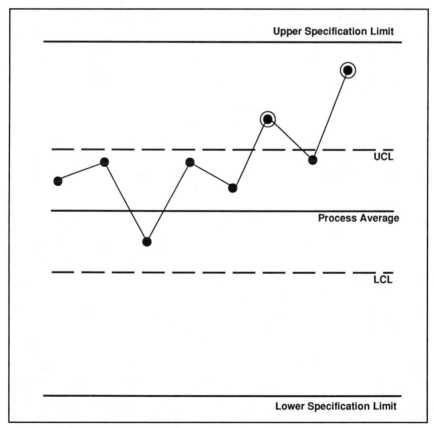

Figure 7.2 Control limits versus tolerance limits.

A quiet dinner followed. As the ice cream dishes were being collected Bob flipped his paper placemat over and began to draw lines. The first set of lines were the control limits. Outside of these he drew the specification limits.

Bob explained that the control limits on the chart Leon was using tracked averages. Because averages represented the center of a set of data, the actual variation of the parts would be greater than the variation of averages. In other words, the sizes of the motor shafts would vary farther than the control limits. Therefore, it was not unusual to see control limits that were smaller than the tolerance limits.

"Let me tell you a story," Bob continued. "You can tell it to your people to help them understand the importance of both control and tolerance limits.

"Let's draw a picture of a process that is so capable that the control limits are very small in comparison to the tolerance limits. As you can see, the control limits in this drawing are only a tenth as wide as the tolerance limits.

"The obvious questions for the machine operators will be: 'Why should we adjust the process when we lost statistical control?' and 'Are the parts still within tolerance?' What you should do, Leon, is point out to them that the control limits make no judgments about the usability of the parts. Instead, they detect problems with the process as they begin to occur. Thus, if they wait until a tolerance limit is exceeded, it might take several problems piling up to cause the faulty parts. In contrast, the control limits will detect each problem as it begins to occur.

"Then all you have to do is ask them, 'What would you rather do, solve small problems as they occur, or wait until several have combined to create a serious problem?' Obviously, the easier method is to solve a lot of little problems, instead of facing the frustration of having to untie a knot of problems."

"I see," Leon said. "The control limits are really a gauge of the quality of our processes. The tolerance limits are a guideline for the quality of the part. If we pay attention to both, we can better assure the success of getting the job done."

"Precisely," Bob responded.

Everyone at the table was interrupted by the president of the organization calling the meeting to order. After the usual formalities, the guest speaker was introduced. It was Bob Barley. Breton was surprised. The meeting announcement had listed an SPC expert from Chicago.

Bob quickly explained that the original guest was delayed by a snowstorm in Chicago and that he would fill in. He also noted that he would talk about the roles of different factory people in SPC.

Bob began with a story of his own company's implementation of SPC. One machine operator wanted to know what his role was in the new SPC system. Bob quickly outlined that a machine operator has three basic tasks to perform as a participant in continous improvement through SPC.

1. Fill in the chart. Each machine operator in an SPC system must complete a control chart for each job run.

2. React when necessary. When the control chart indicates the loss of statistical control, it is up to the operator to react first. The operator usually has only a few minutes to try and locate and correct the source of the problem. Only upon failing to correct the problem in the first few minutes does the operator alert a supervisor for assistance.

3. Contribute ideas toward the solution of problems. It is the operator who is closest to the production process. Therefore, every operator is the source of a wealth of information about the little quirks in a process. This information could be vital for finding a solution to a common manufacturing problem.

Bob next turned his attention toward the role of management.

"It is the job of management to listen to what the machine operators are saying about the quality of the process," Bob explained. "Management has the resources to make major corrections to a process.

"An interesting story is told of a welding shop during the early 1980s. For years the management of this shop had been frustrated by a high scrap rate among their welded products. Several investigations had all indicated that poor quality welds were a major cause of the high scrap rate. Thus, management issued a welding standard, told supervisors to watch the workers more closely, and they introduced rewards for work teams that could cut their scrap rates.

"No matter what management did, the scrap rate remained high. Then one day, they decided that SPC might be worth a try. A consultant was hired. He interviewed many plant employees. The consulant was getting ready to launch an intensive training program in SPC. As part of the training, he selected the weld quality problem as a class example.

"During the first class he asked the participants to list possible sources of the welding problems. One student mentioned something about how the type of wire used in the MIG welding equipment was never reliable. He said it was unreliable because he got a different brand of wire every week.

"The consultant went to find the welding wire purchasing agent after class. It was quickly learned that this agent bought up to fourteen different types of welding wire — whatever was on sale.

"The consultant and the class located a single brand of wire and had one of the welding teams use it for a week. Their scrap rate that week was less than half of the plant's average. Clearly, using so many brands of welding wire was hurting the quality of the welds.

"The cause of the high scrap rate was only discovered because the knowledge stored in the minds of the machine operators was tapped.

"Management also has a second major role in an SPC system. They must support it with time, money, and people. Most SPC systems fail without clear upper management support.

"Management must develop a long-term quality plan for the company. Then they have to back the plan *and* be active participants. One major corporation in Detroit clearly demonstrated how this was done. The top managers of the corporation drew up a quality plan that gave specific assignments to the middle managers.

"Part of this quality plan was training all employees in SPC methods. When the first class was held for the machine operators, the chairman of the board and the president were both in attendance. They sat at the front of the class and took notes. Clearly, this showed that the SPC program was very important."

Bob then told the group how SPC is also unique as a technology. SPC teaches all employees within a company to cooperate with each other in solving problems. Furthermore, everyone has to track the quality of various processes using a common tool of information, the control chart.

In many cases, this is the first time that a company has engaged in such teamwork. The lessons learned by this teamwork can lead a company into easily implementing many of the better-known technologies of manufacturing. Examples include just-in-time delivery systems, computer aided design and manufacturing (CADAM), participative management, and computer integrated manufacturing (CIM).

"Therefore," Bob explained, "SPC is really more than just a method for controlling quality. It is a system of collecting information to support a philosophy of continuous improvement."

Bob summarized, "We have seen that SPC is a method of gathering information about manufacturing processes. The key tool for this method is the control chart. It tracks critical characteristics of a part as it is being made. Should a problem in the production process begin to occur, it is usually detected by the control limits on a chart.

"Once detected, it is up to the operator to react to the problem by testing possible solutions. It is up to the management of the company to meet with the operators and discuss the problems the charts detect, but the operators don't have the resources to correct."

At this point, Bob finished his speech and took questions. Breton was impressed; several hands immediately appeared around the room.

The first question was on whether the state of Michigan would pay for SPC training. Bob outlined a new program where half of the cost of training is picked up by the state.

The second question was on how to chart several critical dimensions at the same time. Bob suggested that each person go back to his or her respective customer representatives and petition for the selection of single critical characteristics. Another person near the back of the room suggested the use of short-run SPC charts that can handle several dimensions at the same time.

More questions were asked, and Bob handled each one without hesitation. Breton realized that Bob Barley would be an excellent contact person to know. In fact, he waited until all of the questions had been asked. Then he was first to applaud as Bob left the podium.

As Bob came back to his seat, Breton leaned over and said, "Great speech, Bob."

Bob nodded in response. Any further conversation was interrupted by another member of the organization beginning a slide show on his trip to Japan. Breton would have normally moved closer to Bob to ask some questions, but the first slide caught his attention.

It was a photograph of stamping presses very similar to those used at ROB. What caught his attention was that the floor beneath the presses was white. There wasn't a trace of hydraulic fluid. The speaker pointed out that this particular machine was over thirty years old and showed no signs of neglect. Breton was impressed. If he could keep his equipment that well maintained, he knew half of his production problems would never occur.

After the slide show ended, the president of the organization made some closing remarks and asked the current members to continue their recruiting drive. A board member stood up and announced the current job opening in the quality field. After that, the meeting adjourned.

About half of the people in the room left right away, while Breton cornered Bob Barley. "Where can I get a person who can teach SPC to my people? You know, someone who can talk their language and make them understand?"

Bob responded with a list of the consultants in town who taught SPC. However, his enthusiasm for these people was obviously missing. Breton pressed him further. Bob tossed out a few random names of people from industry that might be good at teaching. Then Bob paused. "Well..." he said hesitantly. "There is one other possibility."

"Yes?" Breton responded eagerly.

"This guy isn't for everyone. I mean, he rubs some people the wrong way, but he knows his stuff."

"Can he talk nose-to-nose with the shop people?" Breton asked.

"Yes, and I've seen him teach SPC to people who couldn't write."

"Sounds perfect. Where can I meet him?"

Bob pointed toward a knot of people standing near the door. "He's over there telling stories again."

With that both Bob and Breton walked toward the group. As they approached, Breton could see that the person they were interested in was completely surrounded by people. Breton couldn't see his face yet, but when he saw the tennis shoes his heart sank.

Bob made a hole through the crowd and took Breton up to the center of attention, Jack King. "Breton, meet Jack King." He smiled at Breton and held out a hand.

"We've already met," Breton said sheepishly.

"What can I do for you" King asked.

"I'm looking for an instructor to teach my production people the principles of SPC."

"Well, let me buy you a drink. You're going to need it after I tell you something."

King grabbed Breton's arm and waved good-bye to his group, as he lead the confused production manager to the bar. King slapped down a ten-dollar bill and ordered two drinks. He turned to Breton. "Your boss, Mr. Mead, has the same idea. I'll be at your plant on Monday."

Breton looked at King and then his drink. After some thought he downed the drink. It looked like he was going to need another before this was all over.

CHAPTER 8

Control Charts
for Measurements

The Monday morning meetings in Mead's office were not becoming routine. Instead, each week saw surprises and new tensions rising among the managers. None of them were used to the rigid schedule of change Mead had imposed. Frank Graves was actively complaining of the whole project whenever Mead was out of earshot.

Mead, however, never felt better. He could see the first evidence of change taking hold. Breton and Brenda actually talked to each other once in a while. The union was more than enthusiastic about the idea of change. But, he still faced the audit coming in two months from his top customer.

"We must implement SPC as soon as possible." Mead began. "We only have a few weeks before we will be audited on our SPC system."

Immediately Breton and Frank raised objections. They were quickly quelled when Mead pointed out that this was not a topic for discussion. The angry silence that followed was quickly broken by King coming through the door. "I hope I'm not late." he said.

"Not at all." beamed Mead. Then Mead turned toward the managers. "Ladies and gentlemen, I give you Mr. Jack King from our local community college. If you have questions on how we will implement SPC, this is the man to ask."

Breton held back for a moment because of the conversation he had with King a few nights before. Brenda was quick to raise a single finger to indicate that she had a question. "Mr. King," she began. "How would you recommend that we implement SPC in the little amount of time that we have?"

"I wouldn't," responded King. Blank stares greeted this response. He noted these and continued. "To be specific, you won't be able to implement a complete SPC system in the few weeks that you have. However, you can plan and begin the implementation. Your customer should take this as a sign of good faith in meeting their requirements."

Breton noted that King was a different person alone in a room of managers. The joking and tricky demonstrations were missing; however, the tennis shoes were still there.

"What do you mean plan the implentation?" Anna Fitzhugh asked.

King responded immediately, "You have several key decisions to make that will determine the success of your SPC program."

"Such as. . .?" she inquired.

"The most important of these will be to leave this room today with a unanimous decision about what you will do. If a single person in this room harbors doubts, it will split loyalties and confuse the work force."

"Speaking of the work force," began Harris Harrison, "what's the union's role in an SPC system?"

"You," answered King, "are the keystone of an SPC system. The workers will be the ones to collect the data and fill in the charts. They will be the people to react to problems detected by SPC. It will be critical that the work force sees SPC as a job skill. It's not a requirement being forced onto the people. It's a tool to help them do their job better."

Other questions were raised, but Breton felt that something unusual was going on here. In a few minutes he had figured it out. King had never been to ROB nor had Mead introduced him to anyone in the room. Yet, King knew what positions they all held. There was more going on behind the scenes than he had suspected.

After about ten minutes of questions Mead suggested that the managers discuss what type of SPC system they wanted. This discussion became quite lively and spirited. After an hour they had to take a break to let things cool down.

When they returned, King had placed a flip chart of blank paper in the room. He started the second part of the meeting by asking each person to state his or her vision of SPC. These were duly noted on pieces of paper. As one large sheet was filled, King tore the sheet off of the pad and tacked it to a wall.

When he had finished this exercise the various ideas were spread across the room. The managers now could discuss the merits of each. Another hour passed, and Mead finally called a vote. The decision was to start small with only one or two work areas. The people in those areas would be trained and control charts placed in their work areas. As problems were encountered the proposed system would be modified.

Frank Graves got his opinion in last. He wanted the system to be cost effective. He wanted each team's time spent of SPC tracked and compared to any improvements that would be achieved. Both King and Mead agreed.

Personnel diretor Leon Marsden and Breton Rhodes were assigned the task of scheduling time for the workers to attend SPC training. They decided to select thirty people in two groups of fifteen to be the first SPC teams. Breton said that he would select work areas that had histories of product-quality problems.

A week later the first group of fifteen were assembled in ROB's lunchroom. These were the workers from the automatic screw machine area that had passed the screening for reading and math skills. Among the machine operators was the line supervisor and the setup mechanic. Each had been given a training manual and a calculator. Breton was also there.

King entered the room at exactly seven o'clock that morning. He introduced himself and explained the need for SPC. After his talk, Breton rose and explained why it was important for everyone at ROB to learn SPC.

Breton said, "You people have been chosen as the first SPC work team. You will be the test group. I want to hear about any problems this effort creates. You will help to design the final SPC program for the whole company. And, as an added bonus, your work quotas will be suspended during this test period."

The first work team nodded its approval. A few people were already nervously leafing through the training manual. Then King spoke.

"Before we begin, I want to assure you that what you are about to learn is very important for every working person in this country. In addition, this is not a class. I won't give you tests or call on you for answers. Feel free to cheat with your neighbor all you want. This is much easier to practice with a friend.

King glanced around the room for any questions. The hum of the ventilation system and the vending machines required him to speak louder than he normally did in a classroom.

"A lot of you are worried about the math involved in this method of SPC. Well, stop worrying. See this calculator?" King held a simple four-function calculator over his head. "This will do the math for you.

"Now, let me begin by explaining what SPC really is. Not some textbook definition, but what it really means."

He turned on an overhead projector that had been placed on one of the tables. A home slide projector screen stood behind him. He placed a clear sheet of acetate on the projector and wrote *SPC*.

"SPC normally stands for statistical process control. I want you to remember a different phrase, Stable, Predictable, and Capable." He wrote this on the sheet.

"What SPC does is check to see if your production process is stable, predictable, and capable of meeting your quality requirements. Think of control charts as another gauge attached to your machine. This gauge is read just like the gauges for pressure, temperature, rate, speed, and so on. This one will be just a little different."

King showed a transparency of a completed control chart. He pointed to the dots flowing across the page. "See how this process is stable? These dots represent the average diameter of a part being ground to shape. They all stay near this center line. Do you see these dotted lines? These are the control limits. Because all of the points stay inside of these limits, we can predict the behavior of the machine."

He paused. "Now, let's turn to page four of your training manual and begin to learn how to fill in one type of control chart. As I go along, I will note how the chart applies to your own situations.

"The first chart is called a control chart for variables. Specifically, it is called the average and range chart. It tracks anything that can be measured. You know, things like dimensions, strength, and flexibility. There is another family of charts that we will look at in a few weeks that covers attributes. Attributes are things that you count, like defects and scrap."

King reached into his briefcase and drew out a long metal object. "Does anyone recognize this object?" he asked. The team responded with dissatisfied agreement.

"Who can tell us something about it?" King inquired.

Steve Norwalk, a screw machine operator, put his hand up in the air slowly. King read the name tag on his shirt and said, "Yes, Steve."

"That's the hydrotransmission shaft that we turn in our department. It's been nothing but trouble since we got the job."

"A thirty percent plus scrap rate problem," Breton chimed in.

"Yeah," Steve acknowledged.

"Okay," King responded. "Let's see if we can determine how SPC will help improve the manufacturing of this shaft. The first step in any control chart is to find a critical characteristic. This is the one dimension that is more important than any other."

Without raising a hand or being prompted, Ken Verspries began talking. "We got seven outside diameters in different locations to turn on that part. If we have the slightest error on that first diameter, the rest will never work."

King looked over his glasses at Ken. "Thank you, Ken. Would you agree that the first diameter turned is our critical characteristic?"

The team nodded its agreement. King continued, "Our next step would be to study the specification and setup for this job." He looked over his shoulder at the nearby lunch table. Sitting on it was a short stack of papers. "Oh!" he exclaimed mockingly. "Look here, I just happen to have all of that information right here."

King set down the shaft and picked up the papers. He unfolded a blueprint and began to study it. "It says here that the first part of the shaft you turn is the power end on the left of this print. And it says that the diameter should be two inches, plus or minus 0.005 inches. Sounds like a tight tolerance to me."

The team immediately agreed. King glanced up briefly before he continued. "Our next step then is to see what your turning process is capable of producing. To do that, we will turn thirty shafts while leaving as many variables as possible constant. You know, things like the material used, the tools involved, the operator, and things like that."

He paused to place a new clear sheet on the projector. "This procedure is called a process control study.

"What do you know, I just happen to have thirty shafts lying right here in a box. Let's measure the diameter on these things and see what we find out."

The teamed moaned slightly at the thought of measuring shafts they had seen too much of already. King handed calipers to the five people at the front of the class. Then he gave each of them six shafts to measure. The five quietly measured the shafts and wrote down the measurements. King collected these figures as they were completed. He wrote down all thirty on the transparency.

"I don't want you to think that you have to do capability studies. The quality people should be handling that task. I'm doing it today so that you will understand where the numbers came from to create the control charts."

King calculated the average for the thirty readings. It turned out to be the required two inches. Then he calculated the standard deviation. With this he estimated that the variation in diameters was too high. He worked silently. He stood back and mentally double-checked the figures. He then turned toward the team and explained how this was a good place to start.

"What we have found out by examining these thirty shafts is that some of them are outside of the tolerance. In addition, we are safe in assuming that more will made out of tolerance. And, once out of tolerance, all of the future turnings will never correct the problem. The high scrap rate you have is probably due to the fact that parts start out bad."

"Been saying that for years," mumbled one of the team members.

"Well," continued King, "let's see how a control chart can help us correct the problem." He turned back toward the projector and displayed a blank control chart on the screen.

"Our first step is to study the process over time. What I want you to do this week is pull a few of the shafts you turn every couple of hours and measure this diameter. Then take this chart and write down what you found. This chart is called the average and range chart. It is meant for situations where you take measurements from a continuous production process.

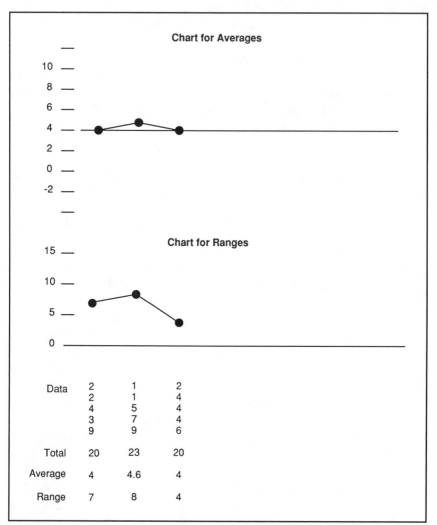

Figure 8.1 The first step in creating a control chart is to gather data.

"Continue to do this until you fill the data columns here at the top of the page. What we will do with this information is create control limits. Control limits are a prediction of how much variation we should see in future runs of these same shafts."

King then placed a new transparency on the overhead. This one looked like the control chart before but it had measurements in the data section.

"Here's some data from another company I've been to. In this case, the operator of a metal stamping machine paused every hour to measure the location of a hole. She would draw five parts each hour and measure this critical dimension. See how she wrote the time at the top of the chart and then the five measurements?"

King pointed at the chart on the screen as he continued to explain. "You all have calculators. Let's see how the operator found the average of these five parts. All you have to do is add up the numbers and then divide by the number of numbers. This gal had five readings, so we will divide by five. Who has the total?"

For a few seconds everyone in the team looked at each other. Then they realized that this was a hint to start calculating. Several pulled their calculators out from under the training manual and began to add the five readings.

A few minutes later Steve Norwalk called out, "Twenty." Another team member agreed.

'When I divide twenty by five, what's my average?" King asked.

"Four," responded most of the team.

"Good. I'll write that down in the spot below the numbers. The next spot on the chart asks for the range. The range is the distance between the highest and lowest number in our five readings. In this case our highest number is eight and the lowest is one. Just subtract one from eight to get the range."

"Seven," responded the team.

"Right. Now let's assign each of you to the remaining columns of data on this chart. Steve, you take the nine o'clock readings, Tom, you take the ten o'clock..."

King assigned each team member a different column of data. They wrote down the five readings they were responsible for and began to calculate. King took this opportunity to walk over to the soda machine. He pumped in two quarters and got no response. A swift kick to the change box resulted in a paper cup dropping down and being filled with sticky fluid.

A few minutes later the team was done with the exercise. One by one, King asked for the averages and ranges each student had obtained. He wrote these into the appropriate columns.

"Now," he began, "I can plot these averages and ranges on the chart below and look at the pattern that results."

He continued to talk, this time telling an amusing story, as he plotted the points along the two sections of graph paper. When he finished, two zigzag lines crossed the page. He pointed at the first line.

"These are the averages found each hour. Notice how they tend to follow this central line. We call that line the process average. If these points headed uphill or down, we would call it a trend. A trend would tell us that something is wearing out or breaking down. In this case, however, the process follows the center line. Therefore, I'm going to call this process stable. Remember how I said that's the first requirement of SPC?" Many nodded in agreement.

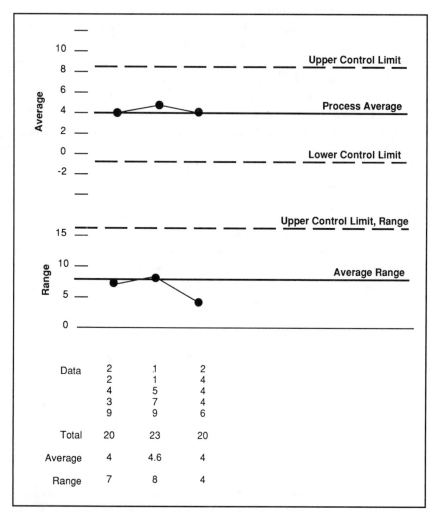

Figure 8.2 A control chart with control limits added.

"Now, look at the range plots. Remember, if the range gets too high, then there is too much variation in the parts. The range also follows the center line drawn on the chart. So far, this process looks pretty good.

"The next thing we have to determine is whether the process is predictable. What I'm going to do is predict the area where the next several plottings are going to fall. To do this I calculate the control limits. Take a moment and look on page seventeen for the formulas of a control limit."

The team leafed through the training manual. A few gave disapproving looks. "The good news is that the SPC coordinator in a plant usually does these calculations. What you will see is the chart with limits ready to be used. However, because you are the first team to use SPC here, I want you to see how the limits are created.

"Let's look at what we have so far. We have twenty-five averages and ranges. If I added all of these averages together and divided by twenty-five, I'd have a grand average, wouldn't I?" A few nods.

"And if I added the ranges together and divided by twenty-five I'd have an average range. The grand average would be written as an x-double bar. It means average of an average. The average range would be an R with a bar over it. That means, average range.

Control limits for averages:

$$\text{Upper Control Limit}_{\bar{x}} = \bar{\bar{X}} + A_2\bar{R}$$

$$\text{Lower Control Limit}_{\bar{x}} = \bar{\bar{X}} - A_2\bar{R}$$

Control limits for ranges:

$$\text{Upper Control Limit}_R = D_4\bar{R}$$

$$\text{Lower Control Limit}_R = D_3\bar{R}$$

where, $\bar{x}$ = average of the averages
$\bar{R}$ = average of the ranges

Sample Size	A_2	D_4	D_3
2	1.880	3.246	0
3	1.023	2.574	0
4	0.729	2.282	0
5	0.577	2.114	0

"Take a look at page seventeen and you will see the x-double bar and the R-bar in the formulas. All that's left to find are these other terms, A-two, D-three, and D-four. The good news is that these are listed in a table on page eighteen."

The nervous flipping of pages created a shuffling sound. The facial expressions of several students relaxed noticeably.

King proceeded to demonstrate how the control limit calculations were made. When he completed the control limits for the average, he drew them as large dotted lines above and below the center line on the chart. The points plotted for the average fell inside the lines. When he calculated the control limits for the range, the lower limit was zero. Therefore, he only drew the dotted line for the upper limit above the center line of the range chart.

"Normally," he explained, "we would calculate the grand average and plot it as the process average on this chart. In other words, we would draw this dark line across the page as the center line of the process. We would also draw the center line for the ranges using the average range. I knew these in advance, so I drew them in to show how the plottings would follow these lines.

"Now for the predictions." King pushed the finished control chart to one side so that only the last half of the plottings showed. Then he placed a second chart against the edge of the first chart. In the data area were more readings.

"These," he accounced, "were the readings taken the next day at the same machine, running the same part. Let me extend the control limits onto this chart and see if the averages and ranges continue to fall inside the control limits."

King drew the limits on the new chart and began to calculate and plot averages and ranges. He only tried the first four columns, but all of the points fell inside the lines.

"This is the predictability we are looking for. Now, let's review for a moment.

"We are using this piece of charting paper to track the measurements of a few parts pulled at regular intervals. In our example, the parts were checked every hour. The average and the range of the sample were calculated. On the chart are center lines and control limits for the average and the range. If the plotted location of these averages and ranges stay within the control limits, then the process is stable and predictable."

King paused. "So, what's the big deal, you ask?" Several people nodded.

"The importance of this chart is that it shows you in real time when a process is behaving well. If the points stay inside the control limits, then the process is behaving normally. As soon as a point falls outside of the limits, you have lost statistical control. That means that the process has changed a little bit. You might have a problem starting to occur. This would be a good time to stop and fix the situation."

King pointed at the chart still on the screen. "The chart is detecting something more subtle than scrap. It detects the small problems before they build into large problems that create the scrap and rework you experience.

"Let's look closer at your particular situation. You have to turn a lot of shafts in a day. A control chart could monitor the success of these turnings. Suppose I turn a shaft and it's 2.002 inches in size. Do I call this bad and try to fix it?"

Many students shrugged their shoulders. King turned toward Breton. "How about it, Mr. Plant Manager. How far can a piece or the average piece deviate before it's a problem?" Breton shrugged and turned away.

"You see, the control chart gives you a statistical standard for when to react. It tells you when a problem is starting to occur. The points inside the control limits vary, but this is the variation that is normal for the machine. A point outside of the limits indicates that is different. This is the time to take action.

"As we will see in our own tests, the control charts will detect other events as well. Everytime we lose statistical control we will look for the cause. Slowly, we will build up a list of causes. Then, if we can, we will eliminate as many of these causes as possible. Sure, it will cost us some time now, but the increased production and quality in the future will more than pay for the effort."

A student in the front row was making the signal for time-out. "I see we are getting near the end of this first session," said King. "I want you to monitor the shafts over the next three days until I come back. We'll use that data to calculate control limits and post your first control chart. From that point, we start looking for the cause of your troubles."

The first meeting of an SPC team had ended. Enthusiasm was not readily evident. Breton stopped King and asked him how to get the troops fired up for SPC.

"Just have one small success," replied the teacher. "Those people know the score on the factory floor. They're waiting to see if this is for real, or if this is just another management fad. If you want to get them excited, shoot down some long-standing method of doing something as soon as the chart shows that it does not help the company. You're paying them for productivity now. They don't get one dime more for quality."

King then left Breton standing alone in the lunchroom. Breton drifted over to the coffee machine. He was thinking. He bought a cup of the acrid drink and sat down to think some more. After fifteen minutes he reached a conclusion. He got up and headed for the production offices.

A few days later the first work team was in the lunchroom waiting for King. When he arrived on time, as usual, he was surprised to see a large sign hung at the front of the room. It read, FIGHTING FIRST. This was a curious development indeed.

As King scanned the class he spotted Breton in the front row with his notebook open. This was quite a change for the man that had stood to one side during the first meeting. Something was going on here.

"Good morning," King said.

"First!" shouted back the team.

King looked genuinely surprised. "What is going on here?"

"We had a little meeting of our own," Steve Norwalk answered. "We decided if we're going to be a team, we're going to do it right." Applause followed this remark.

"I see," King said. "And where is your control chart data I asked you to collect?"

Steve drew an overhead transparency out of his notebook and strutted to the front of the room. He placed it firmly onto the overhead projector and switched it on. The entire chart was filled with data. The averages and ranges had been calculated and control limits added to the plotting area. King was impressed; "Nicely done."

"There's more," responded Steve calmly. "We filled two and a half charts since you left." Ken Verspries brought up two more transparencies and laid them on King's table. King held these up to the light and inspected them. On the whole they were filled out correctly. However, a few points were outside of control limits.

"Nice job," King remarked.

"Yeah!" shouted the team.

"You are out of statistical control in a few places."

Ken answered, "So, tell us what to do."

"Hmmmm," said King as he turned toward the projector. "Let's start with the reaction plan." With that, he placed a new transparency on the projector. In bold letters it said:

> 1. Stop production.
> 2. Find the problem.
> 3. Try to fix it.
> 4. Locate supervisor if you can't fix it.
> 5. Write down what happened — no matter what.

"This," he began, "is a crude, but effective reaction plan. What it tells operators is that when a point lands outside the control limits, they should stop the production process and look for what caused this problem. If they can fix it easily, they do so, and write down how they did it. If it's not so easy to fix, then they look for a supervisor or setup person to help fix it. After that, everybody records what was tried and what finally worked."

King put a different control chart up on the projector. "This is the front of another control chart. It has the usual plottings and data. However, this is the back of the same chart." He placed a new transparency on the screen.

"Notice how any changes in the process have been noted. Look at this entry. It says here that at 10:10 P.M. the roll of steel was changed. Now look at this entry below. At 12:45 A.M. of that same shift the average size of the part got too large. They determined that the new steel was too thick, and they had to shim the stamping die to fix the problem."

Looking at the team he continued, "Now think about how important information like this is to yourself and a company. Imagine that you are transferred tomorrow to a stamping job like this one. What would you rather do, spend weeks learning all the ins and outs of this particular process, or read the back of these charts to see what commonly goes wrong with the machine and the most common ways to fix those problems?" The unconscious nodding of heads indicated that the team was beginning to grasp the importance of reaction plans and the documenting of the process changes.

King continued, "Now think about the company. If the company assigns you to problem-solving teams, wouldn't the information on the back of these charts be a wealth of ideas for what problems to solve? Wouldn't you be able to document the problems that management has ignored all of these years. More nodding and more looks toward teammates.

"Did you know that without these notes on the back of a chart, SPC is nothing more than some pretty pictures on the factory floor?"

King paused to let this sink in. "Now let's look at your charts again." With that he placed the first chart back on the projector.

"Your first chart went pretty good. However, what happened here at two o'clock when these points went out of statistical control?"

"Henry," Steve called out. "That was your shift. What happened?"

"I'm not sure. It was out for two hours, and then it came back into the limits."

"Ah," said King. "See how not keeping a log of process changes cripples our ability to learn from these two points?"

King placed the second chart on the screen. "Take a look at the pattern from the start of this chart to nine o'clock on Wednesday. See how most of the points are below the center line? Now look at the rest of the points. See how they are all above the center line. Would you say that the average size of the part shifted at nine o'clock on Wednesday.

"Sure would," responded an operator.

"What happened at that time?" King inquired.

"That's easy," Ken responded. "That's the time we had to replace the cutting tool head because it cracked. I bet the change in the average size happened because we didn't calibrate the cutting tools back to the center line."

"Very good," said King. "This is the type of thinking that goes along with SPC. If the tools had been set to reproduce the same average piece as before, this shift would not have happened. And, when we look at the shift, we can see that his change increases the variation in the final batch of parts.

"To see why you're having scrap and rework problems, let's look at the capability of the process." King showed the team how the samples they took were a limited amount of the variation in all of the parts produced. He repeated the same lecture on variation that Breton had heard in his class. However, Breton noted that King altered the presentation of the lecture to better fit the type of people now in the room.

King showed how a few simple calculations could create what he called a *Cpk Index*. When the Cpk was under 1.00, the process would produce scrap. The idea was to get a process as far over 1.00 as possible. The team quickly calculated that the Cpk for the turning process they were monitoring was 0.67. It was obvious that improvements in variation were necessary.

Steve Norwalk had looked puzzled throughout King's explanation. King finally asked, "So, Steve, what's your question?"

"Well," responded Steve, "I've been trying to figure out the relationship between the control limits and the specification limits."

"How do you mean?" prompted King.

"Well, look at our control limits. They're way beyond the specifications. Why wouldn't we react when the specification limit is exceeded and just ignore the control limits?"

"Good question, Steve. I'll tell you why. You see, the specification limits were established by an engineer sitting far away from the production area. He probably calculated that the plus or minus 0.005-inch tolerance was best for this part. Unfortunately, he also probably has never been here to see if such a tolerance can be held."

Many of the students' eyes widened with agreement.

"What a control chart does is sample the actual production process. From each small sample we get an average and a range. The control limits show us how far these averages and ranges will vary in this process. That's reality. The specifications are the ideal.

"A capability study helps us to compare the ideal to the reality. The role of the control chart is to monitor what the process is capable of doing."

"So," ventured Steve, "the specifications are a target we try to achieve, and the control chart is one of the tools we use to guide us."

"Bingo," responded King.

"Returning to his original topic, King outlined how the reaction plan for the team's chart would help them to make adjustments as the process began to change. They learned how trends or runs of averages could occur on a chart and why these required a reaction. The example King gave was the tool wear on the screw machines. As the tools wore out, the dimensions on the part would probably change. This would usually be detected as a rising or falling trend in the points.

King told the team to start tracking process changes, especially tool wear. If they saw seven points in a row forming a trend, they were to react, even if none of the points were outside of the control limits.

The team seemed very enthusiastic at the idea of attacking production problems directly. King noted the obvious change in their attitudes. He waited until this meeting adjourned before asking Breton about all of this.

"Oh, yeah," said Breton. "I had a little talk with the crew a couple of days ago. I told them that if we didn't attack this as a team and have some kind of success, then management would go back to quotas and layoffs as a way of life."

"Kind of a risky statement, isn't it, Breton?" King asked.

"True, but if we don't have SPC in four weeks, it won't really matter what I say."

With that Breton forced a smile and left the room. King stayed behind long enough to pack his papers and overheads. This could be fun, he thought.

The next day the members of the Fighting First team were at their work stations. They weren't setting any production records, but they were noting the changes in their machines and materials. Steve Norwalk had to prompt a few people to be briefer in their writings and faster with their work.

During the afternoon Ken had a point on the chart go over a control limit. The range was too high. "Yo, Steve," yelled Ken over the noise of the machines. "What does it mean when the range is too high?"

Steve walked over taking care not to slip on the oil covering the floor. "Let me see your parts." Steve grabbed a spindle Ken had just turned. The part was still warm to the touch. Steve placed the spindle into a small measurement fixture at the inspection station. By this time several team members had wandered over to watch.

As Steve rotated the spindle in the fixture, the dial gauge set to measure diameter swung up and down violently. "Ken, you're cutting them out of round. Take a look in the machine."

Ken pulled open the shield door and was met with a boiling cloud of heated oil. He peered through the mist and saw a wad of spiral cuttings jammed near the cutting head. "Here it is," he called out. He grabbed a long hook-shaped tool and picked the metal bits out of the machine. Then he closed the door and started the machine.

The first set of parts produced were carried in gloved hands to the inspection station. This time they were round. Ken measured the diameters and plotted the range on the chart. This time it fell within the control limits.

"Damn," he said as he turned over the chart to note the events of the last ten minutes. "This chart really works."

Later that night, Breton was leaving his office and cutting through the screw machine area. He wanted to see if the second shift was keeping data on the chart correctly. As he passed one machine, he saw a woman duck behind one of the stock piles. Breton made an abrupt turn toward the pile to see if this operator was sneaking a smoke or something.

"What's going on here?" he demanded.

The frightened woman was crouched down on a small pile with one of the SPC training manuals and a calculator. "I'm trying to figure out how this control chart stuff works," she said nervously.

Breton was embarassed. He apologized. "That's all right, you practice it all you want. Just don't hide when you do it. If your supervisor doesn't let you do it in your spare time, tell him to see me."

Geesh, thought Breton as he continued to his car. The world is sure becoming a different place.

The following week King held his third meeting with the Fighting First team. They had begun to record more information on their chart. They had completed four charts now. King talked to them about the results and what could be learned. Eventually, the conversation turned to the future.

"The next step in the SPC process is to keep this chart in statisticial control for thirty days. That will assure both you and management that you understand how to maintain variation on the parts. You see, you are no longer guessing how to fix problems. You are detecting them earlier and correcting them quicker.

"At the end of thirty days, we will perform another Cpk calculation. That will tell us the process capability when it's running under statistical control. You can see already that the Cpk is rising since the first chart you recorded. It's up to 0.80 on this newest chart."

"And our scrap rates are down by a third," added Breton.

"Have we told Mr. Management?" quipped King.

"The memo's on his desk now," Breton responded.

"You're learning," said King. Then he turned toward the rest of the team. "When the thirty-day period is over, your SPC team is in place. The chart is used forever. As you reduce variation, the control limits will have to be changed inwards to reflect the improvement.

"If you start new jobs with similar requirements, you will now know what you should be able to produce in the way of quality. As we will learn in future meetings, we can also use this historic information to do a more aggressive form of problem solving. What we will do is first eliminate the easy and obvious situations with the control chart. Then we will select those problems that are more difficult to fix. To correct these, we will work as a team to find and eliminate the causes of the problem."

Pointing a single finger in the air he said, "This is what I mean by continuous improvement. Everyday you work to make the job run a little easier and a little better."

CHAPTER 9

Control Charts
for Attributes

It was the third week of SPC training at ROB, Incorporated. King had left his home early that morning due to the eight inches of snow that had fallen the night before. Although the roads were difficult, he arrived ten minutes early.

King didn't want to appear in the classroom early, so he took a detour through the production area. He was crossing one of the elevated catwalks over a conveyor line when he sighted Breton several yards away yelling at a line supervisor.

King stopped and leaned against the railing on the catwalk. He watched Breton first point at a piece of paper and then at the face of the supervisor. The supervisor was nodding in agreement and making every effort to look away from Breton. Neither of them had spotted King watching.

After a few minutes the supervisor grabbed the piece of paper from Breton and scrambled off into the gang of machinery. King picked up his briefcase and continued walking. Breton saw him coming and waved.

"Good morning, Mr. King. Have any problems driving in today?"

"Not much. I took the pickup today. Anything new?"

"Oh," said Breton. "I had to chew out one of the off-shift supervisors just now."

"What happened?" probed King gently.

"He took down the control chart so that his people wouldn't waste time on it."

"I take it that you corrected his attitude," King suggested.

117

"Actually, I threatened to introduce a new entry way into his body."

"Why," asked King, "have you taken such an interest in the SPC program? It hasn't demonstrated any benefits to you yet."

Up until this point the two men had been strolling slowly toward the lunchroom. The last remark made Breton come to a stop. He glared at King for a moment. Then his facial expression relaxed.

"Insurance," he replied.

"Insurance?"

"Yeah. Look at it from my perspective. If we don't pass our SPC audits with customers, we lose business. And I'll be one of the first managers to get the ax. If we sort of try and we don't get much in the way of results, then everyone is unhappy and we wasted a lot of money. However, if the program succeeds, I'll get some of the credit."

"I see," responded King.

The two men continued into the lunchroom without exchanging another word. Inside the room the second work team assigned to training was waiting. A few people snuffed out cigarettes that weren't allowed in the lunchroom. The rule was not strictly enforced, but Breton had been cracking down on other rules lately, and no one was in the mood to take a chance.

King set his briefcase on a table as he switched on the overhead projector. Brenda Patterson sat near the back of the room. She had been assigned to follow the progress of this group. Breton was supposed to watch only the first group, but he seemed to drop in a lot on Brenda's group. She was aware of his desire to see SPC work and to grab a large share of the credit.

"We have a problem," began King. "We have learned how control charts work, and we have looked at the average and range chart. However, the bulk of what you do involves attributes, such as defects and defectives.

"Basically, you people are responsible for the injection molding of parts. Let's take the example of the NC-234 computer cover job." King picked up the cover to a personal computer. "This cover has some critical dimensions, but as we learned last week, you do not have the authority to make the changes necessary to control those dimensions. Instead, you are expected to prevent visual defects on these covers."

Things had not gone as well for this second team as they had gone for the first team. The management at ROB was convinced that this group could control the dimension problems with the computer covers. However, the attempt to keep an average and range chart on the molding process failed. The operators could track the dimensions, but they could not alter the molding machine controls.

Further investigations discovered that most of the dimensional problems resulted from plastic resin mix variations used in the process. In addition, a quick check of the mold showed that it was not made to specifications.

These were serious problems beyond the authority of a handful of machine operators. King suggested that Mead assign the engineering staff to the task of correcting the dimensional problems.

The previous session ended with the second team demanding that they be given a project that was more within their grasp. King agreed and promised to find a better problem for the team. The computer cover was still a good choice. In addition to the dimensional problems, it also had several quality attribute problems.

"This plastic computer cover," continued King, "has several attributes that must be corrected. Before we discuss these, I want to explain a few definitions."

King wrote *Defect*, *Defective*, and *Checklist* on an overhead transparency. "A defect is some sort of flaw in the product. Take a look at the computer cover. What are some of the defects you have to watch for while this is being manufactured?"

"Flashing," called out one team member.

"The presence of excess plastic along the edge of the part, right?" King asked. The group agreed. He began to write the defects.

"Cracks," chimed in another team member, while his companion said "sinks."

Peeling, scratches, short shots, delamination, and warp, added other people. After only a minute or two, Kings screen was filled with possible defects.

"A lot of defects are possible," King stated. "It would be in our best interest to classify each of these. The traditional approach is to use levels of severity. For example, would I count a scratch that can barely be seen on the same level as a scratch that is large and wide?"

"No way," responded the group.

"That's right. Instead, I create three categories for defects. The first category is called a critical defect. These are defects that are dangerous to the people that use the product or the people that make the product. For example, a car with brakes that don't work has a critical defect.

"Any critical defects on our list?" asked King. After a moment of examining the list the group decided that there were no critical defects shown.

King continued, "A second category is the major defect. That's a defect that would affect your ability to sell this cover. Which of these defects would be considered major?"

The group decided that some forms of scratches, peeling, and cracks were major defects.

"A third category is the minor defect. That's a defect that isn't so severe the customer will reject the product, but it is still noticed by the customer. Generally, these are the annoying types of defects. We don't like them, but they don't affect the performance of the product. For this cover that would include very small scratches, dents, and other such defects."

King circled the word *defective* on the transparency. "A defective part," he declared, "is one that has one or more defects that make the part unusable for its intended purpose. For example, this cover is meant to be assembled onto a personal computer. Because it makes up most of the exterior of the computer, it has to be both functional and attractive.

"If a customer sat a monitor on this cover and it collapsed, the cover is said to be defective. If the cover has a very large scratch or sink, the assembly plant you sell this to may call it defective."

King began quizzing the group. "Can a single defect make one of these covers defective?"

"Yes," answered the team.

"Can a cover have many defects and still not be defective?"

The team hesitated.

"It is possible if all of the defects are minor," King replied.

"What is the maximum number of defects allowed on a part today in manufacturing?" he asked. Silence.

"The answer for today's manufacturing systems is zero. Companies are actively seeking zero defects in their products. Why? Because if all products are free of defects, then they should be usable and saleable. That means greater profits for the company."

"What is the cost of a defective cover?" King asked to end his quiz. More silence.

"Say, I don't know," instructed King.

"I don't know," responded the group.

"Neither do I, and that's a big problem. Nobody knows what it costs to have defective covers. I can tell you that most companies find that it costs several times the expense of the material wasted." A few surprised looks appeared among the group members.

"In fact, the average company in America throws away about 15 percent of its production. If you multiplied the cost of each part against a 15 percent scrap rate, you would find that it doubles the cost of production." More surprised looks appeared.

"The first step in attacking the problems associated with defects and defectives is to develop a checklist." King now circled the words *defect checklist* on the overhead transparency.

"A defect checklist," he explained, "is a description of each possible defect and its levels of severity. Here's an example." King withdrew the transparency and replaced it with a new one. This one had neatly typed descriptions.

"This is the defect checklist for maple syrup. I got it from a small food producer on the other end of town. I like it because it's a short list. The first item is contamination. At a critical level it describes large pieces of foreign matter and obvious mold growths. Notice how it takes pain to define *large foreign pieces* as any contamination of one millimeter or larger. This helps the people looking at the syrup to know when contamination is bad enough to be called critical.

"Major contamination is defined as pieces of foreign matter less than a millimeter in size. See how there is no definition for minor contamination. The manufacturer feels that if it's not visible, then it's not going to annoy the customer.

"For the computer cover, you would have to go through a list of possible defects and develop these types of descriptions. In addition, you would want to present a description of the product when it's done right. In other words, a perfect part. The best way to present all of this information is to draw pictures or save samples of the different types of defects. This helps all of you to count and classify the defects accurately.

"I'm sure that you have all seen the case of disappearing defects. You know the situation. You've made a thousand covers that are badly needed by the customers. However, there are severe defects on many of the covers so the lot is rejected by quality control. A few minutes later the marketing people are down on the production floor looking at the covers. Slowly they discredit enough of the defects to make the lot acceptable. Disappearing defects." The group chuckled in recognition of the situation. They had seen it happen many times before.

King continued, "The advantage of a defect checklist is that this game cannot be played any longer. Instead, the focus shifts to monitoring the process and preventing the defects in the first place.

"What we will learn today is how to track and correct the process to reduce the number of defects that occur. Of course, before we can do that, we have to have a defect checklist."

King reached into his briefcase and drew out a collapsible Polaroid® camera. "We are going on a beauty search. We are going onto the floor to find examples of each of the defects you listed. Then we will try to find one perfect part. We will have a beauty contest for the best-looking part. Then I will photograph it and the defects. These pictures will make up the core of our defect checklist."

The group was organized into two-person search teams. They were led into the plastic molding area. Several skids of computer covers were waiting for the team. Each search team was assigned a particular defect. Their job was to find a good example of the defect. Once that was accomplished, they then had to find what they thought was a perfect cover.

Within a few minutes, each team had found its respective defect. These were labeled and lined up on the factory floor. King walked from cover to cover photographing each. Each picture rolled out of the camera and was placed on the matching cover.

The search for a perfect cover consumed much more time. King could see some team members arguing with each other over the merits of a particular cover. In the end, each team presented its cover to the group, now standing in a circle. The covers were given numbers and scraps of paper were passed around the group. A quick vote was taken and the perfect part selected. King also photographed this part.

Notes were added to the back of each photograph and the covers were placed back onto the skids. The team returned to the lunchroom in time for a brief break.

Afterwards, King began explaining how attribute control charts work. "There is a whole family of control charts designed for monitoring attributes, like the defects we just hunted down. There are four that are the most commonly used in industry. The c-bar and u-bar charts monitor the number of these defects per part. The p-bar and the np-bar charts monitor the number of defective units a process produces. We will start with the p-bar chart as our first example."

King reached into his briefcase and drew out a piece of twenty by twenty-four-inch paper. He snapped two pieces of tape off of a nearby roll and posted the blank chart on the wall.

"All attribute charts," he announced, "use this type of charting paper. On the bottom you will note an area for listing the possible types of defects for the product you are monitoring. A count is kept of each occurrence and totaled at the very bottom of the chart. That total is plotted on the graph paper that fills the middle of the chart. Nothing could be easier.

"Let's start with a specific example. I have six months of scrap reports for the computer cover. Every week the number of covers that had to be scrapped was recorded on these reports. What a p-bar chart does is track the percentage of parts scrapped. The p in p-bar represents percentage. The bar over the p means average percentage."

King placed a clean sheet of acetate on the overhead projector and wrote down the scrap numbers for the first twenty-five weekly reports.

	Production	Scrap
Week 1	1,200	130
Week 2	2,000	175
Week 3	1,500	200
and so on . . .		

"These are the reported numbers. To create a p-bar chart we translate each week's scrap count into a percentage. We do this by dividing the number of scrap pieces by the number of covers produced that week.

"Take the first week for example. If we divide the 130 scrap pieces by 1,200 production pieces we get 0.108. That number is called a proportion.

If you multiply it by 100 you get the actual percentage. You can save the batteries on your calculator by moving the decimal point two places to the right. In this case, it represents 10.8 percent scrap.

"We will use the proportion on our chart. What I want you to do is calculate the proportion for each of the twenty-five weeks. Now, there's a dozen of us here so I'll assign two weeks to each person."

King pointed to each student and called out the weeks they were responsible for calculating. The team dug into the assignment and was ready with answers in only a few minutes. King listed the answers on the overhead projector.

He finally declared, "These are the plotting points for our chart. Let me draw them on this chart I've taped to the wall."

King proceeded to write the proportions along the bottom of the chart and to plot the corresponding point on the graph paper. He connected the points with lines and the results looked a little like a seismograph readout during an earthquake.

"To find the process average, I merely total all twenty-five weeks of production and scrap. I divide the total scrap figure by the total production figure."

He quickly totalled the figures on his calculator and announced a process average of eleven percent. Walking over to the p-bar chart on the wall he drew a single bold line across the page at the eleven percent level. Half of the proportion plots fell above this line and half below.

King spent the next several minutes explaining how control limits were formed for a p-bar chart. The formula looked intimidating to the team at first, but King showed them how the calculator could make quick work of the problem. When he had calculated the control limits, he drew these as heavily dashed lines above and below the process average. Most of the points fell inside of the control limits.

Now King drew out a second large, blank control chart and taped it to the right of the first chart. The two edges of the charts were against each other. King took pains to line up the graph paper portion of the charts. He then used his black marking pen to extend the control limits from the first chart onto the second chart.

"Now," he said, "let's take the remaining data from the scrap reports and plot them on this new chart to see if they are in statistical control."

King wrote down the new data on a new sheet of acetate on the overhead projector. The team members calculated the proportion for each of the weeks. As a team member got an answer he or she went up to the new control chart, wrote down the proportion, and plotted the corresponding point. After ten minutes the new chart was completed. About a third of the points were out of statistical control.

King paced back and forth in front of the chart exchanging glances between the chart and the team. He drew to a sudden halt and asked, "Is this process under control?"

"Nope," ventured a team member near the front of the class.

"That's right. In fact, there are two things wrong with this chart. One is that we cannot predict where the next scrap rate is going to fall. The second is that we have no idea what made the covers scrap. See this area near the bottom of the chart? We haven't written in all of the possible defects and kept count on which defect made each part a piece of scrap."

King lifted up a cover from under the lunchroom table. The computer cover looked like someone had left it in the rear window of a car too long on a summer day. The distinctive boxy shape of a normal cover had been distorted into something that looked more like a candy dish.

"Is this cover defective?" asked King mockingly. Laughter was the only answer he could get in return.

"Which defect made this cover defective?" he asked.

"I think it's warp," replied a line supervisor. The team roared with more laughter.

"Right. And every time a cover is rejected as scrap, someone has to record on this chart why it became scrap. That's your assignment for next week. I want you to start a tally on why each piece was scrapped. Class dismissed."

Later that Afternoon

Mead was obviously tense. He nervously stood by his desk compulsively rearranging papers and pens. King was seated in a corner chair. He was slowly drinking a mug of ice tea with a slice of lemon hanging precariously from one side of the glass.

"We only have two weeks before the SPC survey," Mead said.

"Relax. Your teams are coming along fine. Just make sure that you have a documented plan of training and implementation for SPC."

"Have you ever been through one of these things before, Jack?"

"A couple. They can be hard on the nerves, but you usually do very well." King finished his tea and placed the mug on the coffee table well to the left of the nearest coaster. "You should talk to other people who have been through this and get some tips. I've got to go now. I'll talk to you again next week."

Mead sat alone in his office for a moment. Finally, he picked up his telephone receiver and called Ron Headly at the Urn Corporation. Mead wrote down several ideas that Ron passed along. He hung up the phone and stared at it for a minute. He picked it up again, but hung up before he even started to dial.

Mead looked at his watch. Eleven-thirty. As he took his coat out of the reception area closet, he told Sally he was going to lunch early today. He went to his car and pulled out onto Fuller Avenue. A few blocks away he pulled into a gas station. He trudged through the snow to a pay phone on the side of the building. He dialed a number and waited. "I need to talk to you," he said.

After a long pause he said, "I'm having lunch at the club. Why don't we talk there?" After a shorter pause he hung up. A few minutes later he was driving east on Cascade Road. Mead felt a little better.

The following week, King was back with the second team talking about what they had discovered keeping track of the causes of the scrap parts. One team member had brought the list written on an overhead transparency. He placed this on the projector. King looked at the results. He nodded confirmation of its accuracy.

"You have done well," he declared. "See how scratches caused more rejections than any other defect? Once you accumulate several weeks of this type of data, you will be able to see which defect is causing most of your scrap. Then you direct your attention on preventing this defect."

"Let me give you an example." King pulled the first transparency off of the projector and replaced it with a new sheet. This one had several defects listed and their frequency of occurrence.

"This is a list of the defects car dealers have reported from new car deliveries. Notice how scratches and dirty cars are the two most frequent problems reported? Take a second look at the two leading defects again. Do you suppose that they might be related?"

King paused to survey the room. A few people were making facial expressions of agreement.

He continued, "When the cars are delivered to dealers, they are packed onto carriers. If the car is dirty and an employee has to squeeze between the cars, doesn't it seem logical that some scratches will result?

"What the car dealers did was to wash the cars before unloading them. They would take a high-pressure hose and squirt down the cars right on the carrier. The number of dirty cars dropped to zero, and the number of scratches fell as well.

"You see, when we can find the cause of the scrap, then we have the power to attack it." King answered a few questions about the p-bar chart before he continued with his discussion on how to use an attribute chart for finding and fixing problems.

"The attribute chart is a powerful tool for continuously improving a process. Let's take the example of the computer covers. Right now you have to scrap about 11 percent of them for one reason or another."

King placed a transparency of a p-bar chart on the overhead projector. He drew a heavy line at the 11 percent level. He added a zigzag line over the left side of the line to represent data points.

"If we do nothing, the process will continue to produce 11 percent scrap. In fact, that's the capability of the process, to produce a lot of scrap. Now, what makes attribute charts different is the fact that we want statistical control at first, but we don't want to maintain it.

"Think about Breton coming out to your work station and asking how everything is going. You turn to him and say, 'Great. Just look at this control chart. We're producing 11 percent scrap with high predictability.'" The team members chuckled.

"As you could imagine this is not the answer any manager wants to hear. So once we have statistical control we know that we understand how the process works. Now we have to improve its performance. After all, what is the maximum amount of scrap we can tolerate?"

"Zero," shouted the team.

"Correct," responded King. "Therefore, we want to drive these plotted points down to zero on this chart. First, we solve some of the problems and the average plotting should decrease."

King continued his zigzag line, but this time it was on a downward trend. "As we solve more problems we can see if we are making real improvements by watching how far down the plottings go. Eventually, we will reach a point where we start to hit zero a couple of times. Do you know what we do then?" No reply.

"We circle the zero point and try to find out what went right that day. We would do the same for any point that landed below the lower control limit. This shows that a significant decrease in scrap happened that week. The trick is to find out why and try to repeat those conditions the next week.

"Eventually, the plottings will all fall to near zero. At that point you can discard the control limits and circle any point that is above zero. If I go three weeks without scrap then even a single piece of scrap means the process might have changed.

"This is how we interpret and use an attribute chart. Any questions?" There were none. "Let's take a break, and then I'll show you another type of attribute chart."

The team moved quickly from their seats into lines already forming at the vending machines. King turned toward the p-bar chart hanging on the wall and hoped that this company was indeed ready for an SPC audit.

The second half of that day's session was spent discussing the c-bar chart. As King explained, c-bar charts track defects on each part.

King said, "The procedure for the c-bar chart is to take a fixed number of parts at regular intervals and count how many defects you find. The automotive companies do this at their assembly plants. They take a car at random every day and pour over it looking for even the tiniest defect. The thinking is that if the assembly plant workers are tougher about defects than any customer, then they will produce cars that will satisfy every customer."

"They didn't check my car," mumbled a team member in the back of the room.

King ignored the remark and continued. "I have now hung a new blank control chart on the wall. To create a c-bar chart we have to calculate the average number of defects we find in a fixed sample size. Any suggestions on how many computer covers we should examine, say, every hour?"

"Two," suggested Brenda. "Our floor inspector is already looking at a couple every hour."

"That's what I like about attribute charts," remarked King. "The data for them usually exists before you start charting. Brenda, do you have that floor inspector's reports?"

"They're in my office. Do you want me to get them?"

"Please."

King entertained the team with a story while Brenda walked the short distance to her office. About two minutes later she was back in the lunchroom with the needed data.

King put a new sheet of acetate on the overhead projector and began listing the defects that were listed on the reports. The number of these defects found over a period of several weeks was also listed. He then totaled all defects and calculated the average number of defects per every set of two covers. The answer was 1.6.

King said, "What we see here is that the average cover will likely have some sort of defect. We can see by the list I just made that most of these defects are very minor. However, they are still there and like I've said before, you cannot tolerate any defects.

"Take a moment now and look at the totals for each type of defect. Do you see one that stands out?"

"Sure," replied a molding machine operator. "It's scratches, just like on the other chart."

"That's right," confirmed King. "This tells us that scratches occur frequently. We can see that on our c-bar chart. The p-bar chart tells us that the scratches get bad enough to cause many covers to be rejected as scrap.

"What we need to do is to use the c-bar chart as a monitoring device to see when and where the scratches occur. If they are occurring with each sample, we will know that there is a consistent cause. If they occur every now and then, we will know that a special cause comes and goes. Either way, we will begin to track down the cause and eliminate it.

"The p-bar chart will be our scorekeeper. As we attack these problems, it will tell us whether we are winning in the big picture of scrap rates. Once we force those down, we will be able to demonstrate real savings in hard cash." The team seemed pleased with that idea.

"Now, to help us find the cause of the scratches I want you to complete the c-bar chart using regular samples from the production line. In addition, I want you to fill out a special piece of paper."

King put a new transparency on the projector. It was a perspective drawing of the computer cover. "I figured that the scratches are only important on the outside of the cover. Therefore, I want you to mark on this drawing where the scratches are found."

Brenda's brain sent a signal that something was wrong here. Why did King have a drawing of only the outside of the cover? How did he know that scratches would be the most frequent defect? Somebody has showed him the defect reports before class. But who? The records are kept in her desk. She would have to think about this after class.

King continued, "What a map of the cover does for us is look for a consistent cause of the defects. In industrial terms we call this lift truck disease. The term comes from a study done on the dents being found in large metal stampings.

"What the study team did was map the location of dents found on the parts. It seemed that they were all located on the same edge of the part. They traced the handling of the parts and discovered that the dents occurred when a lift truck packed the parts onto a train car. Drivers couldn't see when the parts were tight up against each other, so they just went forward until they heard the distinctive crashing noise."

The team winced at this story. They could envision the metal parts being slammed against each other.

"The study team suggested that protective cages be placed around the parts during shipment. Do you know what? The dents along the edges suddenly disappeared.

"This is what we are going to do. I want you to keep track of how many types of defects you find. I want you to track the location of scratches in particular. Then next week, we will start talking about what we can do to improve the situation."

The team broke up at the end of the session and headed back toward the production area. King and Brenda were chatting at the front of the room.

"Mr. King," began Brenda, "how long before we are going to see benefits from SPC?"

"Maybe next week, maybe in a year," he answered.

"What can we do to speed the results?"

"Teach them how to work in teams to solve problems, support them, and encourage them."

"I'm trying," sighed Brenda.

"Good, because I've recommended that you teach the group how to do group problem solving in a few weeks."

"What?"

"See you next week," King said as he hurried out the door.

Brenda was stunned for a moment. She was spending every hour at the plant preparing for the SPC audit in two weeks. Now she would have to find time to put together an instructional program in group problem solving. She was thinking this dilemma over when she noticed a file folder King had left behind. She picked it up and discovered that it was his lesson plan for problem-solving methods.

Inside the front cover was a note. It said, "I hope this will help you. JK." Who is this guy? Brenda thought as she thankfully placed the folder in her notebook and headed back to her office.

Two weeks later the customer representative arrived. His overcoat and suit both had that crumpled look of a man who spends his life on the road. Before he was fully into the reception area, he had lit a large cigar. He announced himself to the receptionist as, "Fritz Wolf, customer representative."

As the receptionist dialed Mead's number, Fritz glanced around the area. One of the few satisfactions he got from his job was playing the part of detective. He knew that most companies tried to fool him by pretending they were doing things that in reality they never did. For example, he saw no quality awards hanging in the lobby. That was one point against ROB. However, the operating philosophy of the president was framed and hanging where everyone could see it.

Fritz leaned closer to this document and examined the signature for age. It was still fairly fresh. This wasn't hung on the wall yesterday for his benefit, but it couldn't have been there more than a month or two.

Fritz was ushered into Mead's office. Breton and Brenda were standing in the room to receive the visitor. Fritz shook their hands and sat in the chair closest to Mead's desk. He snuffed out his cigar in the large ashtray on the corner of the desk. It was then that Breton noticed the ashtray. Mead never smoked in the office, and he didn't remember ever seeing the ashtray before.

"Herbal tea?" Mead asked as he picked up a teapot from the side of the desk.

"Yes, I'll have some."

Breton and Brenda were both confused now. Mead always drank coffee. Where had this tea suddenly come from?

Fritz poured himself a glass of tea and sweetened it with the honey on a tray near the teapot. He then launched into his speech on how he was there to help ROB, Incorporated improve its quality. He knew the speech by heart. It was the 175th time he had said it.

The group decided that Fritz would start working with Brenda and look over the progress the company had made on SPC. Then he would meet with Breton and check on production-related issues. Finally, Mead would take him to lunch at the club. After lunch the group would meet back at Mead's office. There Fritz would debrief the group and prepare his report.

Brenda was wound up with tension. However, she did notice that Mead seemed unusually calm. He, too, had been a nervous wreck a few weeks ago. What had happened to change him? Unfortunately, there was no time to worry about such questions. A few minutes later Fritz and Brenda were strolling down the factory floor on a tour.

Near the plastic molding area Fritz spotted the c-bar chart King had started there two weeks before. Without even looking at the front of the chart, Fritz turned the piece of paper over to read the notes on the back. The second note down caught his attention. It read, *Technical stuff.* Another point against.

Fritz then turned the chart back to the front and looked at the data. It was written in both pencil and pen. It was obvious that several different people had written on the chart. Greasy fingerprints were in every corner. It seemed genuine.

"Hey, put that down!" shouted the operator of the nearest machine. "I need that information. We're trying to find out what's causing all of the scratches on these parts."

A startled Fritz set the paper down immediately. Brenda wanted to scream. Didn't that idiot operator know who this was? She knew that it wasn't a good start to the audit. However, she was wrong. Fritz was impressed. The operator's anger confirmed that this was a genuine control chart being used by the people on the line.

"Shall we?" asked Fritz as he motioned to Brenda to continue the tour. As she turned to walk on, Fritz glanced at a caliper lying on the table. A calibration sticker was attached to the back. Another point for ROB.

CHAPTER 10

Group Problem Solving

It was over. Fritz Wolf had left an hour before, and his preliminary report was sitting on Mead's desk. ROB had failed.

That was the pessimistic view. What Fritz had said was that the SPC program was still too new to determine if it was effective and met their requirements. He also said that the company should be watched closely over the next six months for signs of real improvements.

Mead knew what that meant. The customer would watch every shipment they sent. If any of them were rejected, the purchasing people would slow down orders. He knew that they could forget about any new contracts for at least a year. It was time for damage control.

Fritz identified four areas that ROB should immediately direct its attention: reliability testing, problem-solving teams, research, and a system of quality cost tracking. Frank Graves was already working on the cost system. The other three areas would require outside help and training.

Mead decided that this would be a good time to get an early start on the weekend. He packed his papers into his briefcase. He pulled his overcoat and scarf from the closet and headed out to his car. The steps down to the parking lot seemed awfully lonely to him. Once in his car he turned to the local jazz station.

The drive home seemed longer than usual. Once in his house he settled down in his favorite chair and watched the snow falling in his backyard and on the wooded lot beyond. He promised himself that he wouldn't think about the week, but he did.

After about an hour he phoned his stockbroker and instructed him to sell half of his shares. Mead was not going to take chances. He paused and called the plant.

"Sally?" he asked. "I want every manager in my office on Monday morning. Have them read the audit report and prepare a plan of action." Without saying good-bye he hung up. He wasn't going to take any chances.

Monday morning the managers were sitting glumly in Mead's office. They were expecting the usual chewing out when things went badly. They were not disappointed. Sally shut the door to the office, because the noise distracted her from her work.

Finally, Mead lowered his tone and said, "You all were asked to prepare action reports on how we can deal with this situation."

They had all lost a weekend preparing their reports. A few began to reach for their reports when Mead continued, "Whoever thinks they have written the best action report possible, please hand it to me."

Everyone froze. Nervous glances were exchanged. No one handed Mead a report.

"Good," replied Mead. "I want you to all modify your report as follows."

Mead picked up a pad of paper from his desk, put on his glasses and began to read. "Brenda, I want you to train all personnel in the techniques of problem solving. Breton, you and Harris work to make sure that SPC is the buzzword on the factory floor. Frank, I want to see a cost system by Friday. Lee, I want your people to start reliability testing on our critical jobs. You can also start scheduling your people for training in experimental designs.

"Wherever possible, we will automate where you can demonstrate a cost benefit. I've asked our attorney to meet with us next month to discuss liability issues. Anna, I want you to submit a proposal for the restructuring of our vendor and customer relationships. People, we have about six months to change our skins or we will be working somewhere else."

As if on cue, the managers rose and left the office. Each was glad to be out of the confined space, but at the same time they realized that the road ahead was now going to be much tougher.

Brenda hurried back to her office. She tossed her action report into a corner and picked up the phone. "Hello, Bob?" she asked the quality manager at Urn Corporation. "Do you have some time this week?" A pause. "Well, I need to learn about problem-solving teams."

Bob and Brenda made immediate arrangements to meet that afternoon. Brenda called in her quality supervisor and instructed him to revise the action plan to include more on the use of problem-solving groups. She then headed out toward the lunchroom for a much-needed cup of coffee. On the way she passed Breton standing among a group of workers. They were all joining hands in a circle the way a football team does at the beginning of a game. What the hell is that man up to now? she wondered.

At one-thirty that afternoon, Brenda stepped from her car parked at the Urn Corporation. Although four inches of new snow had fallen the night before, their parking lot was swept clean by plows. After the ritual sign-in with the receptionist, she was given safety glasses and an I.D. badge. Bob Barley was soon at the front desk ready to guide her through the plant.

The two made their way to a room sitting in the middle of the production floor. "You may remember this room from the first time you were here," Bob said.

"Yes, I remember."

"Step inside." As soon as Bob closed the door, the noise of the production area was snuffed out like a match in a hurricane.

"Amazing," remarked Brenda.

"Not really. This is a modular, soundproof room. We had a truck deliver it right to this site. It gives our problem-solving teams somewhere to meet that's quiet."

"What will the team we are observing today be working on?" Brenda inquired.

Bob walked over to one of the cork boards that surrounded the room. He picked out some large sheets of paper carefully pinned to the wall. He dug down a couple of sheets. While placing a finger on the page he said, "This is the blueprint for a part we make in our metal stamping area. It's a hinge for a coffin." Brenda shuddered.

Bob continued, "The problem is that it squeaks a lot when placed under a load. The engineers told the group that it was probably caused by the variations in the two hinge halves. What this group is trying to do is find and eliminate the sources of variation in the stampings."

"Interesting."

"It's almost two o'clock now. Why don't you take a seat and the team should be here shortly."

Brenda settled into a comfortable chair near the back of the room. When the first team member entered the room, the sudden increase in noise made her jump. No wonder everyone turned around and looked at them when they had intruded on a team meeting on their first tour. Bob walked over to this first member and introduced her to Brenda.

"Margie this is Brenda. She's here to watch our group." Bob turned toward Brenda and announced, "Margie here is the leader of the group."

Margie said a few pleasantries and then went to the stack of papers Bob had leafed through earlier. She selected two and placed these on a large clip located above the dry erase board. Within a few minutes the room was filled with the nine members of the problem-solving group.

Margie lead the group in discussion. "Leon, what's the status on part variation this week?"

"The standard deviations are down to fifteen thousand, but we're still short of the target," replied Leon DePaul, the line supervisor.

Margie pointed toward a short woman sitting next to Brenda. "Carla, any feedback on the squeaking problem?"

"Field service says that the complaint rate is down five percent, but they don't know if that was by chance or if they are seeing a real improvement."

Margie frowned. "Well, let's look at our fishbone chart and see if there is anything else we can try." She held the chart on the wall down with one finger and stared at it intently.

"What have we tried so far?" asked someone near the front.

"Well," Margie said, "we tried the shims in the presses, a more consistent quality of steel, maintenance of the dies, and adjusting the stroke height."

"I say we should try less tension on the steel feed," someone else suggested.

"No, it's the feed rate," replied another team member.

"Wait a minute," commanded Margie. "Let's list these ideas, discuss them for ten minutes, and take a vote."

The group proceeded to do exactly that. Brenda was impressed. A line worker was successfully leading a group that included supervisors. In about fifteen minutes they had discussed their next course of action, voted, and left the room. Margie stayed behind to make notes.

"What are you writing?" asked Brenda as she approached.

"I always write down what we discuss and what we decided after every meeting. That way, if weeks from now someone disputes what we said, I can show them what really was decided."

Brenda was impressed. This had been a very beneficial observation. She'd had a rough idea of how to teach problem solving, but she had needed to see the mood of a properly run group. Now that she had seen it, she knew exactly how to proceed at her own company.

"Let me buy you a cup of coffee," Bob said.

Brenda agreed and they headed for the break room. For a moment Brenda wondered if Bob was always this cooperative or if he had an attraction toward her. Unfortunately, this was neither the time nor place to find out. Brenda had too much on her mind and another interested party to worry about.

On Wednesday, Brenda was ready to teach the first ROB team all about problem solving. She had gone through a complete ritual of preparation. She had studied the subject, collected a couple of amusing, but related stories, taken notes on three by five cards, and just before going to the lunchroom, she paused in the restroom long enough to vomit.

"Problem solving," Brenda began, "is the most crucial link in the system we call SPC. You people have already spent weeks filling in control charts. Some of you have found problems. However, you know as well as I do that the problems will not go away by themselves.

"Instead it takes a team effort to locate and eliminate the problems. That's what I am going to talk to you about today. We are going to learn the basics of problem solving as a team. Then we will pick a couple of problems and attack them head-on.

"A lot of you have complained to me and the other managers about difficulties on the factory floor. In the past there was very little we could do. However, we are in a new era at ROB. Now we want to listen and help. Our very future as a company will depend on the actions we all take toward continuous improvement."

Brenda thought her speech was sounding a little too preachy, but she was happy that she was able to speak without stuttering or shaking. She flipped on the overhead projector and placed a transparency on the glass.

"Focus," yelled the team. This startled Brenda for a moment, but she soon had her composure back and adjusted the focus knob.

She continued, "The way we will attack problems is called PDCA — Plan, Do, Check, Action."

Brenda glanced up to see if the group was taking notes. "The procedure is really quite simple. We begin by looking at the overall situation in your area. From this overview we develop a plan of how we will work on problems. From a list of possible problems, we will pick one. As we attack the problem, we will frequently check our progress against a target or goal. When we find the solution, we will take action to ensure that the problem stays eliminated and that other related groups learn of our success.

"Plan, do, check, action," Brenda repeated.

"To accomplish this we will need to learn the basic tools a problem-solving team uses. These tools give us a common approach to looking at problems. I thought it would be best if we pick a particular problem you are having now and use it for an example."

"Shaft diameter," shouted out one of the members.

Breton stepped forward to explain. "We have been having a problem getting the first diameter we turn on a shaft to be consistent. Right now we have too much variation."

"Is that the chart you are keeping out there now?" Brenda asked.

"Yep," Breton replied.

"Okay. Let's start with the shaft diameters. The first technique we will have to learn is the one you will be using most frequently. It is called *brainstorming*. This is a method of letting a group of people freely express their ideas on a particular topic. The way it works is that your team leader picks one person at a time to speak. If that person has an idea, the leader writes it down. If that person wants to think about it for a moment they say, 'pass'.

"The leader continues around the room until all ideas have been stated. Now, there are some rules about this that you should know. The most important is that no one can comment or criticize another person's idea. Even if it sounds like the dumbest idea you've ever heard, don't say things like, 'Wow, that's a stupid idea.' The point is we don't know where a dumb idea might lead us. All ideas are important.

"A second rule is that you can hitchhike on other ideas. That means that you can add to what someone else has already said. In a lot of problem-solving meetings it is surprising how many times two people had half of the answer to a problem. The full answer wasn't learned until these two people were able to talk freely.

"Now, let's try this with the shaft problem. I'm going to go around the room a couple of times and ask each of you to think of anything that might be causing the problem. Even the most trivial answers, I want to hear them. Bruce, let's start with you."

"I don't know," mumbled Bruce. "Maybe the tool wear." Brenda wrote *tool wear* on the board. She pointed to the man next to Bruce.

"Steel quality," he said firmly. Brenda noted this. Brenda made three trips around the room until most people were asking to pass. The board was filled to capacity with ideas.

"Do you see how this creates more ideas than a single person could have?" Most members of the team nodded their agreement.

"What we would do now depends on what we are trying to accomplish. Right now we are in the planning stage of our problem solving. We are trying to pick what we are going to do. Therefore, we need a second tool to help us organize our point of attack."

Brenda placed a new transparency on the overhead. She handed copies of it out to the team. The screen showed a long arrow with six other arrows pointing toward the large arrow.

"This is a fishbone chart," Brenda said. The class could now see how it roughly looked like a fish's skeleton. "Its formal name is the cause-and-effect chart."

Brenda walked back to the overhead projector and began to write labels at the end of the six arrows. "The large arrow going across the page signifies that bad shaft diameters are the result of some process during production. These other six arrows represent where the source of the problem may originate. The six forces are man, machine, method, material, management, and environment.

"If we examine the list we created with our brainstorming, we can start to organize our thoughts better by placing each possible cause on a bone connected to each appropriate arrow." Brenda glanced up to see what looked like a confused team.

"I think an example will help us to see how this works better. Bruce, you said that tool wear might be a problem. Which arrow would you

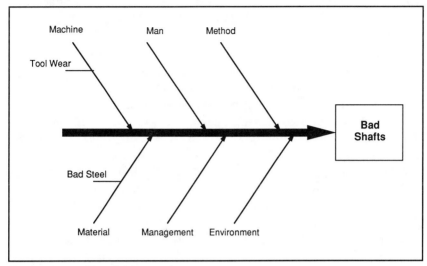

Figure 10.1   The fishbone chart.

place that idea on?"

Bruce studied the fishbone chart for a moment and said, "Machine."

"And," Brenda continued, "where would we put poor quality steel?"

"Material," responded the team. Brenda then drew a small line out from the material arrow and labeled it *poor quality steel.*

Brenda proceeded to fill in the rest of the fishbone chart as the team members suggested where each potential problem should be located. There were brief arguments over some of the ideas. A couple were placed on two arrows to settle some of the disagreements.

"Now what we do," Brenda announced, "is discuss the merits of each idea and whether some of the ideas should be combined. Now remember, this is not a life and death discussion. We are trying to compromise and agree on these causes and how important they are to the problem."

The team promptly launched into a spirited discussion of the merit of each idea. Breton and Brenda both had to wade into the arguments that broke out to calm feelings and emotions. Brenda made a mental note to spend more time during the next session discussing how to criticize someone else's idea politely.

After about twenty minutes of mostly feuding, the team was given a five-minute breather. When they had returned to their seats, Brenda continued her lecture.

"Now what we are going to do is vote on which possible cause of the problem we will attack first. I am going to pass out small slips of paper to each person. I want you to list your top three choices in order of importance. Remember to stick to things you feel we can attack as a team. The things that are too big for a team the management group will have to attack."

For a few moments the group sat quietly filling in the sheets of paper. Frequently, the various team members glanced up at the fishbone chart. A few crossed off something on their lists and wrote down something new. Brenda collected the papers and tallied the scores.

Then she announced that tool setup was the favorite of the group. Therefore, the team would now have to try new methods of setup and see if the results improved the diameter problem.

"This is the *do* phase of problem solving," Brenda explained. "We will now brainstorm some ideas for how to improve the setup."

The group was at no loss for ideas on setup. Apparently they had these ideas pent up for years. It quickly became clear to Breton that several setups were being used on this job. He finally suggested that a single setup procedure be written for the job and that it be followed religiously for the next couple of weeks. The team shouted agreement.

Although this violated the orderly method of reaching a decision, Brenda decided to let the group implement their plan. "Now," she said, "before you try the consistent setup procedure, you have to establish some sort of target to meet. In your case that will be easy. You already have a control chart on the machine. I also saw today that a capability study was done on the first diameter you turn. We can measure improvement against the variations we are already documenting. In other words, if the variation in the diameters decreases significantly, then your new method works. And what would we do with that method?"

"Keep it," shouted the team.

"Right. And if the method makes things worse or shows no improvements?"

"Dump it," responded the team.

"Good. I think it's time to try your idea and see what happens. Whether it works or fails, we will continue on and pick the next most popular idea and test. All the successful ideas will be used. In fact, we will do this until we either are told to stop because there is no more room for improvement or until the job is phased out. That's why they call it continuous improvement. We work everyday to make the job run just a little bit better."

Brenda dismissed the team. She let out a deep breath of air. She had made it all the way through two hours of talking to a group. If her nerves held out, she should be able to complete the next several meetings that lay ahead. For right now she had to worry more about the second team that would be meeting tomorrow.

The Next Day

The second team was definitely more subdued than the first. As Brenda waited for the session to begin, a couple of the machine operators came up to the front of the room and asked her questions. One even tried making some small talk.

Brenda called the meeting to order. "Let's begin with the attribute problem you have been working on recently. Mr. King tells me that you are keeping track of both the scrap rate and the types of defects you are finding." The team confirmed this. Brenda continued.

"Good. What I want to talk about today is how to use this information to solve problems in production. Now, I'm going to assume that the computer cover is the problem you want to address. The first thing you have to do as a team is describe the situation so that everyone has a good understanding of the problem. To accomplish this, we will fill in what's called a flowchart. It shows the production process step by step. Let me show you a typical flowchart."

Brenda placed a transparency on the overhead projector. It was a copy of the flowchart for the grinding of steel parts. She took a few moments to point out how each new operation or movement of the product was portrayed as a box on the chart. Arrows connected various processes to show the flow of production.

"By filling in one of these flowcharts, we can see where potential problems may begin. Take the example on the screen. See how the grinding process begins with the cutting of steel stock? What would happen to the quality of the final part if the steel was miscut in this first step?"

"Wouldn't be any good," replied an unseen member of the team.

"Right. If the quality is bad early in the process, then no amount of work down the line is going to fix the part. Therefore, a flowchart can also teach us how important some problems are by how they affect the rest of the production process. The more we can make these early steps perfect, the higher the final quality of the parts."

Brenda noted the general agreement with her last statement. She then quizzed the class to describe the actual production process of the computer cover. There were some brief disagreements over what came first and how far the chart should go, but on the whole the team had a pretty good idea on how the cover was made.

First, plastic resin was cleaned and checked at the raw materials receiving area. Then reground plastic was mixed into the resins at the beginning of the molding process. The plastic resin mixture was placed into molding machine hoppers, and the parts were molded. Then, an operator removed the parts and placed them on wooden fixtures so they would cool with minimal distortion.

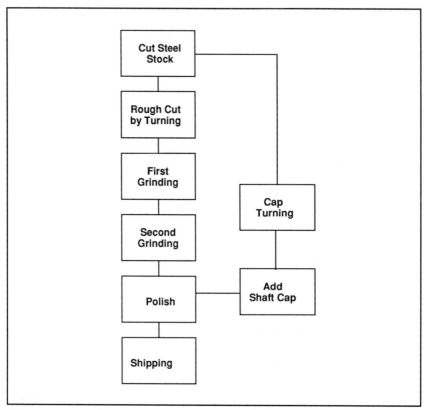

Figure 10.2   A flowchart for grinding a steel part.

After a few moments, another person removed the cooled cover and trimmed off the flashing. This person then tossed the cover onto a conveyor belt. Several yards down the conveyor line stood three people. The first snapped on a metal faceplate. The next person inserted several mounting points. The last person drove in screws to secure the mounting points.

After another trip on the conveyor, the covers were stacked to await packaging for shipment. The packing person wrapped the covers in plastic bags and then placed them into large boxes. Sixteen covers were placed in each box. The box was then carried by a lift truck to the shipping area. When an order was filled the paperwork was completed and the covers were loaded onto a truck.

When Brenda had finished drawing this out on the overhead projector she said, "Now, does anyone see a point in this process where scratches might occur?"

Quickly, the team identified several stages. "Our job," continued Brenda, "is to find the areas that cause the most trouble and eliminate the sources of the damage. It's just that easy."

Brenda then reviewed the plan, do, check, and action steps of problem solving. She showed the team that a systematic approach that takes a lot of small steps would probably be more successful than throwing money and people at a problem. For her example, she returned to the problem of the scratches on the computer covers.

"Let's start with confirming some of the assumptions you have made so far. The next tool I want to show you is called Pareto analysis. Pareto was an economist who did studies on the distribution of wealth. What he found was that a very few people usually control the bulk of the country's wealth. This principle applies to defects as well. The bulk of your defect problems will belong to one or two types of defects. Eliminate those defects, and you will have eliminated the majority of your problems.

"I'll show you how we check for the Pareto principle. I'll take your defect counts for the past week and total them by defect type. Then I will create a bar chart that shows the number of each defect in descending order."

Brenda placed a new transparency on the overhead projector. It was a bar chart of the defects the team had been tracking. Scratches had the overwhelmingly highest defect count — a total of 179 in one week. The next most frequent defect was cracks. There were forty-three of those. Then there were over two dozen defects that had occurred, but none had been seen more than seven times.

"Here's what the Pareto principle looks like physically. These first two defects cause most of the problems. We call those the vital few defects. These dozens of other problems occur very rarely and are mostly little trouble. We call them the trivial many.

"We have both confirmed and defined the importance of the scratch problem. The next question I have is where on the flowchart are you counting the scratches?"

The line inspector raised his hand. "Well," he said, "we've been counting them as they wait for the packing person to bag and box them."

"So any of the handling done from molding to packing could be causing the problem?"

Several people in the room nodded their agreement.

"I also hear that Mr. King had you keep a defect map showing where the scratches occurred. Who has that map?" Nobody volunteered. "Good thing I made an overhead of it, isn't it?"

The team laughed and Brenda felt good that her first attempt at humor had worked. She continued, "I notice that this map shows that the majority of the scratches are occurring on the top edges of the cover. It's almost like the edges are being banged or dragged over something rough. What I need to know from this group is, where are there situations in the process where such scratching could occur?"

Brenda proceeded to introduce the team to the concept of brainstorming. They freely suggested several ideas on how the scratches could have occurred. After a vote and some discussion, a couple of ideas were combined.

One person suggested that laying the covers top down on the conveyor belt might be a cause. Another person said that the metal staples holding the belt sections together might be a cause.

Brenda hinted to the team that both causes might be working together to create some of the scratches. The team quickly deduced that one change would address both possible causes. The team decided that turning all covers top up on the conveyor belt might be a solution. Therefore, the team voted to have each person working the conveyor line turn the covers up whenever they were placed or replaced on the moving belt.

To help create a list of other actions to try next, Brenda showed the team the cause-and-effect chart the first team had created.

"This is called a fishbone chart. It not only lists possible causes of a problem, but it also places those problems into groups. This helps to see how a possible cause would affect the production process. Why don't we complete a fishbone chart for the scratch problem so that we can have a list of possible causes we will correct until the problem goes away?"

The team agreed and dove into the task. In fact, they were concentrating on the problem so much they were fifteen minutes past break time before anyone noticed.

After the break they completed the fishbone chart. The rest of the session was dedicated to discussing which possible causes would be addressed next. The end result was a brief list of ten possible causes the team felt necessary to investigate. The list included factors such as covers bumping each other during handling and the effect of worker's jewelry scratching the cover surface.

Brenda felt a lot better when this session was over. She felt that the two teams had understood how problem solving worked. The second team was assigned to monitor the number of scratches as they changed their method of placing the covers on the conveyor belt. Brenda was anxious to see the results of this change.

She didn't have to wait long. The next day she was finishing lunch when the line supervisor from the plastic molding area came running up to her table. "You've got to see this," he exclaimed.

Brenda threw what remained of her lunch back into the brown paper sack and followed the supervisor onto the factory floor. Over at the computer cover manufacturing area several people were looking at the SPC chart hung near the packing area. Brenda recognized that two or three of these people belonged to the other SPC team. Something had drawn their interest to this chart.

As Brenda and the supervisor approached the chart the group quickly broke up and disappeared. The supervisor picked up the chart and handed it to Brenda without saying a word. Drawn down the middle of the chart was a vertical line marked with the words *begin new procedure.* The number of defects plotted after that line were well below the lower control limit.

"We normally see a couple of dozen scratches on our midday check," said the supervisor. "Today we only found three, and they were minor."

Brenda was impressed, however, she cautioned the supervisor. "Good work, but you're going to need a few more checks before we can be sure that the new method really works. Make sure that you circle this point and note the new method on the back of the chart."

Brenda turned toward the several workers peaking at them from behind their machines. She gave a thumbs up. The team cheered. Inside, Brenda was cheering too.

A few days later Brenda checked the chart again. The number of scratches found had rebounded slightly, but the majority of the points plotted were below the lower control limit. She smiled and took the chart back to her office for copying.

The next day she met with the first SPC team. She had the obviously successful second team chart on the overhead projector. The team did not look at all happy. Brenda said, "I wanted to show you what a successful countermeasure does to an attribute chart when it solves some of the problems."

"We'll kick their butts," blurted out one of the operators.

The competition between the teams was suddenly obvious and stronger than Brenda anticipated. She hesitated while she decided whether it would be better to feed or retard these feelings. She decided that they didn't need to be fed and made a mental note to remember the emotions of this group.

When Brenda met with the second team the next day they seemed very pleased with themselves. Brenda decided that they needed to be brought back to reality.

"You did well on your first try," she began. "However, that doesn't happen very often. Don't be surprised if the next problem you take on requires more effort and time." This seemed to quiet the group down a little bit.

"Now, let's look at your c-bar chart. See how you have a string of points near or below the lower control limit? Do you know what you have to do now?"

"Celebrate?" someone ventured.

"Nope," replied Brenda. "Your process average has dropped because of your new method of handling the covers. Therefore, you have to re-establish your control limits and process average downward. Before you were finding about one defect per cover. Now you are down to one defect for every three covers. Therefore, I move the process average down to this new average and recalculate the control limits."

Brenda went through this calculation and created a new set of limits. These she drew on a new piece of chart paper. "Remember," she said, "our objective is never-ending improvement. What we do now is try the next possible solution on our list and see if it improves the situation. We continue to test ideas until we get down to zero defects."

Later that day, Brenda was sitting in Leon Marsden's office. "Leon," she asked. "Aren't you planning to start an in-house newsletter for all employees?"

"Sure, I've got my staff assembling stories for the first issue now. Why?"

Brenda placed the second team's SPC chart on the desk and replied, "I think I have your cover story."

Leon looked at the chart and the clearly marked point of improvement. "Yes" he said. "I think you do."

CHAPTER 11

Reliability

Brenda Patterson was walking down the hallway of ROB, Incorporated. It was an early spring day. The last of the snow was melting outside, and the sunshine poked out from occasional clouds. Inside she felt better than she had for several weeks. The SPC program was finally getting off the ground, and the damage from the recent customer audit was being repaired.

As she turned the corner near Mead's office she saw Breton Rhodes and several line supervisors gathered in a group near the entrance door to the factory area. Brenda noticed that they seemed to be talking nervously. When she turned the corner they had all swung around to look at her. Then they resumed their conversation.

As she approached the group they quickly broke up and retreated to the factory. Only Breton remained behind. She began to greet him, but noticed that he was looking past her and down the hallway. As she got closer Breton motioned for her to follow him behind a nearby filing cabinet. Before she could even ask what was going on Breton blurted out, "Frank's been fired."

"What? What happened?"

"His cost of quality system was really a fake. Old man Mead had an outside auditor come in this weekend and go over the books. Frank had been making up the cost of quality reports and a few other choice numbers."

Breton suddenly straightened up and walked boldly from behind the filing cabinet. Brenda peeked around the corner and saw Mead walking toward his office. Breton leaned back as he buttoned his coat and said,

"I've been called in."

Brenda watched as Breton headed down the hall and into Mead's office. She felt a little silly hiding like this, but there was no telling what was in the wind if a member of the management staff was so suddenly terminated. Brenda decided that this might be a good day to keep a low profile. Of course, the management meeting in half an hour would prevent that.

When the staff meeting was finally convened an hour later than usual, Brenda searched Breton's face closely for clues as to the mood of the day. Breton had been with Mead since early that morning. The other managers had waited quietly in Mead's outer office. No one dared to make a protest that morning. The absence of Frank Graves was all too obvious. Mead was playing for keeps in his bid to save ROB, Incorporated.

Breton talked to no one and seemed lost in thought. This was a bad sign. Mead briefly reviewed why Frank had been fired. He assured the rest of the group that their positions in the company were safe and that this was probably an isolated incident. No one was reassured.

The bulk of the meeting involved progress reports from each of the managers. Mead outlined that he had been able to keep the customers at bay over the past several weeks, but it was time to make some real progress. He picked up several letters from his desk.

"These," he began, "are the Material Correction Notices we received over the past six months. First, we have to reduce the frequency of these. I propose that we work as a team to create a reaction plan for squelching these as they occur. Second, it seems that the reports are equally divided between dimensional problems and reliability problems. We can assign the dimensional problems to the SPC teams. Breton and Lee can tackle the reliability issues."

The group sat and furiously jotted down notes. Sally had prepared copies of the MCNs for each team member. The discussion period was very quiet on this issue. For one thing, few dared speak today. For another, the antagonistic voice of Frank was missing.

The meeting quickly broke up, and the managers scrambled back to their respective offices. Breton and Lee went to the engineering department. Once there Breton called Brenda and invited her to the office. "Mr. Mead seems to have forgotten that quality control has something to do with reliability," he said over the phone.

This comment had reassured Brenda. Only a few months ago it was unheard of for one manager in the company to look out for the concerns of another manager. It would seem that the management team was beginning to truly cooperate.

Once the three managers were together they sent out for lunch. This working session was going to last a while, and they didn't want to be interrupted. Lee Enfield pulled out a stack of papers from his desk and began.

"Let's start with the basics. Reliability is really quality assurance set in motion over time. Quality assurance checks the quality of parts as they are being produced and readied for shipment. The task of reliability testing is to monitor the quality of those same parts over time."

"This stack of papers represents the sum total reliability engineering done at ROB since I was employed eight years ago. At the place I worked before, this would have been about a month of work. Obviously, we have a lot of ground to make up."

Breton and Brenda nodded in agreement. Brenda had petitioned for increased reliability testing to no avail for the first three years she was at ROB. "Where do we start?" she asked.

"I think," replied Lee, "that we should start with a reliability testing procedure that spells out the methods we use, definitions of common terms, and the goals of testing."

Breton added, "Let me get Colleen in here to take notes so that we can get this typed up right away." With that Breton darted out of the door and flagged down Colleen as she was running a stack of files up to the front office. In a few minutes she was sitting in a corner of Lee's office hurriedly taking notes.

Lee spoke first. "Let's start with definitions so that everyone is clear on what we are talking about. The most basic term in reliability is *failure rate*." Lee wrote this term on the small dry erase board he kept on the wall above his desk.

"A failure rate is how often a product fails over time. The usual standard is to express this as the percent of products that fail during a one-thousand-hour period. Do we agree on that?"

"Sure," both Brenda and Breton said at the same time.

"Colleen," said Lee, "let me give you an example you can use after we make the definition. We have that engine clutch plate we make for generators. What we do now is watch about a hundred generators in the field where we can track how many hours they are being used. After one thousand hours of use we count how many clutches have failed."

Breton interjected, "What about products where we count the number of cycles instead of the hours used? We have a door-lock assembly that we make for automobiles. In a reliability test we would mount it on a machine that would open and close the lock a hundred times a minute."

"Good question," Lee said. "In that case we would adopt a standard number of cycles. For example, after a hundred thousand cycles we could count how many locks have failed. Thus, we might get some figure such as failures per 100,000 cycles.

"Now," Lee continued, "we can also use the mean time between failures or the mean time until failures as additional measurements of reliability."

"This is getting confusing fast," said Brenda. Colleen was still writing rapidly and nodding in silent agreement.

Lee responded, "I've got just the machine to illustrate what I'm talking about." And with that, Lee jumped up and headed out into the engineering development area. Breton and Brenda scrambled to keep up with him. Colleen continued to write as she followed the group.

Lee went to the far corner of the prototype room and dug under a tarp covering a strange machine. "This," he announced, "is what I like about reliability work. I get to break and pull and destroy all sorts of stuff. This machine is built to flex our motor base plates a quarter of an inch in two directions."

The three companions looked at the machine. It had a large steel bar with vicious looking alligator clamps about three inches long. Lee was digging in a box of parts. He produced five thin steel plates and clamped them into the machine. With the flip of a switch, the electric motor on the machine leaped to life, and the steel arm began to move back and forth. With each swing of the arm the five plates were first flexed forward and then backward.

Lee turned up the speed of the machine as he began to explain. "Do you see this counter on the side of the machine?" he shouted over the noise. "It records how many times the plates are fully flexed. When the first plate fails we record the number of cycles and restart the machine. We do that for every piece until they have all failed."

Lee reached behind the machine and switched it off. He then took out a note pad and began writing down some figures. "Suppose, that the five plates failed after the following number of cycles." He wrote: *12,000, 15,000, 16,000, 19,000,* and *22,000.*

"These are the times until failure. In this case we express time as the number of cycles. If I average these numbers together I would get the mean time until failure."

"It's 16,800," announced Breton as he put his calculator back into his pocket.

"Right," confirmed Lee. "What this tells us is that the average mounting plate will last about 16,800 cycles of flexing. The only way to know if that is good is to know more about the type of conditions the part will experience. For example, this mounting plate is flexed as part of its job in the product. Whenever the generator this is attached to is moved or bumped, the plate flexes to absorb the shock. As engineers we have to estimate how often that will happen to a portable generator. Luckily, some field studies have shown us that it only happens six or seven times a day in the construction industry."

"So," interrupted Brenda, "if the average plate survives more than sixteen thousand flexings, it is very unlikely that you will get a mounting plate failure."

"That's right," confirmed Lee. "However, there is even more involved in knowing that for sure. For right now we'll just outline the basic concepts. Take mean time between failure or MTBF."

Lee moved to the other side of the lab and pulled out a box containing the newest product ROB was developing, an anti-theft lock for car doors. "This new lock is quite an improvement over our last design. However, we still worry about failures. In this case we measure failure a little differently. There are several parts that can fail in this lock. A failure of one of these parts requires the customer to get the lock repaired. Thus, we look at the time between failures. When we average these, we get the MTBF. In other words, we get a good estimate of how often a customer will have to bring the car in for lock repair.

"Our problem right now is that we have a MTBF of two thousand cycles. With average daily use of car locks, that means a customer would need a lock repair once every eighteen months. That is just too frequent."

Colleen was now bracing her note pad on the measuring surface plate as she completed her fourth page of notes. "Any other definitions?" Breton asked.

"Well," Lee responded, "there are things like the mean time until repair and availability. I think it would be best if I just summarize those for Colleen and save her some note taking." Colleen returned a grateful smile.

"However, we should discuss the idea of B10 and B50," Lee said.

Breton and Brenda looked at each other and then at Lee. "Go ahead," they said.

"Well, B10 refers to how long it takes until 10 percent of the products fail. We have been talking more about B50, the time until half of the products have failed.

"The time until 10 percent failure is sometimes used as a product specification. Take the case of the motor mounting plate. The average plate may last 16,800 cycles, but the specification is directed at the time until 10 percent of the plates fail."

"But we only sampled five parts," Brenda injected. "How can we accurately estimate when 10 percent will fail with such a small sample?"

"That," said Lee, "is why I thought we'd better talk about B10 because to estimate the time until 10 percent fail, we have to outline the various forms of reliability curves."

"Like the curve of normal distribution," Breton added.

"Right," Lee responded. "But there are families of the other curves that describe failure rates." Lee walked over to a flip chart near the door and tore off a large blank sheet of paper. He placed this on the surface plate and withdrew a large black marking pen from his pocket. On the paper he drew a horizontal line marked *time* and a vertical line marked *failure rate*.

"You see," he said as he drew a straight line parallel to the time line, "we have been assuming a constant rate of failure over time. In reality, the majority of parts and products we test have changing rates of failure over time. The classic example of this is the bathtub curve."

"Draw it," Breton commanded.

Lee began high on the failure rate line and began drawing a dipping curve across time. "When a new product is introduced, say a computer, there will be some immediate failures due to things like defective electrical components or connections. This is called the infant mortality phase as defective goods fail early.

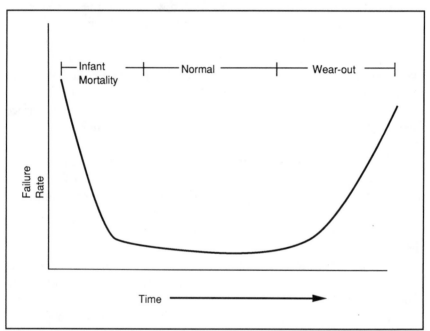

Figure 11.1   The bathtub curve.

"Now as time proceeds, the failure rate will fall because the defective products have been eliminated. A good computer company will turn on newly built computers for twenty-four hours straight to find the defective machines. Anyway, after a week or two of use the surviving machines are in good shape and usually don't have problems until parts physically wear out. That can take months or years. Thus, the rate of failure flattens out at a low level."

Lee continued to draw the line across the page, but at a level very near the time line. He explained. "As the products age, the failure rate will start to increase again as things wear out." He now drew the line up away from the time line. The resulting picture looked like the cross section of a bathtub.

Lee pointed at the flat portion of the curve. "Do you see how the failure rate is constant during the middle phase of a computer's life? It's very easy to make estimates. However, this first part of the curve is decreasing exponentially. To estimate when 10 percent of the units will fail requires me to fit an exponential curve to the date.

"In plain English, a decreasing exponential curve means that it will take very little time for 10 percent to fail, but much longer until the 50 percent level is reached. If that's what's happening with the mounting plates, the mean time until failure figure will be deceiving."

"So how do you make the estimate?" Brenda inquired.

Lee opened a drawer under the measuring surface. He pulled out a dozen varieties of graph paper and spread these out onto the surface. "These are probability plotting papers. Each one is capable of helping me determine different characteristics of failure rates."

He sorted through the pile and pulled out a single sheet that was crisscrossed with lines. "If I plotted my times to failure for each part on this sheet, the resulting slope of the line will tell me the type of failure rate curve I have."

Colleen pushed her note pad to one side and gave up on trying to take notes. This entire conversation was eluding her. The two observers were also facing the same problem.

"Hold on, Lee," Breton said. "This is getting more complicated than it has to be. Our job today is to outline only what is possible and how we are going to use it."

Brenda added a similar remark, and Lee reluctantly agreed. Breton summarized for Colleen. "We have some reliability testing equipment to allow us to test a few of our products directly. We also have a little bit of field information coming in from our warranty claims and direct observations, correct?"

"Right," Lee said.

"Now," Breton continued, "it would seem to me that the first thing we would want to do is expand our ability to collect this information. In addition, we want to collect the information that relates directly to the customers' requirements."

Both Brenda and Lee thought that would be a good idea. "Colleen," said Breton, "make a note that we wish to form a group representing marketing, sales, engineering, and quality that will determine what reliability information is needed and how we will gather such information." Colleen made the note.

"Furthermore, we are going to have to determine additional uses for the information other than making sure we meet specifications. If I understand you correctly, Lee, this is good information for designing better parts and processes to produce those parts."

"It is possible to tie our results into other activities," Lee confirmed. "That's where I'm lacking experience. I can do the tests and analyze the data, but this company has never made any attempt to put that information to good work."

"We can change that," Breton replied. "I think we should visit another company at a later time to see how they use reliability information. We'll schedule that later. For right now we have a third issue to clarify. From what you are telling me, we can describe the reliability of a single product in several ways. There's the MTBF, the mean time until repair, the availability of the unit, and the time until a certain percentage of units fail."

"Plus some other terms," Lee added.

"I think it would be best if you drew those up in a list that both define the terms and told when they were appropriate for use."

"Sounds like a good idea," Lee confirmed.

Breton continued. "It seems to me that the critical component in the analysis is to determine the curve of the failure rate so that accurate predictions can be made for reliability. Should we settle on a single method to be used first?"

"We can," responded Lee. "The Weibull curve is a good starting place. That piece of paper I was showing you tests for a Weibull curve."

"What does a Weibull curve look like?" Brenda asked.

"That's the beauty of a Weibull," replied Lee. "It can assume many different shapes." He wrote out a formula on a piece of paper. It was logarithm e raised to the power of another formula. He pointed at the beta character in the second part of the formula and said, "The value of the beta in this formula determines the shape of the curve. Thus, we can create an exponential curve or a normal curve from the same formula."

Breton didn't fully comprehend what Lee was saying. He said, "We'll designate that Weibull analysis will be a preliminary step in reliability testing. Now what do we want to accomplish with reliability information?"

Brenda and Lee began to rattle off a string of possibilities. Breton stopped them and suggested that they use the flip chart to record each idea for discussion. Later they could decide on which applications would be listed in their preliminary report.

"Obviously," began Lee, "we need reliability information to see if we are meeting customer requirements. We have switches that have to survive so many cycles, welds that have to survive stress over time, steel that has to survive salt spray for a week,..."

Breton interrupted, "We get the idea. Brenda?"

"I need the data to see if our SPC information confirms the quality of a part."

Breton added, "And I need to know information on welds, connectors, and fasteners to know that our assembly operations are successful." Breton wrote these ideas down on the flip chart.

The three managers were suddenly startled when Colleen said, "Of course, reliability information is needed to prevent liability suits."

The other three paused in surprise at Colleen's nonchalant remark. They wrote it down as well. So the page was filled with ideas on how reliability information could be used to help the company stay competitive. Lee's ideas focused on the testing of new designs to make them more durable for customers' use. Brenda was worried about product quality. Breton wanted to know if a product could be made more reliable as well as manufacturable.

After another hour of discussion the group settled on several goals for a regular system of reliability testing. Their initial report to Mead suggested that two reliability engineers be hired to conduct full-time testing. In addition, the information from the sales force and customer surveys would be added to the test results. This bulk of data would then be used to improve designs and seek cheaper components that would have high levels of quality and reliability.

Breton, Brenda, and Lee took their ideas to Mead for approval. The three suffered a setback when the budget-conscious Mead spent ten minutes shouting his disagreement about hiring new staff. Instead, he reminded the group that there were already several engineers on staff, and one could be trained to do the job. In addition, he wanted to see actual data on how many parts required reliability testing. He also wanted to see the cost justification for performing the tests.

As the three dejected managers later sat in the break room sipping coffee, they came to an immediate conclusion. They should never make a proposal to Mead without hard numbers and cost estimates. And, they should never forget to estimate the cost reduction of the proposed action. That was an easy decision, because Mead had done everything but stencil it to their suits.

The next decision was not easy at all. How could they plan a successful, profitable reliability testing system when they had so little hands-on experience? "It's time to visit Urn again," Breton said.

"Who do you know over there in reliabilty?" Brenda asked.

"There's Carol Beignet," Lee answered. "I've met her at professional meetings a couple of times. I don't know if she remembers me."

Breton slipped a quarter across the table toward Lee. "Call her and see," he said.

Lee went back to his office and spent several minutes on the phone. Outside the plate glass dividers stood Breton and Brenda. They watched anxiously for any positive signs from Lee. None were seen. Lee hung up and walked out into the hall.

"I hope you're free next week Tuesday, we've got an appointment," Lee said. The two breathed a collective sigh of relief.

The following Tuesday found Breton wedged sideways in the back of Lee's Alfa Romeo convertible. It was a fairly warm spring day, but Lee had left the top up. The space behind the front seats was barely large enough for a couple of bags of groceries. Breton easily filled the space with his large frame. Brenda rode with the window down oblivious to Breton's lack of comfort.

Breton welcomed the solid bump that marked Lee's rapid entry into the Urn Corporation parking lot. After extracting Breton from the back seat, the group headed into the reception area. In ten minutes they were ushered into Carol Beignet's office.

Carol's office was really just three partitions and a desk parked near the end of a long workbench in the reliability laboratory at Urn Corporation.

"Welcome to the reliability lab," she said to the group. "I hear you want to see some reliability tests in action?"

Lee introduced each member of the team and confirmed that they needed to see how a successful reliability program was run. Carol directed them to a nearby booth built into the corner of the large laboratory. Brenda estimated that twelve hundred square feet was dedicated to reliability activities.

In the side of the booth was a heavy glass window. Carol explained, "This is one of our environmental test chambers. Many of the products we make are exposed to some pretty harsh conditions. Today we are testing a part we make for the auto industry."

Carol picked up a console piece that was waiting for exposure in the chamber. "Do you see this piece of carpet we glue to the side of this metal piece?" The group nodded and Breton touched the carpet.

"Once glued on, the specifications say that it should take five foot-pounds of force to tear this carpet away from the metal. Our SPC system tells us that the average piece requires almost twice that force, so we aren't worried about the pull strength. Our problem is this."

Carol suddenly opened the door to the chamber. A large cloud of steam rolled out as a wave of heat hit the group in the face. She led them into the chamber. Inside were half a dozen parts suspended from the ceiling. Lying below the parts were the carpets that had fallen off.

"I put these in here last night. You can see how well the glue held up to heat and humidity. By exposing these to high heat and humidity, we are simulating actual conditions in a car over a longer period of time. This is called accelerated testing."

The group was impressed. It was quite clear that if a part couldn't survive a day in the chamber, it obviously wasn't going to survive years in a car parked in the sun everyday.

"What environmental testing does for us is confirm that the part will remain reliable under extreme conditions. As you can see our pull test is successful in the plant. After all, it remains near room temperature all year with only moderate swings in humidity. However, when temperature and moisture extremes are introduced, the parts fail."

Carol led them out of the environmental chamber toward a box in the corner. Brenda asked, "What are you doing to prevent the glue from failing?"

Carol replied, "For right now the best we can do is try the different types of glues that are readily available at a reasonable price. Those pieces of carpet lying on the floor were attached with the last of the glues available in our current price range. What we will do next is look at how the glue is applied during production and see if we can find a method of application that will survive the environmental chamber."

The box in the corner was a stainless steel container about three feet to a side. In the middle of the top surface was a small window. Inside were three metal parts apparently being steamed.

Carol explained, "These metal parts are being exposed to mists of salt and water. This test simulates about four winters of driving a car over salted roads. As you know, states like Michigan dump a lot of salt on the roads in the winter. The automakers want their steel part to stand up to the salt."

Carol motioned toward a technician monitoring a machine making a rapid series of clicking sounds. "This is something I think you will find interesting." The group walked over near the machine. A dozen hinges were mounted on the machine as a mechanical arm swung them open and close in unison.

Carol said "These are the hinges we mount on our line of coffins. We test their reliability to open and to hold the lid of the coffin open. The clicking sound you hear is a mechanism in the hinge built to hold one hundred pounds in the open position. The arm on this machine applies the force. The clamps holding each hinge are wired to detect when a hinge fails."

Brenda felt an uncontrolled shudder. She doubted whether she would ever get used to the Urn Corporation's product line.

"There's a similar test going on over here." Carol waved the group toward a similar machine clicking small switches in tandem. "This is a test on a switch we build for the government. The switch is electrical, but the switching arm is built of a flexible plastic that we form here at the plant."

The three managers watched as the machine continued to push up and down rapidly on the switches. Carol continued. "It takes three days to reach the 100,000 cycles the government specifies for these switches. Right now we average 315,000 cycles until failure."

Carol noted the looks on the faces of the ROB visitors. She could see that they were impressed. "Of course, this is still not good enough."

"Why is that?" Lee asked.

"Come on, I'll show you why," Carol responded. She led the group back to her desk. There she took out two pieces of paper. Each had the same set of lines the group had previously seen on the Weibull analysis paper. "This is the failure curve of the average switch we produce now. What we found is that we had an exponential curve of failure. Although it took an average of 315,000 cycles for a typical part to fail, it only took 79,000 cycles for 10 percent of the parts to fail. Clearly, this would not meet the specifications."

Carol held out the second piece of paper. "What we did is try a new form of plastic resin for the switch arm. The plastic maker claimed that it was more resilient. When we molded new switch arms with this plastic we got an average part to fail after 350,000 cycles."

"Is that really an improvement?" Brenda asked.

"No," Carol replied. "However, look what happened to the slope of the curve. It got larger. In other words, the first serious failure occurred later. In this case 10 percent of the switches would fail after 133,000 cycles. That's well above standard, yet the average changed very little."

"So," Breton observed, "reliability data is like any other statistical information. A single piece of information is usually meaningless unless other supporting information is known. For example, an average means nothing unless we know how much variation is also occurring."

"That's right," Carol confirmed. "And the mean time until failure means very little if we don't know the shape of the curve or the failure rate over time."

The three managers all made notes. This was the type of information they had been seeking.

Carol reached across her desk and drew the computer keyboard toward her. She typed a few keystrokes and then began to maneuver the mouse. In a few seconds the same graph appeared on the screen.

"This," she announced, "is the same information in a computer program written for reliability analysis. The graphic capability of this computer allows us to quickly translate the data into the appropriate model of the curve."

A steep curve was drawn on the screen. Superimposed in a lighter color was a more gentle slope. "Here are the two curves as they look in normal perspective on a time line. You can see how the earlier curve quickly rose to a high failure rate."

The group was impressed, but they had dozens of questions for Carol on how the information was used for Urn Corporation's benefit. She explained the importance of testing for failure under extreme conditions to correct problems before customers found the same problems. She talked about the need to protect themselves against liability suits. However, she spent the greatest amount of time discussing how examples like the switch helped the company find improved methods of designing and making their products to increase their quality over time without raising the cost per unit.

"You have to realize something," Carol said. "Reliability is not another form of quality assurance. Instead, reliability is something that begins with the design of a product, goes through the manufacturing process, and continues into the use of the product by the customer. Therefore, reliability testing is a joint venture of engineering, quality assurance, and production. It is critically important to have a product engineer that thinks out the design of a product well into its life cycle."

"How do you mean that?" Brenda asked.

"We encourage our product engineers to become married to the product they design. Reliability has to be a consideration in all stages of the design process. First, the actual design of the part should reflect the need for reliability. Second, the product engineer should review similar products for their performance record from customers. Unreliable components must be replaced by higher quality parts. Finally, the design must remain durable enough to survive the variations that normally occur during production.

"For example, we once visited an anti-aircraft gun maker down South a few years back. The engineers built a whole bunch of backup computers into the sighting system to ensure that the gun would not break down in combat. Unfortunately, it made the construction of the final gun so complicated that many of the computer systems were wired wrong. It would have been easier to design a single computer that could have taken the shocks and rough environment such a gun system would encounter."

"Bottom line?" Breton asked.

"The bottom line," Carol said, "is that if you want a successful reliability testing program someone had better be in charge that will make sure that the tests are done as part of your continuous improvement strategy."

As the three drove back to ROB, Incorporated, Breton pondered who would be best for the job. Crammed into the small backseat area he studied Brenda closely. Lee already had his hands full. Brenda only needed some additional training to be competent for the job. The hard part was figuring out how to slip this suggestion to Mead without the other two finding out.

Several jarring bumps in the road occurred from the combination of potholes and Lee's obsession with always going twenty miles an hour faster than the posted speed limit. Breton hardly noticed because he was lost in thought. Brenda was wondering what the mean time until failure was on Lee's shock absorbers.

CHAPTER 12

Quality Costs

The following Monday morning Breton, Brenda, and Lee were walking to the weekly manager's meeting discussing their plans for reliability testing. It would be another week before they presented their proposal to the group. To slip the idea of having Brenda lead the reliability testing effort, Breton had bribed Mead's secretary, Sally, with a dozen roses.

As the three entered Mead's office, they all stopped at the sight of a new face in the room. Sitting in one corner was a tall, young man in a dark blue suit. He couldn't be out of his twenties. Before the startled group could say anything, the man was on his feet and extending a hand.

"Hello," he said. "My name is Vincent Snow."

The three managers exchanged handshakes and greetings. Without being asked Vincent explained, "I'm the new accounting manager. I'm looking forward to working with all of you."

The three were still embarrassed by the sudden departure of the previous accounting manager. For a moment they didn't know what to say to a man who could easily be out of a job within months. Finally, Breton suggested that they sit down since the meeting would soon start. Breton also noted how Vincent was taking particular notice of Brenda. He made a mental note of this for later reference.

Mead and the other managers swept into the room just as the meeting was supposed to start. His first order of business was to introduce Vincent to the group. Mead explained that Vincent was a graduate of the University of Michigan Business School and had spent the last few years studying the new economics of industry. "Vincent's first job is going to be to restructure our cost accounting system to match our quality objectives," Mead stated.

"Yes," Vincent confirmed. "I would like to gather some ideas from this group a little later in the meeting. It's absolutely vital that this cost system matches your needs closely."

Breton had never gone to college and the articulate nature of Vincent's speaking set off a defensive feeling. He distrusted someone who had not cut his teeth in the real world of manufacturing.

Mead went through the usual progress reports and reviewed a couple of pending proposals. After about twenty minutes he turned the meeting over to Vincent.

"First, it's a pleasure to meet all of you. Please keep a lunch hour free this week because I would like to meet with each of you and learn more about your particular situation."

Vincent glanced around the room for signs of any reaction. He saw none. "Anyway, my job will be to create a quality cost system that will accurately tell us the cost of making a mistake. Part of continuous improvement is the ability to know what each mistake costs and what each correction of this mistake costs. After that, it's only simple mathematics to see if the correction costs more than the original problem.

"In addition, a quality cost system will allow us to monitor how much money we save by finding and correcting small problems in the manufacturing process. Let me show you an example."

Vincent walked over to the dry erase board mounted in Mead's office. He uncapped a marking pen and tried to write down some numbers. The pen was dry so he tossed it over his shoulder and tried another. This one worked.

"Suppose," he said, "that we make a million dollars worth of a product. About $250,000 dollars goes toward fixed costs, like insurance, heating the plant, and so on. Another $700,000 goes toward the cost of production, things like wages, material, and scrap and rework. This leaves $50,000 in profit."

The group of managers agreed with this calculation.

"Now if I institute a program of continuous improvement that reduced the amount of scrap and rework, the cost of production is lowered. Let's suppose that it drops to $650,000. That increases my profits to $100,000. Now how much more would I have to sell to make the same gain?"

The group of managers paused a moment before a couple of low whistles were heard. It was now easy to see that they would have to almost double sales to double profits. However, the improvement of their own processes internally would create the same increase in profits with the original level of sales.

"I think you can see the benefit of a good cost accounting system," Vincent said.

Without raising his hand Lee asked, "What kind of accounting system are you thinking of using?"

"Well," replied Vincent, "we have a few choices. That's why I need to talk to everyone. The system we choose will depend on what we want to accomplish."

"Why don't you briefly outline our choices?" Mead suggested.

Vincent began by erasing the figures on the board and then dividing the white area into three columns. "Our first choice is the traditional approach used for quality improvement plans. It is called quality costs. It divides the expenses associated with maintaining quality into four groups."

Vincent wrote *Quality Costs* at the top of the first column and then listed the following:

1. Internal Failure
2. External Failure
3. Appraisal Costs
4. Prevention Costs

"Internal failure," he explained, "is the cost due to scrap, rework, downtime, paperwork, and other expenses related to things going wrong. External failure is the costs we incur after the product is shipped. This includes things like warranty expenses, returned material, and so on. Appraisal costs are the expenses of testing and measuring. This includes the internal inspection systems, as well as SPC. Prevention costs include things like advanced quality planning, training, process controls, and continuous improvement teams.

"By dividing the expenses into these four categories, we try to reduce the failure expenses without raising the prevention expenses proportionally. In other words, we don't just throw money at our problems.

"The advantage of this system is that we can break out a problem's expense into line items. Both cost reductions realized from a solution and the expense of implementing that solution appear on the same piece of paper. That makes it easy to see if we are really improving the situation or not."

"Could you give us an example?" Brenda asked.

"Sure." Vincent drew out a stack of papers from the top of Mead's desk. "Here's a case study from where I used to work as an intern." Vincent passed the papers around the room to each manager. "This particular company printed the labels that go onto commercial batteries. The largest customers were companies who made batteries for lawn and gardening equipment. If you look at page one you can see that the cost of quality was broken down into line items by source."

Brenda glanced at her copy and saw the following:

Losses (in thousands of dollars)	
Warranties	$45
Failure of Glue	$33
Scrap	$22
Returned Goods	$12
Misprints	$7
Appraisal Costs	
Proofreading	$15
Inspection and Testing	$22
Other	$11
Prevention Costs	
Quality Planning	$3
Problem-Solving Groups	$5
Training	$2
Total	$177

Vincent continued. "As you can see a cost of $177,000 is high enough to catch the attention of any management group. Especially when this represents about 20 percent of the sales volume to these customers.

"At the same time, take note of the low amount of funds being dedicated to the prevention function. The management team that looked at this problem decided that an increase in preventive measures was called for. They assigned a larger budget to the problem-solving teams and directed the quality manager to guide the groups.

"The quality manager pointed out that warranties, glue failures, and scrap were the major problems to overcome. The initial study of what caused the scrap and warranty costs found that they too were mostly the fault of bad glue. Therefore, the teams investigated new forms of glue. Eventually, they found a glue that survived reliability and accelerated life testing."

Breton interjected at Vincent's pause, "What kind of cost reductions did they realize?"

"Well, the external and internal failure costs were reduced by $50,000. However, take note of the fact that the prevention costs rose by $10,000 dollars. A common mistake many people make is to look only at the cost reduction. They ignore the fact that it usually takes money to correct a problem."

"But it paid off in this example," Mead added.

"Right," Vincent responded. "The benefits outweighed the added cost by five to one. In the end, the company was ahead by $40,000."

For a moment everyone in the room sat silently and absorbed the significance of what Vincent was saying. Anna eventually interrupted the pause by saying, "You said there were other choices in how we track costs."

"Oh, yes," answered Vincent, as Anna's comment jogged his memory. "There is also the cost of quality or COQ. It tracks the cost of doing things wrong. We would list out the internal and external failure costs and assume that inspection and testing was a normal expense of business.

"The end goal is to drive the cost of doing things wrong down to as close to zero as possible. As management you would look at the magnitude of the problem and budget accordingly."

"Can we have a quick example?" Breton asked.

"Sure," Vincent replied. "Take our last example. We would look at only our losses. That would be a total of $119,000. The cost of appraisals and prevention is $58,000. That leaves a $61,000 difference. Thus, you can budget a fraction of $61,000 for fighting the problems. Hopefully, your budget will be more than matched by improvements.

"You can also look at your return on investment. A $100,000 for a more efficient gluing machine may eliminate $50,000 in problems every year. Therefore, it takes two years to realize the return on your investment."

"These two systems seem awfully similar," Lee commented.

"In many ways they are," Vincent replied. "There is a third and newer choice still under development. It looks at the life-cycle costs of each product. Instead of just looking at annual internal expenses, it also monitors the increases in market shares and competitive position as important factors."

"Would you recommend we look into that system?" Mead asked.

"Not at this point," Vincent answered. "We are not a large company, and we should wait until this method has been tested and proven by the Fortune 500 companies."

"Questions?" asked Mead, turning toward the managers. There were no replies. "Okay, where do we go from here?" Mead asked.

Vincent cleared his throat. "I suggest that we adopt the quality costs method of tracking improvement. Also, I need to establish some standard costs for scrap and rework."

The room remained silent for a moment. "Vote," Breton suggested.

"Hands," commanded Mead, "for those in favor of Vincent's suggestion." The vote was unanimous. "Fine. Let's move on to the next point."

It was only twenty minutes until the Monday meeting broke up. Breton was instantly at Vincent's side offering to buy him lunch as an official welcome. Brenda disliked the way Breton muscled in to make points with every new person. When Breton left Brenda walked over to Vincent and asked if she could watch him calculate some standard cost figures.

"Of course," he responded. "Why don't you come to my office about two this afternoon. I'll be calculating scrap costs for the major products."

At noon Vincent and Breton sat in a booth at a local seafood restaurant. Breton wanted to pump Vincent for information about the new cost accounting system. He knew, however, that this restaurant was a dangerous place to talk. Many company officials came here because it was just a short walk from the plant.

When Breton made the reservation he specified a special booth in a corner, far from prying ears. Upon entering, he primed the palm of the hostess with ten dollars to make sure that they were alone.

Vincent was toying with the idea of a swordfish steak when Breton began the questioning. "So Vincent, how do you like the company so far?"

"Well, I've only been here a few days but it seems a nice enough place."

Breton ordered the fried shrimp before continuing. "How long is it going to take before the new cost accounting system is in place?"

"Actually," replied Vincent as he indicated to the waitress that he preferred an iced tea, "the system is already in place."

A look of surprise crossed Breton's face. "I thought that Frank wasn't able to create the new system."

"He wasn't, but the accounting system he did use can be modified into what we need."

"I don't follow you," Breton said.

Vincent's iced tea came and he poured an entire packet of sugar on the top of the ice but did not stir it. Vincent liked to let the sugar melt slowly into an iced tea. "The budgets you get right now have lot of line items for your various expenses, right?"

"Sure. Right now I get items like labor, equipment, support services, and stuff like that."

"That's your current cost accounting system. The system is fine, but it doesn't have cost breakdowns for quality-related items. I don't need to develop a new system, I only have to add a new list of items to track." Vincent paused to pour dressing on his salad. "Like the cost of quality items I listed in the meeting this morning."

Breton could only pick at a paper cup of cole slaw as he waited for his lunch to arrive. "I see," he said. "But, how will you calculate scrap, rework, and defect costs when we've never kept any records on those expenses?"

Vincent smiled as he squashed a cherry tomato with his fork. "Ahh, but you have kept records. You might not be aware of their existence, but the paper trail is there."

"How do you mean?"

"This is how I earn my salary. Take the case of your returned goods.

Tons of paperwork is submitted everytime inventories are altered. Not only do we get returns because of poor quality, but we also have other reasons people send our stuff back. It could be that we sent a customer too many parts or that the parts were incorrectly ordered. My job is to sort out the returns due to poor quality and then to sort again by part number."

Breton's lunch arrived before Vincent's. The shrimp were dark brown and greasy. The french fries under the shrimp were already absorbing the excess fat. This was the way Breton liked this lunch served, just the way he had gotten food when he lived in Chicago. "How are you going to do that much sorting in such a short period of time? You only have about a month before Ford is going to be here looking us over."

Vincent took a last draw on his ice tea and spit out the lemon seed that had accompanied the liquid. Then he opened his briefcase and drew out a small black metallic box. It was a little larger than a notebook. "With this," he announced proudly. With that he flicked the two locking tabs on the front of the box and swung its lid open.

Breton stopped in mid-bite as Vincent turned the open box toward him to show him the contents. Inside was the gleaming flat display and keyboard of a computer. Vincent pressed another release and a dual disk drive popped open above the keyboard.

"This is the ultimate in laptop computers," Vincent said. "I got it as a graduation present. I have also configured it to talk to the mainframe computer at ROB. I can down load all of the paperwork that is kept on record and sort it inside of this machine. I have sorted more than a million records in only an hour using this baby."

Vincent clicked the machine shut as his lunch arrived. Breton took note of the way Vincent patted the machine as he placed it back into the briefcase. He also noted that Vincent called the machine "baby." Breton wanted to meditate on these points further, but he was distracted as Vincent began pouring ketchup onto his swordfish steak.

Millie, the waitress for their table, saw what was going on and retreated to the kitchen. In the corner of the dishwashing area there was an old greasy table normally used by the busboys and waitresses for their breaks. As Millie entered the room she saw a tall, thin man nervously smoking as he sat on the tabletop.

"Morning, Millie," the man called out.

Millie looked around nervously and walked over the man. "How did you get in?" she asked, but she already knew the answer.

The man drew out fifty dollars and placed it on the table. "Hear an interesting conversation at booth 12 today?"

Millie glanced around before she scooped up the money. Then she related what Vincent and Breton had talked about. The man made no notes. He only nodded his head occasionally. When she had finished, the man thanked her and walked out the back door. Millie was glad that he was gone. He didn't come often and the money helped buy shoes for her children, but she didn't like the way he talked. He was too confident that she would tell him everything. She also didn't like the way she wished she knew him better.

When Vincent returned from lunch, Brenda was sitting in front of his desk. Vincent greeted her and apologized for being late. "The service at the restaurant took forever," he explained.

"Yes, I know," she replied. "What are we going to do first?"

"I am going to calculate the cost to scrap a particular production part. In this case, I have selected your most popular part, the E-2331." With that announcement Vincent drew a metal housing out from behind his desk. "Ta da!"

Brenda was less than enthusiastic. The dreaded E-2331, she thought. She had seen more of these motor housings in the past year than she ever wanted to see in a lifetime. The company had seventeen Material Complaint Notices from customers directly related to the quality of the E-2331. Mead had threatened to fire everyone unless the quality improved. What was done instead was a 100 percent inspection of the housings to prevent the MCNs. Brenda knew that unless real improvements to the quality of the part were made soon, the customers would begin returning shipments again. On top of that, the 100 percent inspection was finding close to 15 percent defective parts.

Vincent seemed oblivious to all of this. However, he had selected the part specifically at Mead's request.

Vincent began by walking over to the computer terminal in the corner of the room and ripping its cable out of the wall. "There," he declared. "We won't need this anymore." Brenda was taken aback by the bold move. The information systems people treated the computer system with such reverence that this, surely, was sacrilege.

Vincent drew his sleek black laptop computer out of his briefcase and unwound a cable attached to the back of the machine. He plugged the cable into the now vacant terminal socket. He turned the laptop computer on and Brenda pulled her chair over as the screen flickered. After a few seconds of beeps and whirring noises, several screens flashed by. Vincent tapped a couple of keys and suddenly the company's mainframe computer screen appeared.

"You've tapped into the mainframe!" Brenda exclaimed.

"Quite so," Vincent responded.

Brenda knew that computers could be powerful tools when properly used, but she was also afraid of the jargon and the confusing commands people used with them. She hoped that she could successfully evade having to learn computer usage at this job.

Vincent logged onto the mainframe computer and brought up the current cost accounting system. He then pressed two keys at once on his computer and a small window opened near the lower right corner of the laptop's screen. Placing a finger on the open window he stated, "This is my database program. It's going to suck the cost data on the E-2331 out of the mainframe."

A few minutes later Vincent logged off of the computer and unplugged it from the wall. He moved back to his desk and placed the laptop so that Brenda could glance at the screen. "Look here," he said. "This first column is the number of units produced during each run. The next column is how much material we bought to make the part. The next column is the number of labor hours billed to each run. All the data we need are in this one spreadsheet."

Brenda was impressed. "How do we determine the cost to scrap the part?" she asked.

Vincent handed her a dry erase pen and directed her to the white board hanging on the wall. "I'll let you make the calculation. Write down each expense as I calculate it and then you only need to add them all together."

Brenda felt that she could handle that task very easily. As she began to write on the board Vincent noted how attractive she was. He quickly filed that thought away to focus on the task at hand.

"First," he said, "I'll calculate the average material cost for each part. I'll take the total number of housings made and divide it by how much raw material we bought." Several clicks of the keyboard later he announced that, "The average part requires forty-five cents of raw material."

Brenda wrote E-2331 at the top of the dry erase board and under that 45¢. She said, "So, we're losing forty-five cents every time we throw away a part."

"Only in material costs," Vincent corrected. "There are other hidden costs most people don't take into account. Take for example the cost of running the machine to make that part. If I add together the depreciation of the machine and the operating expenses and then divide those into a cost by part I get. . ." Vincent pressed some more keys, "about thirty cents per part."

Brenda wrote down that figure under the material costs.

"Now," Vincent said, "I can calculate the labor costs for making each part. On average, we can only make so many parts per hour. That can be divided into the average labor wage plus benefits, insurance, and so on. I get ninety-five cents per part."

Brenda added this to the growing list.

"Next, is the fact that for every part you throw away, you have to make a replacement part. That means that the labor and machine costs have to be spent again making the replacement part. And don't forget that we have to buy more material for the replacement part. Therefore, the cost to make the replacement is the addition of the numbers we have so far."

Brenda did some quick addition and came up with $1.70 per part. Vincent confirmed this and Brenda added the figure to the list.

"Then," Vincent announced, "there is the cost of sorting out the defective pieces. This isn't so bad because I see that you hire temporary workers to do the work at minimum wage. That works out to about ten cents per part." Brenda added the figure to the board.

Vincent continued, "Finally, there's the matter of paperwork and other minor operations involved in scrapping parts. I would estimate that at five cents a part."

Brenda added together the figure and wrote $3.55 per part. She stood back for a moment surprised at the size of the figure. "Are you sure about this?" she asked.

"Quite," responded Vincent. "See how it's easily over seven times the cost of the raw material wasted in a scrap piece? A lot of companies are not aware of how expensive scrap really is. Let me show you." Vincent got up from the desk and walked over to the dry erase board. He ignored the drawing pens on the shelf and took Brenda's.

"I looked up your quality reports on the E-2331. You scrap about 15 percent of all production on this part. It costs us about $1.70 in material, labor, and machine time to create a good part. It also costs us $3.55 per defective part. If I wanted to make ten thousand good parts it would cost me $17,000 if I produced no scrap."

"But we produce a lot of scrap," Brenda injected.

"That's right," Vincent confirmed. "We make about 15 percent scrap. So, we have to make 11,765 parts so that when the scrap is taken out, we have ten thousand remaining good parts. The ten thousand good parts still costs $17,000 to make but, we have to pay for the 1,765 scrap parts. At $3.55 each that's an additional cost of $6,265.75."

"We're increasing our production costs by over a third," Brenda stated.

"Quite correct. And if any of our competitors are operating at a near-zero scrap rate, they can underbid us by a third."

Brenda whistled. Vincent patted her on the back. "Welcome to the world of high finance."

"So," Brenda concluded, "this $3.55 cost to scrap an E-2331 will become part of the new cost accounting?"

"Yes, it will. I'm going to do this for all of the high-volume jobs we currently run using the same calculations we just did. I figure that's going to take me well over two weeks. However, when I'm done I have a feeling that every manager is going to be held accountable for their decisions based on how much we can cut these expenses."

Brenda wasn't worried about how she was evaluated. Her next question was on a different, and to her, more important topic. "How will you get a cost figure for something we have no data on, like a visual defect or a new product?" she asked.

"Well," responded Vincent immediately, "let's look at a part that has both characteristics." He rummaged around in a box near the door and drew out a small plastic part. "Seen this one yet?"

Brenda had to admit that this was a new part to her. Vincent explained that this was a knob that went on the front of a popular brand of home stereo receiver. "We have never run this part before, so it would be a little tricky calculating the quality costs involved."

Brenda had to agree. "What do you do then?" she asked.

"In a case like this, I will develop some standard costs for the various components of the quality costs. Then it will be up to the production people to track the new part. Once they document some costs for me I can refine the estimates."

"Could you give me an example?"

"Sure. Let's take the case of internal failure costs, you know, things like scrap and rework. I can estimate how much these will cost by looking at the cost of a similar part."

"What have we made that is similar to this knob?" Brenda inquired.

Vincent opened his center desk drawer and produced a small square plastic part. "Remember these?" he asked.

"Sure," Brenda repsonded. "That's an AB-998, a fuse box cover."

"Not only that," replied Vincent. "It also uses the same weight of plastic and about the same cycle rate during molding. In other words, it costs about the same to produce the fuse box as it does to produce the knob."

Brenda beamed, "I get it. The cost figures from the fuse box create a rough estimate of the costs we can expect to encounter with the knob."

"Precisely," Vincent confirmed. "The costs of scrapping or reworking the fuse box are already documented. I will use those figures as a guideline for the knob. For example, to perform a sort of the fuse boxes, it cost $500 to hire the people and set up the sort. Then it cost an additional ten cents per part to sort. Therefore, sorting a thousand knobs will probably cost $500 plus $100 more to sort the actual parts."

"Very clever," Brenda responded. "What are we going to do with all of these data when you're done?"

"The first step will be to lay out all of the quality costs for the company as a whole. Using Pareto analysis we will be able to pinpoint the best opportunities for massive improvements. After that, we will give cost breakdowns for each department. I would imagine that every manager will have to continuously justify his job by showing that he is cutting unnecessary expenses every quarter."

"Sounds like a million laughs," Brenda observed. "Is there anything else we should review today?"

"Ever calculated a Taguchi loss function?" Vincent inquired.

Brenda retreated to the door as she replied, "No thanks."

She was already out of sight when Vincent answered, "Hey, it's a lot of fun." But, Brenda was already out of hearing range. Oh, well, thought Vincent. Brenda was a fascinating woman but . . .

CHAPTER 13

Product Liability and Industrial Safety

It was a pleasant summer day in Grand Rapids. Mead paused long enough at the top of Lyon Street to imagine that he could smell Lake Michigan in the fresh western breeze. He took note of the flowers bordering the modern two-story building that housed the law firm of Haker, Marker, Chartes, and Zinger.

With youthful strides he took the steps in twos. A quick snap of his wrist flung open the smoked glass doors of the law firm. The grey and mauve interior beckoned him forward. A secretary directed Mead into the office of Hal Haker.

Hal sat behind a large rosewood desk, his back to Mead. He was busy completing a note on his personal computer. He quickly turned to greet Mead. "Bob, how are you doing?"

"Just fine Hal." They shook hands.

Hal and Bob looked at each other for a moment before Hal suggested, "What can I do for you?"

"Well, Hal things are going great at the company. Ford and General Motors have both been in to look over our progress and they both say that they will continue to do business with us."

Another pause.

"And. . .?" prompted Hal.

"Well. . . I'm worried. I'm worried about product liability."

Hal interrupted, "Whoa, let me put down my meter flag, this sounds like legal advice."

171

Mead was always fascinated that an attorney as successful as Hal Haker could be so frivolous in conversations. "Anyway," he continued, "I was at an ASQC meeting the other night and several people told horror stories about the liability problems they have experienced in the last few years. I was wondering whether you could give me some pointers to lower my exposure?"

Hal smiled. He liked these sorts of questions.

Nothing is better for the law profession, he thought, than fear. "No problem, Bob. I can give you a few basic pointers and that should give you some direction in preventing liability suits."

"First," he began, "the law is quite clear on direct liability. If you make a product that is harmful and you know that it was harmful, when someone gets hurt, you are liable for damages. However, a lot of law cases have been won where the company didn't know the product was harmful, and someone still got hurt. Worse yet, court awards of thousands of dollars have been given to people who directly disobeyed operating instructions on a product and were hurt. The classic example is someone who puts gasoline in a kerosene heater and the heater explodes and burns down their house."

Mead interrupted, "You mean that someone misusing the product can still sue me for damages even though they were acting like an idiot?"

"Not exactly," Hal explained. "You see, my explanations are meant to sound just like the stories you read in the paper everyday. However, the papers usually fail to report two things, the mitigating facts and the actual outcome. For example, in the case of the heater, the manufacturer may have said nothing about the danger of using gasoline in the instructions. Or, the fuel put in the heater was sold as kerosene at the store, but it was really gasoline. See, how these little factors can make a big difference?"

"Yes, I guess I can."

Hal continued. "Another thing to bear in mind is that some attorneys advise clients to sue everyone in sight for damages. The theory is that someone will be found guilty. Therefore, you may hear about companies being sued a lot. But the important factor is how many of those cases are thrown out before a trial takes place. Judges have little time these days for frivolous cases.

"In addition, an initial award is not necessarily what a company will finally pay. A lot of times the case was decided by a jury and the award amount is shot down by an appeal. On the other hand, a lot of companies pay a bunch of small settlements out of court. This is especially true when the company feels that it might be vulnerable in a courtroom."

"So, what can I do?" Mead asked.

"The important first step is to reduce the chance of harm in a product while it is still being engineered. Have the engineers and the product development people sit down and think of the ways a product can fail. Most people use something called Failure Mode and Effects Analysis. Your buddy, Mr. Headly, over at Urn Corporation does it all of the time. You might want to visit him."

"How does this failure mode analysis work?" Mead asked.

"Failure mode and effects analysis," corrected Hal. "The engineers list every possible failure they can think might happen to a product. Then they try to predict how often it might happen. Using this information they select which possible failure will happen too often. Then they improve the design to reduce the chance. Of course, they document all of this so that if you are called into court you can show that you were working to prevent the problem.

"Take care using this method, though. If the engineers fail to list a problem that later occurs it could be seen as negligence on your part."

"You're filling me with confidence," Mead observed.

"Wait, it gets better," answered Hal. "You are a supplier to the automotive industry. In most cases, the automotive company will be sued if one of your products is defective and you knew it. However, your customer, the automotive company can sue you or enforce penalties under your current purchasing agreement. In short, you have several problems to worry about.

"Luckily, there are several things you can do to prevent liabilities. The first is to prevent torts. Torts are filed when personal injuries are suffered. This includes your own workers as well as customers. Therefore, you will want to improve your worker safety programs. In addition, engineer your products to be safe and document your actions.

"As an additional measure, it would be a good idea to educate everyone in your plant on the importance of product safety. Some companies mark safety characteristics on a blueprint with a special symbol so that everyone working on that job knows that this characteristic is critical."

"Should we have SPC charts on safety characteristics, like pull strengths?" Mead asked.

"That would be a good idea. Especially if you also document that you were continuously improving that characteristic."

"Anyhow," Hal continued, "the next step would be to appoint a product review board. This group could conduct two types of studies. The first would be to review the design and failure analysis work from the engineers. They could look for potential problems the engineers missed. The second type of study would be realistic testing of the product. What's a common product you make?"

"Oh, I'd say an automobile fuse box cover."

"Okay. Suppose that it was very important that the cover keeps water out of the fuses. Put those covers on the fuse boxes of your sales people's cars and send them all over the country. Encourage them to remove and replace the cover several times a day. After a few months you can then test the seal and interview the sales people to see if they were cut or injured using the covers.

"Another thing you can do is audit the safety characteristics of your covers on cars that are being serviced at dealers around the country. I know that the cover doesn't seem like a good example, but you can apply these same ideas to more hazardous products."

"Your example is fine, I see your point," Mead assured.

"Good. Now there's a second area of liability to address, the liability of a contract. Like it or not, you have several contractual relationships to worry about. The first is the sales contract to your customers. You have assured a certain level of quality in your product. If the customer finds poor quality in one of your products, you are liable for either fixing the problem or sending better parts.

"In addition, there is the matter of warranties. I don't know if you have written warranties on your parts, but there is always an implied warranty. For example, if you made brake shoes and one failed on a car within the first few weeks of use, you would be liable. The courts would say that the product failed well inside of its useful life span.

"Therefore, you will want to make sure that written warranties are produced for critical parts. In addition, a good reliability engineering program will help prevent many of these problems. However, when problems are reported by your customers or by the end users, it would be an excellent idea to have a formal system of evaluating the complaints. This should include a reaction plan that allows for appropriate responses, from paying for replacement to full product recalls.

"There are other steps you can take as well. For example, you can get your suppliers to certify the quality of their goods. You can also calculate your liability risk for a product and budget accordingly. Instead of recalls, you can specify that a troublesome part will be replaced as part of a normal service plan on a vehicle.

"Whatever you do, be careful. You have to react to every known safety problem. During a court case the plaintiff will have the right of discovery. That means their attorney will be able to look through your records. If they find a history of customer complaints and you did nothing in response, you will be in big trouble in court."

Mead paused in his note taking to reflect on what Hal had said. "How's the meter doing?" he asked.

"Almost half an hour now."

"And there's probably more you can tell me."

"Quite so," Hal replied.

"Let's call this good for today. I'll check on how some of these programs work and get back with you next week. I take it that you have some standard warranty statements we can copy and use?"

Hal took a folder out from the pile of papers on his desk. He pulled out a few sheets of paper covered with very small print. These he handed Mead without comment. Mead took them, thanked Hal, and left.

Once outside, Mead watched a group of college students lying on the small piece of grass outside the community college building. They seemed content. He wondered if the constant need to stay on top of developments in his business was ever going to go away. Maybe he could get some bass fishing in this weekend. He glanced at the notes he had taken. But maybe he would be too busy. Again.

Two days later Mead was sitting in the employee break room at Urn Corporation. He and Headly were sharing a cup of coffee and talking about liability.

"Liability," laughed Headly. "Let me tell you about liability." Mead leaned closer to hear the story.

"When we first went into business we had a motto for our urns. *Urn for eternity*, is what it used to say in our advertisements. Unfortunately, a couple of our customers took us literally. One was a woman from Florida. When her husband died she had his ashes placed in one of our urns. Now, we have tested the daylights out of urns to survive years on mantles, sitting in tombs, and so on."

Headly took a swig of coffee before continuing. "Do you know what this lady did?" Mr. Mead shook his head. "It seems that her husband was quite the sailor, so she had the urn mounted to the prow of his sailboat. Then she took a world cruise for a few years. Well, with all of the exposure to the salt spray and the pounding waves the stainless steel eventually corroded."

"Let me guess."

"That's right, somewhere between Australia and Java she lost her husband again."

Mead grimaced at the thought of the accident.

"Well, she was madder than a wet hen when she got back to the states. She sued us for damages and we lost. We have since issued instructions for usage of the urns. We've even issued bulletins to funeral homes warning them not to use them for unusual purposes. We offer to make more durable urns for those people that are going to place them in harsh environments."

"So," Mead asked, "what do you do about liability now?"

"Bob, as you could imagine we didn't get into too many lawsuits when we only made urns. However, as soon as we began supplying the auto market and some defense contracts, we quickly realized that liability was going to be a major concern. It didn't take long to realize that excellent quality in the product was the best line of defense against liability claims.

"Our first step was the continuous improvement program you've already seen. With excellent recordkeeping and the direct attack of problems as we find them, we have been able to avoid most embarrassments. However, this was not enough. The next step was to perform FMEAs."

"Failure mode and effects analysis?" Mead asked.

"Right. In fact, if you would like to see how one is done we can walk over to engineering and pull one from the files."

"Sounds great."

The two men dumped their coffee cups into a large garbage can near the door as they headed out of the break area. A few steps away was the engineering department. Headly waved to the few people that were walking around. The rest of the department was bent over various drafting boards, and they were obviously lost in thought.

At the far end of the room was a row of four-drawer filing cabinets. Headly quickly opened the second drawer of a middle cabinet and fingered through the files. He found the one he was searching for and pulled it out for inspection. Flipping it open he withdrew a single sheet of paper and left the rest of the file lying on top of the cabinet.

"Take a look at this," he said. "This is an FMEA for an electrical circuit we assemble for the Air Force."

Mead bent over the paper and noticed that it had a dozen or more columns of various widths. He drew his glasses out of a top coat pocket and put them on so that he could read the tiny writing.

Mr. Headly continued to talk. "An FMEA is really a diary of the engineer's every thought about a product. Specifically, the engineer tries to think of everything that might go wrong with a product.

"This particular circuit controls an air conditioning unit for Air Force mobile command posts. The intention of the circuit is to constantly monitor conditions inside and outside the post so that the air conditioning provides the best amount of cooling with the minimal use of energy."

Headly placed a finger on one of the lines on the report. "I can show you how an FMEA is created by using just one item as an example. Do you see this? It's the thermocouple for measuring external temperatures. In the next column the engineer has listed the possible failures that can occur with the thermocouple.

"In this case, he has listed two possible problems. The first is the outright failure of the couple. The other is the misreading of temperatures by the couple device. In this third column he now lists the possible effects of these failures. You can see how a failure will cause the air conditioning to switch to internal temperature monitoring only. In other words, the system is designed with a backup for the failure.

"If we continue across the page for this one problem, you can see how the report gives us a handle on controlling product quality during design.

The next column lists the possible causes of a failure. The engineer has listed things such as a defective thermocouple, extreme environments, mishandling, and so on.

"For each of these he has evaluated three characteristics. The first is how likely the particular cause will occur. This helps us to know which defect is most likely to occur and direct our prevention efforts more effectively."

Mead interrupted. "How do you know how often something will fail if you haven't used it in a design before?"

"Well," Headly responded, "there are several information sources. Sometimes the manufacturer of the thermocouple has reliability information. Sometimes we conduct reliability tests. I've seen engineers create an estimate by looking at the probability of particular parts in a device failing at the same time."

"I see," Mead replied.

Headly continued his description of the three characteristics that are rated for each possible cause of a problem. "The next thing we look at is the severity of the problem if it does occur. In the case of the thermocouple, a complete failure would be severe, but not a total disaster. You can see that it was rated a four on the scale of five for severity.

"The third thing we consider is the possibility that we can detect the problem before it reaches the customer. For example, the incoming inspection of the thermocouples should weed out the majority of defective parts. However, with a little statistical magic we can calculate how many defective units will still get through inspection. That helps us to both determine the likelihood of detection and the chance of a failure."

Mead observed, "Then this type of information helps you to pinpoint potential safety and liability problems before they occur?"

"Sure, that's one benefit of doing this. However, we can derive several other advantages as well. Take a look at the final columns on the report. Here we assign control steps to ensure that the problem is prevented where it is most likely to occur. We also specify who will have the responsibility to make sure that the action is taken.

"The responsibility for incoming inspection is assigned to quality assurance. However, we have also noted that the purchasing department should actively encourage the vendor of the thermocouples to certify the quality of the parts before shipment. That will eliminate the need for an expensive inspection of each shipment."

"But," Mead interrupted, "how will you prevent the defective units from creating a failure?"

"Simple," Headly replied. "We have redesigned the unit to have a dual set of thermocouples for both the interior and exterior sensors. When one unit fails, the other takes over. In addition, a failure light in the main control unit tells the Air Force operator that the sensor has suffered a minor failure. The unit keeps running correctly and repairs are possible without shutting down the unit."

"What if both thermocouples fail at the same time?" Mead asked.

"Our engineers have calculated that the chance of that is less than one in a million. In addition with a double failure, the unit would switch over to using only the internal sensor as a guide. Thus, the failure still has a very small effect. The old design would have required our paying for the repair of the unit, as well as the damage the shutdown caused."

"Damage?" inquired Mead.

"Oh, yes. I should have told you first, these command posts are loaded with delicate electronic equipment that is sensitive to heat fluctuations. If an air conditioning unit fails to keep the internal temperature at sixty-eight degrees, damage is possible. And, our contract with the Air Force specifies that we will pay for any resulting damages. I'd call that a liability cost, wouldn't you?"

Mead had to agree. He could see where the added expense of the redundant sensors was far cheaper than the potential liability problems. "You spoke of several benefits you obtain with this type of analysis," he said.

Headly answered, "You've seen how important a discipline like this is for preventing potential problems before they occur. We also like it because it forces an engineer to think through a product from several different perspectives. Of course, the most important perspective is that of the customer. The engineer has to think about the customer's needs.

"In addition, the FMEA report helps us to document our thinking process on a new product. When we bring a new engineer on board, he or she can review these records and learn about what went into making the product. New engineers don't have to start from scratch to figure out what will be important.

"Finally, the FMEA is a great tool for management. It helps us to plan where SPC should be implemented on the production floor. A critical dimension or attribute is specified in the report. If the quality of that characteristic is important in preventing a failure, we put a control chart on it at the point of production."

"I'm impressed," Mead said. "Can we use this same technique for existing products?"

"Sort of," Headly responded. "For existing products you do what is called a failure mode analysis, or FMA. You don't have to guess at what may fail or how often. Instead, your customer complaints, returns, and warranty costs should give you that information."

"Do you guys do FMAs?" Mead asked.

"Sure do. In fact, I personally review each one myself. I want to know what is going wrong in the field. I want to know what we are doing about it, and I check to see if we tried to prevent the problem. If an FMEA said we should watch out for a problem but nothing was done, somebody in this company has hell to pay."

With that, Headly swung around, dropped the report into the open file he had left out, and deposited it back into the cabinet. "Let me show you the information we gather." Headly strode off toward the hallway. Mead quickly fell in behind him. Within a minute they were in Headly's office.

Mead sat down as Headly sifted through a pile of papers in his out-box. After only a few seconds, he had what he wanted, a two-page memo. He tossed this across his desk toward Mead.

Mead examined the memo briefly. It was from purchasing and quality assurance to the attention of over a dozen people in the company. Listed on the two pages were failures reported on Urn Corporation products.

"That's one of the most important documents we have in this company," Headly began. "A couple of people in purchasing and quality assurance put it together every month. It lists every problem that has been detected in our products after they leave the company. Every field complaint, customer return, warranty call, and product audit is reported on that memo.

"It covers the last month. You'll see a second column of numbers and percentages. Those are the rates of failure for the past twelve months. The report is compiled on a spreadsheet in one of the computers. It gives us precise information on where our customer problems are really occurring.

"Once a year we compare the reported failures against a full field audit of many of our products. This gives us all a complete picture of where the immediate quality problems are located."

Mead said, "I see that the big problem is with the securing of a motor housing you produce."

"Yes," Headly replied with gloom in his voice. "It's part of an engine assembly. What we are finding out, is that the vibration of the engine tends to loosen the bolts that hold our housing together. It doesn't happen often, but the housings are falling off frequently enough that we have gotten repeated warnings from our customers."

"What are you doing to correct the situation?" Mead asked.

"Well, we've already tried several approaches. New designs and locking washers have had some success, but, the problem still occurs. The engineers think they may have a final solution. They've been experimenting with alternative assembly methods. The prototype they developed from the studies has held up in our reliability tests."

"How hard is it to gather this information?"

"Pretty easy to gather, but you need a computer to organize it in any sensible order. We've been using spreadsheets and database software to do our failure analysis reports. Not only does it produce readable

reports like that one, but it also enables us to do some complex compar-
isons that are all but impossible by hand."

"How do you mean?" Mead queried.

"Like the motor housings. We put all of the failure data into a database
and began searching by various conditions. For example, we sorted failure
rates by type of engine to which the housing was attached. We found
that the larger the engine, the more frequent the failures. We also found
that the failure occurred in northern states in the winter.

"To create that information by hand would have taken someone weeks
using pencil and paper. It took our computer only a few minutes. It also
told us that temperature and vibration extremes were the most likely
causes. Thus, we attacked those causes directly with newer designs."

"And prevented a recall of the cars that you would have paid for,"
Mead added.

"Precisely," agreed Headly. "Now you know why that problem is so
sensitive to us. The potential loss is very great."

"Is there anything else I should know?" asked Mead, hoping he could
wrap up this visit fairly quickly.

"Yes, we've talked about liability and failures a lot. However, another
issue too many people overlook is safety. You can get into some serious
liability problems if you don't have an aggressive internal safety program
for your workers. You can easily have a product defect that will injure
a worker as well as a customer. You have to cover both bases."

Headly turned in his chair and picked up an internal phone. "Hold
on a second, I'll see if I can find our safety person to talk to you." After
a brief pause Headly began speaking into the phone. He asked the person
at the other end for a few minutes of time. After a second pause he said
"thank you" and hung up.

"I want you to talk to Karen Solomon, our safety person. She's in her
office right now and can spare a couple of minutes."

"Sounds great," said Mead even though he really wanted to be at a
restaurant right about now eating a large plate of pasta.

The two men headed down the hallway outside Mr. Headly's office.
They took the stairway that led down to the first floor. After maneuvering
around some open office partitions they stopped at a cubicle outside of
the office door of the personnel department. Inside a woman was busy
sorting safety glasses into several piles.

"Karen?" offered Headly. She swung around in her chair and smiled
at the two men.

"What can I do for you today?" she asked.

"This is Mr. Mead from ROB, Incorporated," Headly answered. "He
has some questions about the role of the safety department." With that
Headly turned around and left. Mead found that rather odd, but decided

it would probably make this discussion a little shorter.

"Hi," he began. "Just call me Bob. I want to know more about the relationship between safety and protection from liability."

"Well, Bob, where would you like to start?" Karen asked. Just then Headly reappeared carrying a chair. Mead quickly noted that there were only two chairs in Karen's cubicle. Headly pulled up next to Mead.

Karen continued, "We have the usual responsibilities of a safety department. First and foremost is the security of our workers. I make sure that they are trained in proper safety procedures, like the wearing of safety glasses at all times on the shop floor." Karen's hand made a sweeping motion over the piles of glasses on her desk.

"A good amount of my time also goes into fire prevention activities. I've had the workers practice putting out contained oil fires with extinguishers and I've had them practice evacuation drills."

"What kind of things do workers usually sue a company over?" Mead asked.

"There you have several possibilities. For example, there is a whole set of right-to-know laws in existence. I spend a day each month telling every worker which products and chemicals they are working with that could pose a hazard to their health. We also take elaborate steps to make sure that hazardous materials are handled properly."

"Can you give me an example?" Mead asked.

"Sure, we do metal stampings here and we have a degreasing pit. That thing is loaded with chemicals that create a lot of toxic fumes. We have a written procedure for cleaning the chemical tank that involves two people being suited up in self-contained breathing units. Only one can go into the tank. If anything happens, the other can get him out fast."

"I see," Mead said, obviously impressed with the level of the hazard being described.

"Of course," Karen continued, "there is always OHSA, the Occupational Health and Safety Administration, to keep us busy. Michigan also has an occupational health and safety administration. Between the two of them we have hundreds of regulations to audit for compliance. That includes everything from the type of ladders we have to reporting the number of injuries we experience."

"Oh, yes," interrupted Headly. "We almost lost out during a General Motors survey because we had too many people reporting minor cuts."

"That's right," Karen added. "They wanted to know why we hadn't reacted to such an obvious problem. I formed a problem-solving group that examined the causes of the cuts. It turns out that a lot of our workers that trim parts or open boxes were bare-handed. We fixed the problem by buying cut-resistant gloves for everyone. The rate of cuts dropped from over fifty a month to only two or three.

"Getting back to what we were talking about, I also have to monitor worker's compensation claims. We keep close track of them for two reasons. For one thing, they are usually expensive claims. For another reason, we don't like losing a trained worker. We want to prevent the problems before they occur."

"How do you do that?" Mead asked.

"It's very similar to the SPC system, actually." Karen turned away in her chair and opened a filing cabinet drawer. She drew out a very thick folder and began leafing through it while she talked. "I can show you a specific example, if you want."

"Please," Mead responded.

"It involves back injuries on the factory floor. If I can just . . . ah, here it is. These are the data we kept as part of the problem-solving effort. The first thing I did was to form a team made up of myself and some of the line supervisors off of the floor. We spent a couple of hours discussing the back injury reports and their causes."

Karen drew out a summary report that had obviously been handled many times. The edges were dirty and the pages had been folded in several spots. "By reviewing our past reports on back injuries, we found that we were experiencing three times the national average for a company of our size and type. That alerted us to the problem.

"Next, we discovered that there were three distinct causes for the problems. The first was obvious, people would lift heavy objects improperly. The second was caused by falls. The rest of the injuries seemed to be the result of continual back strain. This group usually involved assembly people that sat hunched over a bench all day.

"A quick Pareto analysis of the causes showed that the third group had the most complaints, but the most severe injuries were from improper lifting. In the end, we decided to attack all three causes at the same time. We notified the custodian to make the clearing of all liquid spills his highest priority. That action all but eliminated the injuries due to falling.

"I took on the job of educating the entire work force on proper lifting techniques. That was a tough job because you've got so many macho guys out there who think they can lift anything. Usually, they are lifting a heavy object and turning their shoulders at the same time. It was important to have the supervisors rag on people who lifted wrong."

"Did the education help?" Mead asked.

"A little. The rate of complaints fell about 10 percent, but that wasn't nearly enough. I had to talk to the packaging engineer. I checked around and found that we had a lot of stuff packaged in small boxes that weighed over forty pounds. I had to reduce the weight of packages where possible and provide small lift trucks and two-wheel carts for the really heavy stuff.

"It took several months for everyone to quit being macho and start using the tools needed to lift the load. What really helped was having a couple of the injured guys talk to their work teams about proper lifting. Especially when Ozzie pulled a muscle in his back."

"Ozzie?" Mead asked.

Headly quickly answered, "Six foot seven and three hundred pounds."

"Yeah," said Karen with some satisfaction. "Seeing Ozzie use the lifting equipment changed a few egos. After that the rate of complaints fell another 60 percent. I'm still working on ways to reduce it further."

"What happened to the people hunching over benches?"

"Oh, that took about five months to fix. We took a manufacturing engineer out on the floor and asked him how we could get people to sit or stand properly while they worked at a bench. He started by raising many of the benches. This brought the work level up to a comfortable level.

"We also tried a few things that failed miserably. The worst was trying to exercise and stretch at each break. We tried the Japanese idea of playing music over the loud speakers while everyone in assembly would bend and stretch. Problem was that no one would do it. Again, pride getting in our way.

"We eventually had to introduce rotation and teams. Each worker belonged to a team that did several assembly steps. Each hour the workers would switch activities with a team member. This made people do some work standing up and then some sitting down.

"Of course, the real help was putting exercise equipment in one of the break rooms. We just put it there one day and said nothing. Pretty soon everyone would drink their coffee and fool around on the equipment. A couple of the people who knew proper exercise techniques began teaching the others, and soon they were having friendly competitions for who improved their abilities the most.

"The end result was that we had fewer reported back injuries and a much more cheerful work force. Also, the amount of workers' compensation we pay out every year has been dropping dramatically."

The three made some small talk after that, but it was clear to Mead that he had the answers for which he was searching. When the liability question first came up, he was sure that it would involve extra and special efforts. However, it was clear to him now that it was really just one more spoke in the wheel of continuing improvement.

As he drove to dinner that night he turned several thoughts over in his head. Mead realized that liability claims were the most serious form of customer complaints and just like defective goods, it was everyone's job to prevent their occurrence. He also noted that problem-solving methods could be easily applied to teams in the front office. And finally, he noted that all of the reports he had seen that day were computer generated.

He turned into a gyros-to-go restaurant and pulled up to the take-out window. Sometime between ordering and paying for his food, Mead made a decision. He had put it off long enough. It was time for a computer revolution at ROB.

CHAPTER 14

Software for Quality

Brenda was surprised to see the boxes on her desk. It was early Monday morning, and she was already drinking her fourth cup of coffee. The weekend had been relaxing, but she knew that as quality manager she was facing another tough week of decision making.

Now she was face to face with the one piece of equipment she always shied away from — a personal computer. This one had a note on it explaining that it was for her work. "This will help you to make decisions faster. You can thank me later." It was signed by Mead.

Without hesitation, Brenda lifted her telephone receiver and dialed a number in the engineering department. "Hello? Lee? Didn't you once say you knew a lot about the right software for a personal computer? Can I see you for a few minutes this afternoon?"

That afternoon Lee stood next to the gleaming new machine and whistled. "This is a beauty of a machine, Brenda. It's got an 80386 processor, 80 meg drive, and tape backup."

"Never mind the technical stuff," Brenda replied. "Tell me what this machine can do for me."

"Well, there's a world of software packages available. What are you planning to use the machine for?"

"Mead says that he wants me to make better decisions."

"Well, the obvious choices would be to look at the software packages that relate directly to quality assurance. You know, like a computer program that can do capability studies."

Lee went on to describe other computer programs that could be of assistance to a quality assurance department. First, he talked about programs for SPC, reliability, and statistics. These made sense to Brenda because these were activities the department engaged in everyday.

Then Lee began to describe programs such as word processors, databases, and desktop publishing. Brenda questioned him closely on how these could possibly help her to make decisions, let alone improve the performance of the quality assurance department.

Lee decided that it was time to take some specific examples and show how they applied to the problems Brenda faced every day. So Lee invited Brenda down to the engineering department. Once there he quickly headed for a similar computer sitting on a lab bench.

He began with a software package the engineering department was already using to create capability studies and control charts. Booting up the program, Lee began to explain that the program could make thousands of calculations within a fraction of a second.

"However," Lee continued, "the real advantage in having a computer is that it can give you several views of the same problem, or allow you to experiment with possible answers. Take the case of a capability study. This software will quickly produce the information I will need to understand the capability of a process.

"When you calculate capability data by hand, you slowly learn about a process. However, a computer can quickly add additional information about a process by doing a series of calculations that would refine your view of the process.

"As you know, whenever you pick up a capability study, your eyes should scout for three important pieces of information — the specification, the histogram, and the Cpk index.

"The first thing to look for on any capability study is the specification for the critical dimension under study. Everything else will be compared to this. Therefore, you will want to mentally or physically draw a picture of the optimal size and its tolerance range. A computer can physically draw the same picture in an instant.

"The next thing to look for is the histogram. A histogram is a bar chart showing how many parts in the sample are of a specific size. This is the picture of the distribution of part sizes. What you are looking for is the bell-shaped curve of the normal distribution. There will never be a histogram that perfectly mimics the normal distribution, but most will display the classic bump in the center.

"The presence of a normal distribution is critical, for it shows that only random, natural forces are at work on the process under study. If an abnormal distribution was present most of the summary statistics would be useless and need to be corrected."

Lee pressed a few keys of the computer. The two sat in silence as a graphic appeared on the screen. "This is the distribution of weights in the molding of door locks," Lee stated. "Notice how the distribution is normal? That means that the machine is doing the best it can."

Lee pressed some more buttons and pointed at the new image on the screen. "This," he said, "is a different machine making the same part. See how the parts are distributed to form two distinct bumps in the curve?"

"Yes," Brenda replied.

"We found that each bump was associated with the two shifts operating the machine. The second shift operator had a different opinion on the weights needed. That created the two bumps. You see, an abnormal distribution means there's an identifiable special cause."

"And," observed Brenda, "that means it can be corrected."

"Precisely," Lee said. "A bimodal distribution is a histogram with two bumps. Whenever this occurs it almost always indicates a process with two events operating out of harmony. A classic example once occurred in a paint shop. This company painted thousands of automotive parts for the assembly lines in Detroit. The line inspector noted that the specifications for paint thickness were never met by the process. Therefore, he conducted a capability study. What he found surprised him, a bimodal distribution.

"What happened was he had sampled the thickness of paint from both sides of the parts. Each part is painted by passing between two air-powered guns. What the distribution detected was that one gun was pouring out more paint than the other. The bimodal distribution was being created by the overlapping of the normal distributions each gun produced.

"Because a computer was used, he was able to divide the data from each gun into separate groups. By analyzing these, he was able to quickly learn that each gun produced a normal distribution. The computer gave him the flexibility to make such an investigation.

"By adjusting the two guns to the same flow rate, a single normal distribution was created. This also reduced variations in paint thickness and brought the parts into the tolerance range."

"Can you give me some other examples?" Brenda asked.

Lee began, "A skewed distribution indicates that an identifiable force is acting on the process to create a scattering of parts in only one direction. For example, an operator adjusting the controls of the machine whenever he felt that it needed adjustment can cause such a distribution. The data are then skewed by an identifiable force, the actions of the operator."

"You said there were three important things," Brenda observed. "What's the third one?"

"Of equal importance in a capability study is the Cpk index. It is a single number that tells whether a process is well centered on an optimal specification and is capable of staying inside of tolerances."

"Wait!" interrupted Brenda. "You're in my territory now. The Cpk index is a measurement of the distribution of randomly selected parts against the tolerance spread."

Lee answered, "The computer conducts this calculation using the specifications, the average from the sample, and the sample's standard deviation. It determines if the sample average is closer to the upper or the lower specification."

"The Cpk is our standard method of recording the capability of a process," Brenda stated. "Other than speeding our calculations, can the computer help us?"

"Well," replied Lee, "the Cpk is a good index for measuring the current capability of a process. It reports the quality of a process in a single number. It is also a powerful tool of evaluation. For example, some managers collect the Cpk indexes for every job in the plant on each machine. This creates a list of processes rated by their capability performance. This is then used as a target list of problem areas to improve.

"By giving some additional instructions to the computer, it will automatically flag low Cpk so that even an untrained computer operator will know that a process has problems meeting its quality requirements.

"The computer could also be programmed to store a list of all processes checked and their Cpk's. We can sort the list from the smallest to the largest Cpk. That would produce the needed management hit list in seconds."

Brenda was beginning to see how the software took away her need to make lengthy calculations. With the free time this created, she could spend it examining the capability calculations more closely. It would also create reports on the current quality status of each manufacturing process. She could then make decisions based on up-to-the-minute data. Already, she was feeling that the new computer may have some use after all. "What else have the engineers found useful in these capability studies?" Brenda asked.

"Just examining the pattern of distribution against specifications and looking for the Cpk index will tell most of the story on a capability study. However, there are other statistics on such reports that could be useful for a more detailed examination of the process."

"For example, look here." Lee pointed to a small box in the lower corner of the computer screen. "This is called the percent above and below. This refers to the percentage of parts expected to be produced above and below the specifications. In a fully capable process both of these numbers will be zero. However, some noncapable processes have to proceed. Therefore, these numbers can be used to calculate how much it will cost to sort or repair the finished production. This can be of great assistance in calculating a bid for a job.

"For example, let's suppose that a company wants to bid on a part that costs $1.00 to make and $5.00 to scrap. They run a capability study on some preproduction parts and find that 3 percent of any production will probably have to be scrapped. The customer wants fifty thousand of these parts.

"The actual cost to the company will not be $50,000 because some of the parts are lost through scrapping. Thus, the company has to run about 51,550 parts so that when the 3 percent scrap is thrown out they have about fifty thousand parts remaining. This creates a production cost of $51,550. In addition, the 1,550 parts that are scrapped cost $5.00 each for an added cost of $7,750. Thus the 3 percent scrap rate increases the cost of this production by $9,300, a cost increase of over 18 percent. This type of information is vital for making profitable bids or determining if corrective measures are affordable."

"So, I can quickly make some cost of quality decisions, because the information I need is at my fingertips on this computer." Brenda observed.

"Right. And a program like this can store the data from the capability study for use by an SPC program."

"Show me how that works, Lee."

He returned to the computer's keyboard. By pressing a few function keys, Lee was back to the part in the program where the data for the capability study had been entered. He showed Brenda that these data were stored in a file called "TEST.DAT," which is short for "test data."

Exiting the program, Lee pulled out the floppy disk and inserted a new program. In a few minutes, they were both looking at the opening menu of a program that creates control charts. Lee selected the menu option for entering data.

A screen of rows and columns appeared. This was the grid that was normally filled in to create a control chart. Usually, a user would feed in the samples of five pieces examined every hour. Instead, Lee pressed a function key and the message "Retrieve File:" appeared at the bottom of the computer's screen.

Lee typed in "C:TEST.DAT," which told the computer to pull in the data file called "TEST.DAT" from the C, or fixed data drive. After a few seconds, the data appeared on the screen. Brenda was impressed. This meant that data which used to be entered each time a calculation was made by hand, could now be entered once and used many times.

Before Brenda can absorb the full significance of this possibility, Lee has pressed another function key and the computer's screen showed the calculations needed to create an average and range chart. At the same instant the printer attached to the machine came to life. Within thirty seconds it printed a blank average and range chart. The control limits were calculated and plotted. The chart was ready for use by the machine operator.

With raised eyebrows, Brenda was thinking of all of the calculation time she could save with this computer. But, Lee had another surprise in store for her. He lead her out to the production line and showed her a small box attached to one of the stamping presses.

Each time a part was stamped, small arms grabbed the piece and then retreated into their protective coverings.

"Did you see that?" Lee asked. "When each part is stamped that small box measures them for three critical dimensions. The data are sent down this cable to the computer in engineering. Not only can we produce capability reports and control charts based on this information, but we can put decision-making abilities into the computer.

"If this process begins to drift away from its target dimensions, the computer quickly calculates that a significant trend has developed, and it flashes this light here on the machine. The operator has just five minutes to correct the process.

"We hope to make it possible for operators to record their reactions to problems on the computer as well."

Brenda was duly impressed. "I see now how these computer programs can help me, but how can those other packages you mentioned be of help?"

A few minutes later, Lee and Brenda were back in the quality department's office discussing word processing, desktop publishing, electronic spreadsheets, and database programs.

"The best example I can give you of a productive program for quality assurance is the electronic database program," Lee stated.

"A database program stores data just like the filing cabinets you see all around you here in the office. In a filing cabinet, the data are written on paper and stored in file folders. When you find something, you have to sort through the information by hand.

"A database program can store the same information, but in electronic file folders that the computer can search through at incredible speed. Take the example of your monthly quality report. To put it together now, you have to pull all the activity files for the past thirty days and summarize the information by hand."

"And that takes my assistant Steve at least three days," Brenda added.

"Sure," confirmed Lee. "But the computer could race through the same information and produce the same report in only a few minutes."

"Show me how."

Lee sat down to a nearby computer and booted up a database program. He soon had a blank screen on the computer. He asked Brenda what information she needed for the monthly quality reports. She listed things such as stock keeping unit number (SKU), date, number of defectives found, the inspector, and the disposition of the material.

Lee quickly created a form on the computer screen for the entry of data. It looked something like this:

```
Quality Information

Date:
SKU:

Number of Defectives Found:
List of Defectives:

Inspector:
Disposition:
```

Lee then picked up one of the daily reports that inspectors had left on the desk. He quickly entered the information on the report.

```
Quality Information

Date: October 7
SKU: ABD-1357

Number of Defectives Found: 7
List of Defectives: Burns marks on seals

Inspector: Lee
Disposition: Accepted
```

Lee repeated this same step for several more forms. Then he showed Brenda how the computer could make a variety of searches. First he told the program to search the data he had entered and summarize the types of defects. Within a minute the screen listed the types of defects found from the most common to the least common.

Next he commanded the program to summarize all of the data into the format of the monthly quality report. A few minutes later the printer had finished the report.

"Although the computer is good at searching," stated Lee. "Its advantage for a manager is its ability to investigate situations."

"I don't understand," Brenda responded.

"Let's use an example. See this report on cracks found in a bracket received last week? I could turn on the computer and tell it to search for all other recorded incidents of cracks being found in this part.

"Within a few minutes I would have the information. However, I don't have to stop there. I could then tell the computer to take this sorted information and divide it by vendor and quantities of the shipments. That way, it would become quickly clear if the problem was unique to one vendor or a common problem."

"I see," Brenda said. "If the problem occurred with a single vendor, they would be listed many times, while the other vendors may not appear at all."

"Sure. And in engineering, we have used the databases we keep to track down suppliers of materials that have had high quality records with low costs. We have also found that the word processing program we purchased was as useful as any of the engineering programs."

"What do you mean?"

Lee explained that much of the communications done by his department uses the written word. In the past, the department would write some messages by hand and others would be typed. Misspelled words and bad grammar were common problems.

A word processing program allowed a person to type out a message on a computer screen before a high-quality printer created the typed message. Before it is printed, such a message can be read and edited by the author. Furthermore, the word processing package they purchased could check the spelling of words.

The results were clearly written messages of high quality and consistent style. This made the engineering department look more professional. It also helped to speed up communications by making written reports quick and easy.

"Just think about the tasks the quality assurance department is responsible for where a word processor would help," Lee said.

At that point, Brenda began to think about the written documents a typical quality assurance department had to produce in the course of a year. There were the inspection instructions and their revisions; the quality plan had to be updated each year; disposition reports were created on a daily basis. And everyday she estimated she wrote an average of five memos to other departments.

A word processing program also stored standard documents or phrases in its memory. For example, Brenda's inspection instructions always had the same opening and closing paragraphs. By entering these once into a word processing program they could be called up for creating any new set of inspection instructions. Thus, the secretary would save time by not having to continually enter the same two paragraphs.

Brenda expected Lee to call up a word processing program to give her another demonstration. Instead, Lee said, "After you learn how to use word processing, you can use this program."

On the screen a blank white rectangle appeared along with a confusing array of symbols along the top and sides of the screen. Lee used a pointing device hooked to the computer to draw three smaller rectangles on the white space. Then with a few commands, words began to fill in the rectangles he drew.

Next, he drew a square in the middle of the text and the words moved out of the way of this new object. A command or two later the drawings for a new part appeared in the square. Before Brenda could comprehend what was happening, Lee had printed the page out on a laser printer in the engineering department.

This page was unlike any Brenda had ever seen a computer create. Instead of the line of dots forming words and pictures she had seen so many times before, the lines and pictures on this page looked typeset.

"This is desktop publishing," Lee said with pride. "It allows us to put our really important documents into near-typeset quality pages. In addition, we have full control over the layout of each page and the style of typeface that will be used.

"Our engineering bids to customers have really improved with this package. We can include drawings from our CAD program and financial data from spreadsheet programs right into the final document. What takes several hours for us to create, used to take a printer's shop several days to create."

"This," declared Brenda, "would be perfect for creating custom forms for our inspectors, dressing up the quality manual, and for making our own training materials for new people."

Lee responded, "The desktop publishing program can draw text and pictures from almost any of the other programs our computer runs."

"Speaking of which," said Brenda, "What is this spreadsheet program you mentioned earlier?"

"Do you remember," asked Lee, "when the guys from finance come down to talk to us about budgets, they always have written spreadsheets? You know, the ones with the rows and columns of figures."

"Sure," Brenda replied.

"Well, each of the row and column totals should add up to the same number. If there is a mistake, they have to go back and add up all of the figures by hand. What an electronic spreadsheet program does is lay out the same rows and columns, but it continuously is adding up the figures on the computer."

"I don't quite follow you."

"Let's take a simple example, your checkbook. The rows and columns are still there. The first column is the date of the check, the second is the note on who got the check, and the last two columns are the amounts taken out or put back into your account."

"So, my checkbook ledger is really a type of spreadsheet?"

"Right. You have to keep balancing the amount of money left in your account by hand. What an electronic spreadsheet does is automatically add and subtract the total as you would enter every check."

"How does that help me in my job?"

"Think about any figures you have to constantly work over every time new data are added."

"Like my record of defects discovered in the production area?"

"Precisely. You could create a row describing all possible defects and another that contains the counts. The total of the defects and the percentage of each type of defect could be created by the spreadsheet program. Thus, all you would have to do is add the weekly figures and the spreadsheet would automatically update the summary. That alone would save you hours each week."

"What about future applications, Lee?"

"Well, Brenda it's going to take about a year or more for your personnel to get the feel of the programs we have already looked at. Once they are comfortable with their computers, the next logical step would be networking."

"Do you mean like the network for the company's mainframe computer?" Brenda asked.

"Yes. There are small electronic circuit boards you can buy for your machine that would allow you to communicate directly with the mainframe. More importantly, you could also tie your department's computers together using a local area network, or LAN.

"An LAN allows two or more computers to share data. Although this permits several possible applications, two are of particular interest for a quality department. The first is electronic mail. The operator at a computer in the production area can send messages back to the quality lab. These messages can contain the data from the production area. The lab can examine the data and quickly send back a reply.

"This saves the quality people working in the production area the time usually spent running between an inspection job and the lab. Also, it allows the manager to make a disposition decision while the production inspector continues to inspect goods.

"The second interesting feature of an LAN is the ability to have a common data storage device shared by several computers. For example, the host computer in the quality office could store all inspection instructions on a word processing program. Anyone at one of the linked computers can call up the inspection instructions they need with just a few keystrokes.

"More importantly, to update a set of instructions, the host computer operator merely updates the document and stores it on the common data device, usually a hard disk. Instantly, the new form is available for all users. The department does not need to print and distribute the revision to each work group. Have you seen the CAD and CMM marriage yet?" Lee asked.

Brenda knew that CAD stood for computer aided design and CMM meant coordinate measuring machine, but she wasn't quite sure about what Lee was saying. "Not yet," she replied hesitantly.

"Come on over to the quality lab," Lee urged. Brenda fell into step behind him. With only a few turns around office cubicles they were standing in the quality lab.

A large gantry was swinging back and forth over a marble table in the center of the room. A single thin probe hung from the gantry. This was the CMM.

"As you know," Lee began, "the CMM can touch off points on a part to determine distances, surfaces, and locations to the ten thousandth of an inch. However, we just bought a new computer program that will expand its capability. Take a look at the part we're checking right now."

Brenda quickly identified it as a prototype for a new transmission housing. The CMM was probing the outer edges of the part. However, Brenda noticed that no one was at the machine guiding the gantry and probe.

"Who's operating the CMM?" she asked.

"No one," Lee responded. "That's the beauty of this new program. What it does is guide the probe around the edge of the new part. Then it predicts the shape of the part. Next it checks across the surface of the part to see if it was correct. It will continue that cycle until it has an accurate map of its shape and size."

"Then what happens?"

"The data are transferred on the network connector to our CAD station in the engineering department. In addition, a first part inspection report is generated here and used by both engineering and quality to assure the producibility of the part."

Lee and Brenda watched the machine for a few minutes. Finally, Lee said, "The CMM is almost done. Do you want to see the results?"

"Sure," Brenda replied. With that the two of them turned and headed back to the engineering lab.

Once there they pulled up chairs behind a man sitting in front of a large display screen. In his right hand was a pen connected by wire to a touch pad. He pressed the pen on several squares marked out on the edge of the touch pad. A few seconds later a three-dimensional drawing of the part in the quality lab appeared on the screen.

Brenda was impressed. A complete drawing of a prototype had been created in minutes, instead of the hours it usually took by hand. Lee interrupted her thoughts.

"Now that we have a precise drawing of the part in the CAD system we can manipulate it at will. This is a good example of what CAD can do for us. That prototype is for a four-speed transmission. We have to design a new casing for the five-speed transmission being introduced next year."

Lee leaned forward and placed a finger on the display screen. "Do you see that area on the right side of the casing? We have to move the outer wall over an inch in the new design. Phil here can do that by moving the wall in the computer."

The CAD operator placed his pen on the touch pad again and a flashing cross hair appeared on the screen. As he moved the pen a box opened on the screen covering the wall Lee had pointed out to Brenda. Phil typed in some commands and the wall of the casing moved over in a few blinking flashes of the drawn lines. The connecting lines distorted to accommodate the move.

"You see," Lee said. "We have now made the change. Phil will print this out as a new set of blueprints."

Before Brenda could acknowledge his comment, a pen-plotter on her right whirred into action. The black pen raced over a sheet of paper that turned back and forth under the plotter. Within a minute Brenda began to recognize the creation of a conventional blueprint.

She looked at her watch. She estimated that it had taken engineering less than an hour to convert the prototype of an old part into a set of blueprints for an entirely new part. Her mind reeled with the thoughts of how efficient this was over the methods they previously used.

"I'm beginning to look forward to learning about my new computer," Brenda said. "I can see where if my staff is properly trained and I plan carefully how it will be used, the computer could be a powerful tool of productivity."

"Absolutely," Lee replied. "Just call me anytime you have questions."

CHAPTER 15

Quality Through Good Designs

"It's just like cooking soup backwards," King commented.

Brenda had now known Jack King from the community college for almost a year. After she had completed his class, they had become good friends. However, he still had that habit of stating things in surprising ways. "Run that by me again," she said.

King drew in a breath before he spoke. "You want to improve the quality of your products constantly, right?"

"Right."

"Okay, your SPC system and your problem-solving groups find and eliminate the obvious quality problems, right?"

"Right."

"So, what they are doing is tracking and correcting the obvious in your quality system, things like visual defects and scrap. You have no problem finding them because they are laying out in plain sight."

"Okay," confirmed Brenda cautiously.

"Now how many times have you seen an operator use a setup sheet to establish proper settings for the machine controls?"

"Every production run starts with a setup of the machine. We have setup sheets for every job we run."

"Good," King said. "And, how many times have the machines been set up one day and everything works fine, but the next day the same setup produces scrap or rework."

"That happens more times than I care to count," Brenda responded.

197

King smiled knowingly. He had someone in a logical corner. "Do you think it's the fault of the setup sheet, the operator, or the machine?"

Brenda paused to think. All three had been blamed in the past, but she knew that King was driving in another point. It had to be something she was overlooking. "Okay," she finally said. "I give up. What causes the problem?"

"Ignorance," King shot back. "Pure and simple ignorance."

It had worked. Brenda's interest was now piqued. "Ignorance?" she inquired.

"That's right. Nobody here really knows why the same setup procedure used several times and followed precisely would yield such different results. For example, I see that you have plastic injection machines running on the floor. How many controls are there on each machine?"

"I guess a couple of dozen."

"And, which control is most critical for the quality of the final part?"

"That would depend on what we were measuring that was critical on the part," Brenda replied.

"Absolutely correct. However, you still don't know whether changes in control settings, changes in materials, changes in the environment, or in the behavior of the operator causes your problems on the machine."

Brenda thought that this observation was true enough, and she nodded in agreement.

King continued, "Therefore, an experiment is called for to answer this question of why a machine fails to produce consistent quality." King sat back and sipped his coffee confidently having made his point.

Brenda asked, "What about the soup?"

"Ah, yes," responded King. "The soup. You see, to experiment with a machine, we have to identify each ingredient that goes into creating the variations in the quality of the product produced. In an experiment we will try various combinations of these ingredients. It's sort of like cooking different recipes of soup to see which one is best. The analysis used is called analysis of variance or ANOVA. It works like cooking backwards. It takes the results of the various soups and breaks down the effects of each ingredient." King paused and studied Brenda's face closely. "Do you see?"

"Not really."

King's expression changed from one of hope to one of disappointment. He wasn't disappointed by Brenda, but by his own inability to quickly describe to someone how an experiment really worked. He decided that visual aids were required. He pulled a dollar bill from his pocket and laid it on the break table they were sharing in the ROB cafeteria.

"I bet a dollar that I can show you how experimentation works and solve any quality problem you name before this week is out."

Brenda quickly accepted and the two were soon on their way toward the factory floor. King folded the dollar bill and placed it in the grip of the teddy bear he was holding firmly under one arm. "Ted can watch the money," he declared.

King then set Ted on a chair next to the door leading to the factory floor. "You don't have safety glasses. You wait right here," he commanded the doll.

Brenda sighed. She had long given up on trying to understand every aspect of this man. Brenda lead King straight out to one of the plastic injection molding machines they had been discussing earlier. "This," she said, "is one of the largest problems we have been unable to solve."

"Tell me something about this product," King commanded.

Brenda reached into a large box sitting on a skid next to the machine. She obtained a piece of black plastic molded into a slightly curved shape about six inches square. "This is the front plate on the ashtray in a car. This is the part you see when the ashtray is closed into the dash of a car."

King took the front plate from Brenda and turned it over a few times. Brenda drew a second plate from the box and walked over to a measuring fixture on the operator's workbench. "This is the measuring fixture we use to test the fit of the piece. It's supposed to fit flush against the dash it will be mounted into. This fixture simulates the size of the hole in the dash where the ashtray goes."

Brenda took the front plate and placed it into the fixture. Then she grabbed a small feeler gauge lying on the bench and began to probe around the outer edge of the part. "You see we have to have no more than five hundredths of an inch of gap all the way around. The ideal is to have a consistent gap size all the way around the front plate."

King studied the part in the gauge for a moment. He signaled to Brenda that he wanted to see something. She leaned closer to him to hear his request over the noise of the machinery. "Where is the setup sheet?" he asked.

Brenda leaned back over toward the operator and shouted into his ear. He nodded and reached under a pile of papers on the desk and drew out a single sheet. It was covered with oil and fingerprints. Brenda took it over to King.

"Here's the setup sheet."

"Can we go somewhere a little quieter?"

"Race you to my office," Brenda said with a smile.

A few minutes later they were comfortably seated, both quietly noting to themselves how much more peaceful it seemed there than on the factory floor. Still, the constant whine and hum of the machinery was easily felt even here.

King picked up the setup sheet from Brenda's desk and walked over to the dry erase board in her office. He wrote the setup instructions. "Inject speed, three seconds. Mold temperature, 350 degrees. Barrel temperature, 360 degrees." He mumbled each instruction as he proceeded. When he was done he had filled the left half of the board. Without pausing he began to fill the right side with very different instructions. "Two peeled potatoes, diced. Four cups of beef stock. One tablespoon of oregano."

Brenda watched this small show with some interest. She had learned from King's class to always study a situation before drawing conclusions. Bias could be a deadly enemy to learning.

In this situation it was obvious that King had written down a soup recipe next to the setup instructions for the plastic injection molding machine.

"Do you see any difference between these two documents?" King asked.

Brenda paused to think. "Not really," she said.

"That's right, there is no really important difference. In the soup recipe we are given a list of ingredients in their proper amounts. Furthermore, we are also given a set of instructions on how to prepare the soup.

"With the setup sheet for the plastic injection molding machine, I am given a list of resins that are mixed and added to the machine along with a list of where each machine control should be set. I also get a short description of how to operate the machine to create the front plates.

"Now, how many times have you tried to follow someone else's recipe for soup and gotten something that tasted very different from what you ate at their house?"

Brenda had had that experience several times. "Not just soup," she replied, "but ribs, cakes, breads,..."

King interrupted, "Why do you suppose that happens? You are using the same ingredients in the same proportions that your host used. I am assuming that your oven works in a similar manner."

Brenda paused again. That was a good question. She had wondered why she never seemed to be able to duplicate some of the recipes she had collected from friends. Before she could ponder this point further King was speaking.

"Let's look at the soup recipe I've written down, and I'll show you why you cannot duplicate recipes. Look at the call for one teaspoon of oregano. This really adds to the flavor of a soup. But, how old is your oregano? One year, maybe two."

Brenda nodded in agreement. She had little choice since she couldn't possibly date some of the spices in her cupboard.

"You see," continued King, "the older oregano gets, the more you have to add to get a similar flavor. Your friends probably bought fresh oregano because you were a guest. That changed the flavor of the soup. When you try to duplicate the recipe with your old oregano you get a much flatter taste.

"An experiment is really a structured investigation of a situation. The idea is to learn as much about how a situation occurs by studying every aspect of the problem.

"The soup can serve as an example of how this is done. We can test the effect of each ingredient by varying its amount in different batches of soup. For example, if I used three potatoes instead of two t probably would not change the overall flavor much. However, if I increased the cayenne pepper from a quarter teaspoon to a half a teaspoon, the resulting taste would be much different.

"In such a case we would say that the factor cayenne pepper has a strong effect on the taste. What we must do for the plastic injection molding machine is look for the cayenne pepper in the setup sheet. Chances are that one of the controls on the machine is very critical to the final dimensions of the front plate. Thus, if it is not strictly controlled, it can throw off the performance of the machine."

"How would that happen," Brenda asked, "if we set the machine to the same setting everyday?"

"I have two ovens in my house," King answered. "I can mix a batch of cookie dough and divide it into two equal batches. I then set each oven to 350 degrees. After ten minutes in each oven I pull out my trays of cookies. From the first oven I get light fluffy cookies. From the second oven I get carbon. They have burned, yet both ovens said they were at 350 degrees."

"I see," Brenda said. "Just because we set a control, say barrel temperature to 360 degrees, doesn't mean we actually get 360 degrees every time."

"You're catching on," King replied. "Our job is to discover if that's your problem. However, before we can proceed, you are going to have to do a little reading."

With that King took one of the books he coauthored from Brenda's bookcase. He handed it to her and told her to read a specific chapter. They would meet again tomorrow and discuss their experiment further. Brenda agreed and walked King out to the parking lot.

Later that same night Brenda cancelled a date and settled into bed with a box of chocolates and King's reading assignment. The chapter he selected was on the method of experimenting.

Brenda skimmed over the opening paragraphs. They were a description of the various methods available to business for conducting research. Besides experiments, there were also surveys, direct testing, literature searches, and other means of obtaining information.

A few paragraphs later Brenda found what she was looking for, a description of experimenting. The book said that an experiment was a structured investigation where the experimenter controls all but a few factors in a process. The factors that are allowed to vary are called *variables*. These variables are changed according to a strict plan, called the *experimental design*. The experimenter then studies the results of changing the variables or factors to determine the effect of each.

That seemed to make sense to Brenda. If she was going to try a recipe to get a better flavor, she would vary only an ingredient or two while holding the others constant.

She next read about the different types of experiments. The first was called the one-factor-at-a-time experiment, or classic approach. In this type of experiment the researcher would hold all the factors in a process constant, except one. The effect of changing this one factor would be studied.

As an illustration the book used the example of a math class. A teacher wanted to test ways to improve the mathematical abilities of her students. She randomly divided the class into two groups. Each group was placed into an identical, but separate room. Each group was given a math test to complete. The first group was called the control. They finished the test under the conditions they normally experienced in school. The second part of the class was called the experimental group. They had one more factor present in their room. The teacher played soft music in the background while the students took the test.

At the end of the experiment, the teacher compared the scores of the two groups. On average, the experimental group did better than the control group. The teacher had earlier formed a hypothesis that playing music would have little effect on math performance. As it turned out, a statistical test showed that the second group did significantly better. Therefore, the teacher rejected her hypothesis and concluded that playing soft music tends to improve math scores. Brenda made a mental note to try playing a radio the next time she had to calculate a capability study.

The next form of experimenting was called the full factorial method. Under this method two or more factors were studied at the same time. The book called these full-factorial experiments because every combination of the factors involved were tried.

The book used the example of a gardener that wanted to test the effect of fertilizer and water on the productivity of his tomato plants. The gardener staked out a square of land. He divided this into four equal sections. All four sections were planted with tomato seeds. The top two rows received twice as much water as the bottom two rows. The left side of the plot received the normal amount of fertilizer and the right side received half as much.

The result was that each of the four squares represented the four possible combinations of the factors under study. When the growing season ended the gardener counted the number of tomatoes produced from each square. The square that received the most fertilizer and water produced the most tomatoes.

Surprisingly, the square next to it that received a lot of water but only half the fertilizer did almost as well. The gardener learned from trying more than one factor at a time, that the effect of water on producing tomatoes was stronger than the effect of fertilizer. In addition, another piece of information was obtained. The gardener was also able to measure the interaction of water and fertilizer working in combination.

The book had a clever method for showing how to lay out and analyze an experiment. It created two columns for the two factors. A low setting, such as little water, received a − sign. The high setting for the factor received a + sign. Thus, the four possible combinations in the tomato study could be written as follows:

Run	Water	Fertilizer
1	−	−
2	+	−
3	−	+
4	+	+

To find the interaction, a third interaction column is created by multiplying the plus and minus signs. For example, the first run has low (−) settings. A negative number times another negative number creates a positive number. This is written in the third column.

Run	Water	Fertilizer	Interaction
1	−	−	+
2	+	−	−
3	−	+	−
4	+	+	+

Brenda thought that this was a particularly clever way to design an experiment. The book showed the data that resulted from the tomato experiment.

Run	Water	Fertilizer	Interaction	Results
1	−	−	+	17
2	+	−	−	30
3	−	+	−	12
4	+	+	+	32

Brenda quickly saw that the large number of tomatoes produced matched the runs with the large amounts of water. Thus, water was the most important factor in tomato production.

Brenda scanned a few more drawings of full-factorial designs for experiments. They all looked like garden plots. Every possible combination was accounted for in the design. She paused and wondered how many combinations would be needed to test the plastic injection molding machine.

She estimated that she would want to check fifteen different controls at three different levels of settings. With a few strokes of the calculator sitting by her side, Brenda learned that it would require just over fourteen million combinations. Brenda decided that a full-factorial might not be her answer. She missed the part in the book that talked about fractional designs and a man named Taguchi.

Next she read about the rules of experimenting. She reached for a yellow highlighter pen. She knew that this was the stuff that King would expect her to learn. Eight steps were listed:

1. Investigate the situation.
2. Form a central question.
3. Design the experiment.
4. Gather data.
5. Perform the analysis.
6. Build a mathematical model.
7. Verify the results.
8. Take action.

After highlighting these steps Brenda went back and read a brief description of each one.

Investigating the situation meant talking to as many people involved in the process as possible. This would give the experimenter important clues as to the actual workings of the machine. It would also help to identify important variables to study.

After interviewing various people, the researcher should perform a search of published literature, interview experts in the field, and look for any data already collected from the process. This helps to define more variables for study and to identify quality characteristics to measure. For example, a capability study will tell the experimenter the current quality level of the process. This establishes a baseline of comparison for future improvements.

From all of this information, the experimenter forms a central question about the problem at hand. That's easy, thought Brenda. Why won't the front plates mold consistently enough so that they are flush when mounted into the dash of a car?

Then Brenda began to read about the design of an experiment. She read that an experiment must have two characteristics, it must be valid and it must be reliable. Reliable meant that others could repeat the results obtained.

The book listed a dozen threats to the validity of an experiment. It mentioned things like bias, mortality, and instrumentations. For example, if the measuring fixture is not properly calibrated, then the data collected would not be valid.

Brenda read that the whole point of any experimental design is to avoid the threats to validity and to make the design repeatable. This was accomplished through the use of randomizing the order of an experiment, blocking out troublesome factors, and selecting legitimate factors.

Brenda was a little lost on how experimental design worked, so she pressed on to the fourth step, gathering data. The book said that an experimental design was nothing more than a set of instructions on which combinations of factors run at a particular time. In fact, the book referred to each combination of possible factors as a run.

After each experimental run, the experimenter would gather the results. These would be analyzed using a variety of statistical tests. The most commonly used test was called analysis of variance, or ANOVA for short. Brenda recalled how King had mentioned ANOVA earlier that day. This was the test that cooked the results backward. In other words, it decomposed the experimental results into the effect of each factor and the effect of each interaction.

Brenda read how the analysis could help the experimenter to form a mathematical model of what the process was doing. For example, the rate of tool wear could be expressed as a line of regression. The experimenter could predict that after, say ten hours of operation, the tool would wear down by so many thousandths of an inch.

To verify the prediction, the experimenter merely ran production for ten hours and measured the actual tool wear. If it was close to the prediction, then the model was supported.

For this point the experimenter takes actions to change the process to increase its performance. For example, if the tool wear using a new type of lubricant is lower than the historic rate of wear, the new lubricant is purchased for general use.

The next thing Brenda was studying was her clock. It was suddenly the next morning. Somewhere after taking actions based on the results of an experiment, she had fallen asleep. The sun was now shining into her bedroom window. The book was lying open, but facedown on the floor. She was already late for work.

At quarter after eight o'clock, Brenda came rushing into her office. She was glad that no one spotted her and that King was not due in that morning until nine.

Three cups of coffee later King was ushered into Brenda's office. "Did you finish your reading?" he asked smugly. Brenda had to admit that she skimmed some of the material.

"Well," began King, "let's take a closer look at the plastic injection process." He quickly laid out a dozen photocopies of articles from trade publications. "The first step in any experiment is to investigate what is already known."

Brenda picked up the first few articles spread on her desk and glanced at their titles. Each one was a report on experiments conducted on plastic injection machines. King handed her the last article. It was a story on one of their competitors' efforts to increase the quality of an ashtray front plate.

Brenda was taken aback. Here the company had been struggling for years to make the front plates fit correctly, but their nearest competitor had discovered answers and moved ahead. "What does this mean?" Brenda asked.

"It means that if you don't improve your front plate process pretty soon your competition is going to take the contract away from you. I would worry more about what they tested and what they discovered."

King left for a cup of tea while Brenda poured over the short, two-page article. The competitor had part of the same ashtray contract ROB enjoyed. They too had problems with the fit of the tray. However, their studies focused on the problem of shrinkage after the plastic was molded. Their study had found that screw speed and injection time were the critical controlling factors for shrinkage.

Brenda saw a glimmer of hope here. The competitor had not mentioned whether the controlling of shrinkage had improved the fit of the front plate. When King returned from the break room she blurted out, "They still can't make the plates fit."

"Perhaps," cautioned King. "They didn't brag about it so there is that possibility. I recommend that you review all of these articles and then call a meeting of the work team for the plastic area. And, don't forget to invite the engineers."

The next day Brenda was presiding over a meeting of the people involved with the design and manufacturing of the ashtray front plate. She began with a short presentation that reviewed the problem. Then she passed out copies of the article about their competitor. The group was impressed by the information.

"What I intend to do is run an experiment on our machine," Brenda said. She paused to look for negative reactions. "Actually, we will probably run a couple of experiments. The engineers have agreed to duplicate the experiment our competitors have conducted to see if we get the same results."

Several people glanced around at the people sitting near them. Brenda picked up on the visual cue that people had questions to ask. "Questions?" she offered.

One hand went up in the middle of the room. "Yes," said a young operator. "What will happen to our production schedule during these experiments?"

"Good question," Brenda responded. "We will be altering the controls on the machine in set patterns. We will change them only enough to get an effect, not enough to cause scrap parts. Therefore, your production quotas will still be met."

Brenda looked around for other questions and saw none. She continued, "I need the help of this group to plan the experiments. I need a list of factors we can change in the process that have any possible relationship to the fit of the part.

"To give you some idea of the type of factors I am looking for, I have researched several articles on plastic injection molding. Let me list some of the factors these studies have found to be important."

Brenda turned to the flip chart nearby and began to write. She listed injection speed, nozzle pressure, program pressure, screw speed, mold temperature, and room temperature. After she explained each one, the group chimed in with other ideas.

After thirty minutes the team had created a list of over fifty possible factors. Brenda then had the groups evaluate each factor to make sure that it was easily controllable by an operator and probably affected the fit of the part.

After another half hour of discussion most of the factors on the list were eliminated. The resulting list had fifteen factors. Brenda thanked the group and dismissed them. After a ten-minute break she met with just the engineers.

They discussed the actual factor settings. For example, injection speed on their particular machine was measured in the time it took the injector to fill the mold. A typical setting was three seconds. The groups decided to try a low setting of three seconds and a high setting of five seconds.

When the group finished Brenda was left with fifteen factors at two levels each. She pulled out her calculator and found that a full-factorial experiment would require 32,768 combinations of the factors.

Luckily, King had been watching from the back of the room. "There's another way," he stated.

"Tell me," replied Brenda in a depressed voice.

"We could use Taguchi's approach."

"Who's Taguchi?" she asked.

King launched into one of his stories. "Taguchi is from Japan. Back in the forties he was faced with this same problem. When you test a lot of factors you have to do a lot of experimental runs. He knew that fractional versions of the full-factorial designs were possible, so he black boxed the process."

"Black box?" Brenda inquired.

"Yes, he created a fixed procedure for conducting fractional experiments. He developed experimental designs into a sort of cookbook that any trained person could just pick up and use."

"Let me guess," Brenda said. "You just happen to have a copy with you."

"Funny you should ask," King replied as he reached into his briefcase. He produced a small grey book of only about fifty pages. He flipped through the pages and opened the book where a large array of numbers were printed.

"I can test your fifteen factors and some of their interactions with only thirty-two experimental runs."

"Show me," Brenda challenged.

"All right, follow me." King led Brenda back to her office. He explained that the array in the book gave the combinations to run and learn only the general affect of each factor. It would not give her every bit of information possible, but it would answer the question of which factors affected the fit of the part.

"Once you know the two or three really important factors, we can test them at three or more levels to get a clear picture of how they affect the process. We may find that one is very sensitive to change. Therefore, you would put all of your efforts into holding that particular control steady using delicate gauges to measure its actual setting."

Brenda could see the logic in this approach. "Okay," she said. "We'll run this experiment after the engineers report back on what they find."

"Sounds good to me," replied King. And with that they both eased back in their chairs and took deep gulps of their drinks.

The following morning a group of excited engineers greeted Brenda at the front door. Lee Enfield was at the front of the pack waving a piece of paper. "We confirmed their results, but they made a big mistake," he said excitedly.

Brenda was annoyed by the way the engineers became so childish in front of her when they found something interesting. This must be what it's like to have kids, she thought. "Show me in my office," she said aloud.

Lee leaned across her desk and flattened out a page of numbers fresh from his computer. "Look at this," he said as he placed a finger on one particular number. "The screw speed is directly related to the shrinkage of the parts after molding." He glanced up to look for Brenda's look of approval. Instead he only received a blank stare.

Retreating a little on his enthusiasm he began again. "We tested different settings on the screw speed and measured the amount of shrinkage in the parts. We found that we could actually predict the amount of shrinkage."

"That's good, Lee," said Brenda. "So where's the mistake?"

"Our friendly competitors never mentioned how they measured shrinkage. We measured the difference between the size of the mold and the size of the part after it had cooled a few minutes."

"So?" prompted Brenda.

"So, when I went out on the floor this morning to show the operator what we did, we made quite a discovery. Fran had written the size of each part right on it so we would retain our data. When I picked up one of the parts to show how we had measured it, the part was even smaller than yesterday."

"Everyone knows that parts shrink over time," Brenda replied.

"Yeah," said Lee excitedly, "but, they don't know how fast."

Brenda was beginning to see Lee's point. Their competitor had been able to predict and control the amount of shrinkage after a part had cooled for a few minutes. However, in reality the parts were stored up to a week before they were assembled. Without knowledge of the rate of shrinkage over long periods of time, the competitor's experimental data was useless.

"Very good guys," Brenda complimented. "I trust you are working on the shrink rate over time."

The engineers nodded in agreement. "Good, because I am going to test all fifteen factors this afternoon."

"But that will take thousands of runs to complete," blurted out one of the engineers.

"I'll be done before afternoon break," said Brenda confidently as she ushered the engineers out of her office.

The scene later that afternoon was very unusual. Brenda and an assistant were organizing the experiment with the plastic injection molding machine operator. On an overhead catwalk four curious engineers watched to see how Brenda could test so many factors in only an hour or two.

Laying on the operator's bench was the experimental design Brenda had selected. It was an orthogonal array. Across the top of the array Brenda had drawn in the name of each factor over various columns. She referred to these as she talked to the other two people.

"Steve," she said to the operator. "When the machine makes a molding cycle it creates four front plates, right?" Steve nodded.

Brenda pointed at the array. "All right, I'll read the combinations of settings to Diane. You help her set the controls to their designated levels. We'll let the machine make a few cycles before we draw our sample of four plates. That will give the machine time to settle into its new settings."

The two eager participants agreed. Brenda pointed out that she had selected a random order for the runs to be conducted. "The first run will be as follows," she called out. "Injection speed of three seconds, mold temperature of 350, mold gap of 0.125 inches, mold delay of two seconds..." Brenda continued until all fifteen factors were properly set.

A few molding cycles later Steve pulled out the parts and laid them on the workbench instead of throwing them into the waiting box. Diane quickly marked the parts for later identification. Brenda began to read off the settings for the second run.

This procedure was repeated thirty-two times. It took a little over two hours to complete. The experimental team was tired at the end of the runs. Diane carefully transferred the parts to a rolling cart and wheeled the parts into the quality lab.

Lee's group was there to measure the actual part sizes. Brenda stopped them by asking, "How fast do these shrink?"

Lee looked around for one of his assistants. The man rushed forward with some preliminary data. Lee read this and said, "From what we can tell the parts shrink rapidly for the first ninety minutes they are out of the mold. After that they shrink at a much slower rate."

"Fine," said Brenda. "We will wait until tomorrow to measure these parts." The group looked disappointed, but they knew the parts had to slowly shrink before meaningful data could be collected.

The next morning Brenda returned to the lab to find the engineers and Diane already hard at work measuring the parts. The engineers had loaded the lab computer with ANOVA software. As they measured each part Diane typed in the results.

Brenda sat and watched the process. When it was done Diane pressed the F4 key and the printer buzzed to life. The first analysis showed that there was no statistical differences between cavities in the mold. That was good news because it meant that the mold itself was not to blame for problems with fit. Mold repairs were always expensive.

The next report gave the results of the experimental factors. Brenda quickly searched out the error information. If this was too high, then she either missed an important factor or the samples were inaccurate.

The engineers cheered when one factor proved to cause 50 percent of the fit variations. Lee quickly looked up which factor it was and found *percent regrind.* That meant the addition of reground scrap parts into the virgin plastic resin was throwing off the part size.

Injection speed proved to be a factor in the size of the parts. The group celebrated a successful experiment by excitedly talking to each other for a few minutes. Eventually, the excitement died down and some practical questions were asked. "How are we going to confirm this?" asked one engineer.

"With another experiment," King stated. No one had seen him come in, but now he was also examining the data. The group became quiet as he spoke. "Take these two factors and run another experiment. The computer suggests that no more than 10 percent regrind be used in the plastic. It also suggests the three-second injection speed. Run a full-factorial experiment where you try settings around these suggestions. That will help you to pin down the very best setting."

"What about the settings for the other factors?" asked another person.

"Brenda?" said King as he deferred the question to her.

"Well," began Brenda hesitantly, "since these other factors have little effect on the size of the part, we could just select the most economical of the two levels we tested."

"What do you mean?" Lee asked.

"Take the mold delay for example," she replied. "We tested it at five and two seconds. It doesn't really matter which of these settings we use. Therefore, we select the two -second setting because it shaves three seconds off the complete mold cycle time. That increases our productivity without affecting the quality of the part."

The engineers quickly saw Brenda's point and dove into the task of selecting economical settings for the machine. When they were done, they had shaved a full eight seconds off the cycle time and had selected some lower machine temperatures that would save energy costs.

King lead an expedition of engineers back to the factory floor to set up the confirming experiment. Three hours later they came back for lunch with a cart full of parts. These parts would have to cool overnight before they could take accurate measurements.

The next day was Saturday and Brenda snuck in a back door to avoid the engineers. Once in her office she looked at her calendar. Today's date was circled in red. There was no note because Brenda knew why this day was important. She would have to tell Mead today. She couldn't delay the decision any longer. However, before she went to see him she wanted to see what the engineers discovered.

The scene in the quality lab was one of pleasant confusion. The parts from the confirming experiment had already been measured. The computer was spitting out reams of information. Diane stood by a dry erase board plotting average results for each factor level. Lee stood near the computer shouting out these figures as they were printed.

"Everything under control I see," said Brenda as she entered. Only a couple of engineers even bothered to look up. Brenda walked over to Lee to see the results. "Did it work?" she inquired.

"You bet," Lee responded. "Take a look at this output. We confirmed the two factors as being the most important. In addition, we tested each of them at three different levels. Diane's plotting a picture of the results now."

With that Lee and Brenda walked across the room toward Diane. Two graphs had been plotted on the board. One was labeled *regrind* and the other *injection speed*.

Lee pointed to the regrind graph. Diane had plotted a straight line. "Look at this," he said. "As we increase the percent of regrind into the plastic, the variations in size also increase. The relationship is direct and proportional."

"Which means what?" asked Brenda.

"It means that we're going to recommend that no more than 5 percent regrind ever be in the resin."

"What else did you find?" Brenda asked.

Lee turned his attention to the chart for injection speed. Instead of a straight line, a sharp curve rose and then fell near the middle setting of three seconds. "It turns out that if we are off by even a fraction of a second for the injection speed, we miss our target dimensions."

"So, this is the cause of our problems?"

"One of the big ones," replied Lee. "We've calculated on the computer that the very best setting for the target dimensions and the lowest amount of variation would be 3.2 seconds. The trouble is that we will have to buy a new type of controller that reads out in hundreths of a second to make a setting that accurate."

"But," countered Brenda, "what will we gain for the price?"

"Well," hesitated Lee. "The computer says that the largest gap we will ever see should be within our tolerance."

"Good fit and no scrap then?" Brenda asked.

"I'll believe that when I see it," said Lee.

"Seems worth the risk of trying," Brenda replied. "Try the new settings for a couple of days and see what happens. Hell, we're running $100,000 in scrap and rework on that job every year as it is."

Lee had to agree. Brenda was proud that she had finally talked Lee into doing something her way. She was also impressed by the effectiveness of an experiment; seeing something that just wasn't obvious to the operators or the SPC system. She would have felt better if she wasn't stopped by King on her way out of the lab.

"I'll take that dollar now," he said.

Brenda reached into a coat pocket and handed over the money without comment. King had been right and should have been congratulated, but Brenda had more on her mind at that moment.

She walked the length of the company and into the front office area. At the end of the hallway she stopped at Sally's desk. "Is the old man in?" Sally nodded and waved her on into his office.

Brenda could remember when it was impossible to get an appointment with Mead. She could also remember that a year ago she would have never spoken to Mead about what was on her mind. She had once hated the man and dreaded to see him. Yet, now she was forcing herself to be honest with him. If he was going to react negatively to her news, she wanted to know now so she could quit.

"Hello, Brenda," Mead greeted. "What's up?"

Brenda closed Mr. Mead's door. A sure sign that what she had to say was sensitive. "Mr. Mead," she began. "I have to tell you something."

"Yes, go on."

Brenda curled her fingers tightly. "I wanted you to be the first to know at the company." She drew in a breath. "I'm getting married."

"That's wonderful," replied Mead with genuine feelings. "Is there a reason you wanted me to know first?"

"Yes. I'm marrying one of your employees."

CHAPTER 16

Vendor and Customer Relationships

Christmas vacation was over. ROB, Incorporated had now been on its quality drive for over a year. The physical appearance of the plant had changed. The floors were swept clean and parts no longer clogged the aisles.

When Breton came in the door that morning, Steve Fisher dropped a bucket of rice on his head. "Hey! Welcome to the married ranks."

Breton faked anger, but inside it was good to know that his people were paying him one of their highest compliments, the factory-floor prank. Breton had taken the Christmas production break to honeymoon with Brenda. He would now take the rest of the day to pick the rice out of his hair.

Brenda was in a meeting with Mead at that moment. As Breton was getting a rice shower, Mead was asking, "How did you two ever get together? You used to fight over everything."

Brenda blushed slightly. "Well, remember when we first starting taking that class with Jack King?" Mead nodded. "That first night of class Breton's car stalled on the parking ramp. I was driving by and he was all alone kicking his car. I felt bad for him, so I offered him a ride."

Brenda paused and looked down at her feet. "We got to talking about the class and the quality drive, and the next thing I knew we were sharing a drink down at the harbor. Pretty soon he's showing me pictures of his kids from his broken marriage and I'm telling him about my family. I guess one thing lead to another."

"And you kept it a secret for almost a year?" Mead asked.
"Yes."

Mead shook his head. Brenda had surprised him with the news a few months ago. Normally he would have been angry that his managers hadn't trusted him. However, he had his own secret to maintain. Mrs. Walker and her son Keith had moved in with Mead. He was embarrassed about the relationship.

"We have to talk about our suppliers," began Mead to break his train of thought. "I've been reading over your reports on the quality of the goods we buy. As close as I can tell, over half of the problems reported by our problem-solving teams are related to supplied materials."

"Not only that," confirmed Brenda, "but we have seen no improvement in the quality of the material despite repeated correction reports and rejected material."

"Any suggestions?" Mead asked.

"I think we should bring engineering and purchasing in on this conversation. Purchasing is supposed to keep the suppliers in line and engineering is supposed to draw up the specifications," Brenda responded.

"I thought you were supposed to work with purchasing on keeping the suppliers in line?"

"No, I only report the problems and it's up to the purchasing agents to transmit these to the suppliers."

Mead looked puzzled for a moment. "How do you know if the suppliers got the message?"

"I don't. It's up to the agents to do their jobs."

Mr. Mead now felt frustration rising. He had learned that this meant it was time to quit talking and take some sort of action. "Hold it," he commanded. "Let's get everybody in one room and review our supplier procedures and settle on a more workable system that will improve the quality of the stuff we buy."

"Agreed," Brenda said, more than happy to stop discussing the sticky question of the suppliers.

"Good. Now tell that husband of yours to be at the meeting as well," Mead said with a smile.

Brenda smiled back and quickly left the room. Mead leaned over his desk and switched on the intercom. "Sally? Call a meeting of the managers for two this afternoon."

"Righto," Sally snapped back.

Mead eased back into his chair and glanced out the window. The new sign for the company had been installed. Along with the neatly trimmed bushes lining the parking lot the old place was beginning to look presentable.

Mead then picked up the morning mail and leafed through the letters glancing at any return addresses that caught his attention. The Ford Motor Company logo was one such letter. He opened it and began to read.

"Congratulations. Your petition for Q1 supplier has been accepted . . ."

Mead exhaled. The last year or so had been hell. This letter was just another reward that made it all worthwhile. However, he also knew that the job wasn't done.

At two o'clock that afternoon the managers were assembled in his office. The only topic for discussion was vendor relationships. Brenda spoke first.

"Mr. Mead and I have been going over the quality reports on our suppliers. We find that there has been no improvement in the quality of incoming parts and material."

"Don't look at me," barked Anna. "We've complained to them regularly without any effect. We are just too small of a company for them to react to our requests."

"Nobody's blaming you," began Mead before he was interrupted by engineering.

"That's right. We write a specification, they say they can do it, but a month later it's obvious that they don't have the capacity."

"As I was saying. . ." continued Mead.

"And the stuff we see is junk," Breton added.

"Hold it!" shouted Mead. All the managers' mouths slammed shut at the same time. Their heads simultaneously turned toward the president.

Mead looked at all of them for a few seconds as he regained his composure. "As I was saying, I know that this is an emotional issue. However, I'm not looking for someone to blame. I want suggestions for how we can get vendors on board with our quality goals."

The room was silent for a few minutes. Then Brenda began softly, "I have a few ideas." She looked at each of her colleagues cautiously before suggesting, "I think we should brainstorm this issue."

A few low grumbles of agreement could be heard. Brenda picked up a black marker and walked over to the flip chart near the door. She wrote *vendor days* as the first idea.

"What's that?" Lee asked.

"I've seen other companies bring in all of the suppliers for a tour and a pep talk," replied Brenda.

"What good is that?" Anna asked.

"We show them their rankings against their competitors in our supplier quality reports. It sends a clear message that if they don't clean up their act they will lose the business."

"But," interrupted Breton, "we need a solid philosophy about our vendor relationships before we have such a meeting."

The group seemed to agree with Breton. Lee piped up with another idea. "Maybe we should think about ourselves as vendors. After all, we have to sell to other companies."

These comments seemed to launch a lengthy discussion of the question of how to improve the performance of the supply companies and ROB's performance with its own customers. Mead finally settled the matter by breaking the management team into two subcommittees.

The first subcommittee was made up of Anna, Breton, and Brenda. They had the responsibility of developing a new approach to ROB's suppliers. The second team would address the question of ROB's relationship to its customers. These two groups were assigned the task of meeting together in a month to discuss how the two goals could be integrated into one plan.

Brenda signaled Anna and Breton into a small caucus. "We need to meet tomorrow and lay out our strategy," she whispered. The others agreed.

"Tomorrow at nine in my office," suggested Breton.

Across the room, Lee, Vincent, and Harris were having the same discussion. Mead did not interrupt either knot of people. He knew that he could now trust them to work out these problems on their own. Instead, he waited a few minutes and then dismissed the meeting.

Mead enjoyed most of the day. He didn't stay in his office or at a golf course as he had just two years ago. Instead he walked the floor of the factory at least twice a day. He also had some pleasant chats with several operators and supervisors. It wasn't until he was finishing his tour did it occur to him that something was different. Today, no one ran up to him with a problem. After a year of watching the manufacturing process up close, everything was running smoothly for a change. He knew that the rough road of changing to a new quality philosophy was almost over.

The next day Brenda, Breton, and Anna met in the production office to discuss supplier relationships. Anna started the conversation with a discussion of the current supplier environment.

"First," she began, "I think we should be aware of the scope of what we buy." The others nodded unconsciously. "Over half of the materials and products we use in this plant are purchased. We buy everything from nuts and bolts to subassemblies and engineering services."

Anna handed Brenda and Breton copies of internal documents. "These are copies of the types of vendor agreements we currently use. We have multiple sources for many of the components and services we buy. Each vendor is surveyed before becoming a supplier, and we perform incoming inspection on all purchased products.

"The contracts you are looking at specify the price, quality, and delivery requirements for the purchase. We track the actual performance of each vendor against these requirements. We have a full range of punishments for those vendors who repeatedly fail to meet the requirements."

Breton spoke up, "Reality time. When was the last time that we actually pulled a contract from a vendor?"

"Never in the twelve years I've been here," replied Anna.

Breton turned toward Brenda, "And, how many people do you have to monitor vendors?"

"One," replied Brenda. "Technically, he works for both Anna and me."

"Is he enough to monitor and survey all of our vendors?" Breton asked.

"No," Anna replied. "I take it that you have a different idea for how we should treat vendor relationships."

"Funny you should ask," Breton responded. "I spent the night reading about world-class manufacturing practices. Some of the stuff I saw made a lot of sense for our situation."

Anna looked obviously annoyed. Breton ignored this and continued, "For example, a lot of companies are forming joint ventures with their suppliers. Take the automotive industry. The top-rated suppliers are able to participate in the design of new products. This lets them have more of a voice in making parts that will work when assembled and that are easier to produce. That creates higher quality at a lower cost."

"How do we do that when we barely trust them to start with?" asked Anna in a hostile tone.

Breton replied without hesitation, "We go to single sourcing." Anna began to voice objections but Breton interrupted. "Let's face it, we don't have enough people or time to police all of the suppliers as it is. Why don't we pick the single suppliers we can trust and work with them on new jobs? It will save money and time."

"How do we pick the best supplier?" Brenda asked.

"We would have to check the quality, cost, and delivery records of each supply company to weed out the really bad ones," responded Breton. "Then we would go in and make a one-time survey of the surviving companies. We would look at management, the quality system, the manufacturing facilities, personnel practices, accounting methods, in short, the company as a whole."

Anna interrupted, "Even if we could get down to single suppliers, what would we do if they had a fire or went on strike?"

"What do you do now?" Breton asked. Anna seemed stunned by this quick response. However, she soon recovered.

"And, how are we ever going to talk them into cooperating with us when we've spent years making them sign adversarial contracts?" she asked.

Now Breton seemed lost for words. He, too, soon recovered. "That's the hard part." Anna seemed as skeptical as before.

"It certainly is," she confirmed.

Breton quickly countered, "But it could be very profitable for all of us."

"How's that?" Brenda asked.

"Well, if we look at the current situation, we spent a great deal of our time telling the vendors that the stuff they sent us isn't good enough. If we took the time to open up a line of communication where they knew in advance what our needs are, then we should have fewer problems."

"Our needs are already stated in the contracts," said Anna sharply.

"Ah," replied Breton. "But do we tell them everything? We only give them a set of specifications and a blueprint for what we want made. Take the example of the bolts we buy for the motor mount. There's a ring of rubber on the shank of the bolt to reduce vibrations in the final assembly."

The two women agreed although Anna had never seen the bolts. Breton continued, "One of our requirements is that the rubber the supplier molds onto the bolt stays off the threads."

Brenda added, "We've had to send back one out of every five shipments because they have too much rubber near the threads."

"That's right," confirmed Breton. "I think that if we brought the operators from the supply company on site and showed them why rubber-free threads were important, they would carry the message loud and clear back to their own shop."

"What are you suggesting?" asked Anna cautiously.

"I think we ought to treat vendors as partners in our company instead of causes of our problems. There's a whole handful of techniques available for companies to work closer together."

"Such as?" Anna inquired.

"Things like advanced quality planning and simultaneous engineering. That's where a supply company's engineers work closely with our own engineers to develop new products. It helps to make the supplied parts more compatible with our own production methods."

Brenda added, "We could also require capability reports on critical dimensions from our suppliers. Maybe even that they use SPC and send us the charts. It makes a lot of sense to prove the capability of a process before we buy what it will produce."

Anna grudgingly began to accept what was being said. The group would work for three more hours. A couple of times cooling off periods had to be declared. At the end of the meeting Anna was distinctly more upbeat.

"I believe," she said, "that our best approach is to send a clear message to our suppliers. We should say, 'Hey, look. We have used SPC and a new quality drive to improve our business. We want to share our success with you.' It would give them a better feeling."

"Good idea," confirmed Breton. "We should emphasize the positive aspects of our new requirements. We should show the suppliers how they could benefit as well."

"Let's do it," Brenda affirmed. With that, the three managers left the room to attend their various duties. Anna called in her secretary to draw up a rough draft of the system upon which the three had agreed upon.

On the other side of the factory, the other management subcommittee was reaching a similar set of conclusions.

"Let me summarize what has already been said," said Lee. "We agree that we need closer communications with our customers. For one thing, the engineering department should be using something like quality function deployment where we evaluate specifications and market requirements at the same time."

"QFD is in the future," Harris countered. "We need more face-to-face meetings between our employees and the assembly people at the automotive plants where we sell our goods."

"I think we need a stronger marketing force," Vincent offered.

"Hold it," commanded Lee. "What we need is direction, a theme." The group seemed to agree with this observation. "Let's look at the big picture. We have done well with our quality drive in reducing the cost of production and improving the quality of our products. Shouldn't we advertise this fact to our customers?"

The other two men paused. Lee had a good point. What was the value of continuous improvement in the plant if the customers drift away to other accounts. They should toot their own horn on their skills and achievements.

"So," ventured Leon. "Should we go to our customers and tell them that we want to work closer with them because we need the extra information to continue our improvements?"

"Precisely," answered Lee. "Take the case of the mounting plate hole locations. We used to scrap or rework 10 percent of everything we produced. Now we ship everything we make and we haven't had a rejection by a customer in six months.

"We should take that data down to Ford or General Motors and tell them that we want further information on the success of the mounting plate during assembly. Their purchasing agents will be impressed with our agressiveness and the engineers will have an excuse to talk to us."

"We all benefit," Vincent said.

"Indeed we do," confirmed Harris. "Let's type this up as a proposal, and we'll refine it before the presentation at the end of the month."

Two weeks later, both subcommittees reported back to Mead on their progress. Both handed in complete proposals on customer and vendor relationships.

For vendor relationships, Breton, Brenda, and Anna suggested that ROB Incorporated begin by requiring capability studies on all critical characteristics of purchased parts. The engineering department would survey the quality and production departments for which characteristics to note on future blueprints. After that, SPC charts would be required from the supply companies for the same characteristics. Then the work teams reporting problems with purchased parts would be able to communicate directly with the supply company.

As an incentive, the suppliers would be brought to ROB to hear about the benefits of the new requirements. The supply representatives would be given a tour of ROB and would see presentations on improvements made by work teams.

As a further incentive, ROB would make it clear that within three years single-source contracts would be signed to those companies that cooperated best with the new requirements. Before the awarding of the contract, the supply company would be subject to a single, but thorough audit of their quality systems.

Mead seemed to like the proposal. However, he was reserving judgment until he saw how well it fit with the proposal for new customer relationships.

Lee made the presentation for the second subcommittee. He began by pointing out that the best course of action was to widely advertise the new quality perspective of ROB. In other words, to cash in on some of the improvements the company had made during the past year.

Lee quickly read off a list of the major customers. The proposal suggested that a closer working relationship be sought with these companies. Lee then listed the companies that would share technology and services with ROB when they reached the higher supplier ratings. Thus, he suggested, management should continue to strive toward these higher ratings.

At the same time, ROB should begin to ask more questions of the customers. The company should invite more customers to be part of the design process for new products. He even suggested that the engineering department be the clearinghouse for communications with the customers. However, he knew that the manufacturing representatives would object to this point.

Lee's next suggestion caught the group by surprise. He suggested that the stories of continuous improvement at ROB be assembled into live sales presentations. Then the sales forces should begin knocking on the doors of companies they have never considered doing business with. Lee listed off Japanese firms such as Honda, Toyota, Nippon Denso, and others. He mentioned German firms such as Bosch. He even named some Dutch, English, and Canadian firms most people in the room did not know.

Mead interrupted at this point. "Isn't that spreading our sales people a bit thin?"

"Perhaps," Lee replied. "However, I feel that we need to exploit the gains we have already made. We won't survive and grow worrying about just our current customer's requirements. Besides it takes years to develop relationships with some of these companies."

Mead could see his point, but hesitated at hiring more sales people to cover a larger market. Lee let only a few seconds pass before he played his trump card. "The state of Michigan has set up a special task force to help companies like ours establish more overseas accounts. They can assist us in meeting the right people and marketing our talents," he explained.

Mead seemed to warm up to this idea a little more. "We'll discuss this separately later today," he said. "I like what the teams have presented. Naturally, we will have to iron out a few of the details, but otherwise, the ideas seem sound."

This comment made the group feel good. Mead knew that and he paused to let the feeling soak in before he brought the group back to reality.

"I have a few questions," he began. "To begin with, what will happen to the vendor rating system we currently have, Anna?"

Anna seemed startled by the question but she responded quickly. "Currently we rate vendors by the actual price we pay for goods, the lateness of the delivery, and the quality of the material. However, after a long discussion, we will modify those criteria to better fit our new operation philosophy."

"Such as?" prompted Mead.

"For example, we are slowly implementing a just-in-time production process. Therefore, we will no longer reward a vendor for being early with a shipment. The new system will not access demerits for a shipment that arrives the day it was due. A supplier receives a demerit for each day a shipment is either early or late. That way we should be able to reduce the inventory at the delivery area.

"We are also going to report quality as the number of parts we had to reject during production. We will continue incoming inspection, but at a reduced frequency for our better suppliers. Once we start awarding single contracts, we will switch to no incoming inspection.

"The cost score for each vendor will now include the cost of quality incurred for defective goods. If we have to sort parts or return them to a vendor, they will be billed."

Mead reflected for a moment and asked, "Do you believe that will send a clear enough message to the suppliers?"

"It should," Anna replied.

"Vincent?" Mead asked. Vincent's head quickly rose from the financial figures he had been studying. "How will we convince a supply company that is no larger than ROB to abide by our rules?"

"You mean someone like Gulf and Western, where we are less than one percent of their total business?"

"That's right," Mead answered.

"Hmmm, tricky," Vincent paused in thought. "I would think our best strategy would be to send them repeated requests for cooperation hoping that other companies are doing the same. Then they should respond. It's not like we can threaten taking the business away."

Breton injected, "Perhaps Mr. Mead could meet with their salesperson one-on-one and explain our situation. If the guy —"

"Woman," corrected Brenda.

"Woman," continued Breton, "had any brains she would realize that she might get increased sales here if she cooperates."

"Maybe," Mead said. He turned to his secretary. "Sally, make a note to discuss this topic further next week." Mead motioned for Lee to sit down before he spoke again.

"Vincent, do we have other options for the smaller suppliers?"

"We sure do. We can give the little supply companies financial and technical assistance as part of the contract. A lot of small companies would jump at the chance to have customer assistance during the production of parts.

"We could also evaluate the cost-effectiveness of making some of our purchased materials inhouse. For example, we are currently sending all of our exterior automotive parts out to a company that paints them. They then send them right back here for packaging. We've been getting a lot of handling-related defects from that process. It would be cheaper and better to establish our own paint line here at ROB."

"Get me a cost report on that by next Friday, please," Mead commanded. "Lee, how are we going to evaluate the final consumer satisfaction of our products?"

Lee was surprised by this question. His group hadn't given it much thought. "Market research, I guess."

Mead made a few suggestions of his own. He thought that the automotive companies might not be the only customer they should worry about. Eventually, a real person buys a car out there, and our parts are put to the test. That car buyer is going to look at the durability of our parts, their visual appearance, and the value of the car.

"I would strongly recommend that we develop a program of being in closer touch with the final customers, as well as our immediate customers. We should be monitoring car sales by model, field performance data of our parts, warranty claims, and customer complaints.

"In addition, we should independently audit the quality of our parts on the cars after they have been used for a few years. At the same time, we should keep one eye on the competition. They won't be sitting still either. If we can anticipate their moves, we can take advantage of upcoming market changes."

Breton interrupted, "I also think we should make our employees part of this process."

"How do you mean?" Mead asked.

"I think that each employee should realize that the next guy on the production line is his own customer. Everybody has to deliver quality goods to the next stage of production. If we share our market information with the employees, then they will know why they need to continuously improve."

"That makes sense," Mead agreed. "Get together with Lee and add that into the plan. Any other comments or questions?"

"I have one," said Vincent. "I think we need an overall measure of the value of the goods we produce. I think we should develop a life-cycle cost system for monitoring the quality of our goods."

"Can you briefly describe to the group how that would work?" Mead asked.

"Sure. Instead of just looking at the cost to build a part, we look at the cost to the consumer over the life of the product. Take the fan cover we make for air conditioners. It costs our customer $3.50 per cover. However, over the life of the air conditioner, the cover needs periodic cleaning and occasional replacement. This adds to the cost of the product.

"If we examine those costs we can figure out ways to reduce the more expensive sources. For example, if we find a plastic resin resistant to static electricity, less dust will stick to the cover and fewer cleanings are needed. That raises the quality of the product."

Mead turned to Sally, "Note that for next week's discussion." He then spoke to the group. "Further comments? Good, meeting dismissed."

A few members of the management team lingered behind to discuss more details of the plan for vendors and customers. Mead was in one corner talking to Anna. "Have you floated these new requirements past any of the suppliers?" he asked.

"Yes. I showed a draft copy to a couple of our better vendors. They reacted positively. They've been hearing the same message from a lot of their other customers. They know that they have to do something to keep the business. The automotive suppliers with high ratings must have a supply base that uses SPC."

"I'd like to talk to one of them," Mead said.

"I'd suggest TLC, our largest metal casting supplier. If you'd like I can arrange a meeting later this week. The salesman will be here anyway."

"Do it."

That Thursday Mead sat down to lunch with Tom Jelsma, the sales representative of TLC. Mead had arranged for the two to have a private lunch overlooking the golf course of the local country club. Mead had been a member for years, but lately he had rarely set foot in the club.

Despite his infrequent visits, the staff of the club had taken pains to meet his lunch requests. First, they had placed a small round table near the picture window in the library of the club. The table was draped with a crisp white linen. The silver was polished and neatly arranged. The staff would bring in their lunches and then leave the two men alone.

"How's your lunch?" Mead asked to get the conversation rolling.

"Very good," replied Jelsma. As an afterthought he added, "It's the best I've had all year."

"Good, I wanted to give you a chance to relax from the restaurant circuit and have time to talk to me."

"What can TLC do for ROB?"

"Well, I need to know some information you would possess from visiting so many companies."

"Yes?" replied Jelsma cautiously.

"As you know, we at ROB have been implementing a new quality drive. We've had many successes. However, some of the problems we have had involve our suppliers." Mead paused for effect. "Of course," he reassured, "you're not one of our problem suppliers."

Jelsma breathed a sigh of relief. Usually, when the president of a company talked to him, it was to chew him out for some slop in quality of their parts or a late delivery.

Mr. Mead continued. "I want to get the suppliers more involved up-front with our needs. I want them to benefit from our gains. However, I'm not really sure how to approach a supply company about things such as SPC and capability studies."

Mr. Mead already had a good idea of how to approach these companies. What he was really trying to find out is how TLC would react to new requirements.

"Well," began Mr. Jelsma, "I've seen a lot of companies requiring SPC and formal quality systems at a lot of places where they don't even have a quality department."

"How's that?" asked Mr. Mead.

"Last week I was at a tool and die shop in Flint. The place only has a couple of dozen workers. The owner has been in the business for years. I asked him how he knows the quality of his dies are right. He tells me that he knows because his people care about their work and that's all that matters. This guy had no quality manual, no operational guidelines, and no inspectors."

"We were trying to sell him special cast steel for small die milling. I tried to tell him that he won't have any customers in a couple of years if he doesn't get a coordinate measuring machine and certify the accuracy of the dies."

"What did he say?"

"He said that his customers trusted him and would never leave him."

"What do you think?" Mead asked.

"I think the bank is going to own a tool-and-die shop in a couple of years. His customers may like his work, but without certification they can't pass an audit by their own customers."

"How would you convince him?"

"There's not much I can do. I'm a salesperson who's got to keep the customers happy. You don't make big sales forcing customers to face reality."

"I see," observed Mead.

"You on the other hand, could lay down the law. He would complain for awhile but he would come around. He's smart enough to know when a customer is serious."

"And," inquired Mead, "will TLC welcome our new requirements?"

"No problem," lied Jelsma. "We already have implemented our own SPC program."

Mead knew that Jelsma was lying. However, this didn't matter. Mead had learned what he was really after. The suppliers would complain at first, try to bluff their way through the requirements, and then finally cooperate.

Mead knew this because it was the same path he had taken with ROB. Jelsma was really Mead two years ago. The tone in the voice and the resistance to change were the same. Even the lie about having an SPC system was the same. The only difference was that Mead now knew what would have to be done.

On Plainfield Avenue, Breton and Brenda were working on an all-you-could-eat Chinese lunch. Neither had said much since they began to eat. Breton was steadily shoveling down Moo Goo Gai Pan. Brenda waited until he paused to sip tea to ask her question.

"Breton?" she asked. He responded with a grunt and didn't even look up from his food. She continued, "I've got a question that's been bothering me for the past few months."

Brenda paused for a facial reaction, but all she got was a wave of his hand signaling, "go on."

"Well, you really did a good job of talking Anna into a new supplier surveillance method." Another pause and still no reaction. She decided to get to the point.

"Look," she said. "I helped you look up a lot of the material you quoted today. I've also helped you on several projects that makes it look like quality is your number one concern."

Breton stopped eating and looked up at Brenda. He could sense her irritation and suspected that he was about to be blasted for his insensitivity again. Instead, Brenda's next question caught him off guard.

"Do you really believe in these quality methods or are you just playing the part of a political animal?"

Breton paused for a moment. He hadn't really thought much about whether he was fully convinced of the legitimacy of the quality improvement program. All he had worried about was his job and his image at the plant.

"Hmm," he said thoughtfully. He wanted to lie to the quality manager, but she was also his wife and he knew the consequences of that all too well.

"Actually," he began, "I didn't have any faith in the program when it first started. I was supporting it because it was all too clear that Mead wanted action, so I gave him action."

"You're not answering my question," Brenda responded.

"How come you women always want to know what men feel?" Breton snapped back.

"Just tell me whether you really think all of this quality improvement stuff has improved our situation at ROB."

Breton knew that he was cornered. At least it was away from the office and his staff. "Okay," he said. "I'll level with you, but don't you tell another soul."

"I promise," Brenda confirmed.

"Up until the last few months I couldn't have cared less about SPC, experiments, or any of the other things we've been trying. But, then I started to notice that some of our long-term production problems weren't showing up anymore."

"How do you mean?" prompted Brenda.

"Well, like the rework schedule. It used to be that I had to schedule 10 percent of our work schedule to reworking defective products. It's been almost a month since anything had to be reworked. That means my productivity is up substantially."

"And that makes you look good?" Brenda asked.

"Me and my team," replied Breton. Without hesitating to realize the sarcastic nature of Brenda's last question, Breton continued. "The rework reduction made me curious, so I compared my daily calendar to one from two years ago, before the program began.

"What I found was that two years ago I was rushing from appointment to appointment trying to fix a series of crises. Our production schedule was a joke. My twelve-hour days were spent on the phone or the production floor fixing problems.

"I still work the long days, but now I'm planning better production methods, monitoring the success of my problem-solving teams, and coordinating our operations with other departments. In short, I'm acting like a damn production manager."

"Instead of a damned production manager," observed Brenda.

"Precisely," Breton confirmed.

"So, you do buy into the idea that continuous improvement has helped you and the company?" Brenda asked.

"There's no denying it," said Breton as he dug into a fresh bowl of rice and went back to eating his lunch.

Brenda still wasn't convinced, but she could see that Breton's attitude toward the quality department had changed for the better. She made a mental note to keep feeding success stories to Breton. In addition, she would keep an eye out for cases where quality improvement also helped the production department.

Breton is still a political animal, she thought to herself. Why are production managers unable to express their real feelings? She knew why.

Brenda and Breton returned from their lunch at two o'clock. They both wanted to be back at the company in time for the employee meeting. Mead had started giving these once-a-month talks a few months ago. The employees were enthusiastic about the chance to ask direct questions of the president.

The couple took their seats in the front row, as usual. Lee, Anna, Leon, and Vincent joined them. Other supervisors were taking up positions near the rear of the room to count heads as the employees entered.

Cigarettes were crushed out near the entrance to the meeting room. A few random employees carried in cups of coffee to sip during the meeting. Their faces were streaked with the dirt and oil of the shop floor.

Mead took the podium and began tapping on the microphone to indicate that he was ready to talk. A few latecomers leaned against a back wall rather than seeking out chairs.

"Good afternoon," Mead began. Several people replied in kind. "I want to take a few moments today to talk to you. I will take questions later.

"To begin with I would like to point out that we are progressing very nicely with the implementation of our new quality program. I believe that all work stations in the plant now have SPC charts." Mead glanced at Breton and Brenda and they nodded confirmation.

"Furthermore, I am sure that many of you have noticed our new reliability engineer testing parts in the quality lab. Also, we have started the first of a series of experiments on the factory floor to create setup sheets that make sense instead of bad parts."

The setup people applauded briefly. Mead continued. "I am also happy to report that the overall scrap rate within this company has been reduced 50 percent over the past year. This means that we are more cost competitive in the marketplace and that should help us stay in business."

Mead paused for a moment. He looked at his notes, then folded them and put them in his pocket. "Listen," he said. "What I really want to do is thank every person in this room." The room was suddenly quiet. Breton was hoping that this wasn't going to turn into an emotional speech. Brenda hoped it would.

Mead was not looking up at the audience. "A couple of years ago I thought we were in serious trouble. I thought there was a real chance of losing most of our business. I decided that the only way to survive was if we all pulled together. I was right.

"We have spent many months learning about the new techniques of quality assurance. We've made a few mistakes, but we have learned from our mistakes. Everyday we try to make things a little bit better for everyone. We also strive to continuously improve our products.

"Some of you are wondering what we do all of this work for. I have the answer today." Mead opened a box sitting next to the podium and drew out a bright blue flag. In the center of the flag was a large Q1.

"Today, we have achieved Ford's Q1 award." The employees began to cheer and applaud. They had been told for months that top supplier awards, like Q1, meant continued business and jobs.

Mead motioned the employees to settle down. "Normally, a company flies this flag outside to show the world that they are one of the best. However, I have ordered a second flag for out front. This one is going right where it belongs, in the employee cafeteria. This is your flag!"

Now the group was clapping and pounding its feet. Mead was smiling. Brenda was fighting back tears. Breton only shook his head.

Mead would take questions and address other business, but as far as he was concerned the real meeting had ended with the applause. Later he dismissed the employees and shook hands with each of the managers before he went back to his office.

Mead picked up a copy of the company's strategic plan and scanned its contents for this quarter. He knew that Xerfer Corporation was still his largest competitor in the United States and Europe. He leaned across his desk and pressed the paging button to Sally's office.

"Sally? Have the new marketing research manager bring the Xerfer file to my office."

"Yes, sir," Sally's voice crackled back.

A few minutes later Keith Walker entered the room carrying a stack of files. "Here's the information you requested," he said with a smile.

"So, Keith," began Mead, "what have you found out on your own?"

"I joined the pool club in Cleveland where their executives hang out. I flew down once a week to hang around the spring water bar. I picked up a lot of interesting talk on their new product line."

"Good work, Keith," Mead complimented.

"It's all in the brown file," Keith responded.

"Thanks, I'll see you at dinner."

Keith strode out of the room. His creaking new shoes showed his inexperience with a business suit. But Mead knew that the tenacity the boy exhibited would one day make him very successful.

Mead swung his chair around and glanced westward. From his office window he could see the dark clouds of a fall shower forming. Winter wasn't far away but he didn't care. He knew that a lot of work still lay ahead. He also knew that for the first time since his father had made him president, he had completed a really difficult task.

In less than two years he had taken charge and brought a company into the modern age of quality and productivity. Being president of a company had created a high cost in the past. He had lost a wife, his children, and the friendship of several people.

Mead's mind began to click off the plus side of the ledger sheet of life. There was a new woman and child waiting for him at home. The managers of his company now respected him. Those same managers were working as a team instead of being constantly at each other's throats.

He picked up a fan motor cover from his desk. This was the real prize. This cover was good and he knew it. No need to sweet talk purchasing agents to buy this part. No need to salt the bad ones in cartons of good parts. All of those days were over. This part was made right the first time and everyone knew why.

Continuous improvement, he thought. Maybe it works in your life as well as it does in a production company. He turned that thought over in his head several times. Then he packed his briefcase and left to go home. It wasn't five o'clock but he wanted to be with his family. His job was done.

Epilogue

It was a windy fall day. Mead had left the company early and drove east out of town. He wound his way through the rolling hills as brief showers pelted his car's windshield.

Near the town of Ada he crossed the Thornapple River and headed north. After a few minutes he was parked in front of a small country bar. The parking lot was empty except for a few pickup trucks.

Mead pulled open the heavy door of the building. The interior was done in a western motif. The bar was mostly empty but the smoking patrons had turned the air blue. Two men played pool in a far corner.

Mead headed for the booths in the back room. It was empty except for a single man sitting in the shadows of the corner booth.

Mead slipped into the booth. "Hello. Nice place."

"It's discrete," responded the consultant. He seemed quite at home in this dingy place.

"I brought the money."

"Just put it on the table," replied the consultant in a soft voice. Mead placed an envelope on the table. Inside were several dozen hundred dollar bills. The consultant picked up the envelope and thumbed past the bills. He was searching for the name and phone number on a small card placed at the back of the package. When he found it, he looked pleased.

"How goes the quality drive?"

"Well," said Mead, "we have been following your instructions ever since we first talked two years ago."

"You have done well," the consultant replied. "A lot of my customers give up long before they even get started." He paused, "And thanks for the name. Is he ready to start on the road to quality?"

"Sure," replied Mead. "Ed's been struggling to meet the new Department of Defense requirements for total quality management."

"And you?" asked the consultant.

"We've got active problem-solving teams, SPC, reliability testing, a solid management team, and a written plan of action to continually improve our quality."

The consultant seemed unimpressed. "Very good. Now you have some further tasks ahead of you. You will have to develop further technologies, such as Taguchi's method of experimental design, quality function deployment, and just-in-time delivery systems."

"Yes," answered Mead. "We are already investigating those possibilities."

"I know." Mead had momentarily forgotten the intelligence data this man had collected for him over the past two years. When the managers needed information on the competitors, this man had found important secrets.

Mead didn't want to know how he had obtained information on the future product lines of his competitors. "Tell me something," Mead asked. "How often do you provide these services to a company such as ours?"

"It depends on the company. We knew you were in trouble but we did not approach you directly. If you remember, your friend Mr. Reed gave you our number."

Mead was taken back for a moment. Now that he thought about it, the consultant was right. Reed had suggested their number even though Mead hadn't been seeking help. No wonder that part of the payment was the name of another company in trouble.

"I asked Mr. Reed to make you aware of our service. We do no advertising, and you won't find us in the phone book. We only work with companies we select."

Mead had another question, "Why do you do this so secretly? If other companies knew how important quality was and how beneficial a continuous improvement program was they would flock to you."

Without hesitation the consultant answered, "Once we did operate in the open. However, we discovered that we could repeat the quality message a thousand times with little effect. Most companies are too busy to worry about it. Others agree and then go back to their jobs. They make no changes because changing things means extra work."

The consultant paused long enough to take a sip from the iced tea he had been coddling the whole time. "People are funny. They figure that it's someone else's job to improve the world. However, if you tell them the quality message in secret, they work much harder to achieve results.

Secrecy gives importance to a simple message.

"I used to work in a company which said that quality was the most important aspect of their operations. However, the quality people were never even allowed to talk to the production people. If outgoing material was found defective, the marketing people would rip off the rejection stickers and ship the product anyway.

"One day I did a study on the quality capabilities and efficiency of the production area. I found that the company could cut its scrap rate to near zero and save hundreds of thousands of dollars."

Mead interrupted. "And you got no thanks."

"I got fired," the consultant snapped back. "I had upset the politics of the company. The agreement had been never to discuss our problems. As far as management was concerned, they didn't exist. So my report got everyone mad. They waited for my first slipup and then fired me."

"So this is your form of revenge?"

"No, Mr. Mead. Revenge benefits no one. I have sworn to show as many companies as possible that quality assurance through continuous improvement is the best competitive tool available. Life will take care of my political friends."

The two men didn't say anything after then. Mead reflected on what he had heard. Normally he would have been offended by some of the remarks. However, he had been down a road very similar to the man sitting across from him.

Mead just got up and started walking toward the door. He stopped and turned back toward the man in the booth. "Thanks."

The man just waved back. Mead buttoned the collar of his coat and pushed his way back into the face of the cold autumn breeze.

Recommended Readings

This book serves as an introduction and overview of the quality sciences. To explore a topic in depth or to find further information on quality assurance, the following books are recommended.

Quality Assurance

Crosby, Philip B. *Quality Without Tears — The Art of Hassle-Free Management.* New York: McGraw-Hill Book Co., 1984. This book presents many stories of companies learning how to improve productivity through better quality.

Goldratt, and Cox. *The Goal.* Croton-on-the-Hudson, NY: North River Publishing, 1987. This book presents a fictionalized look at the process of continuous improvement.

Harrington, H. James. *The Improvement Process: How America's Leading Companies Improve Quality.* New York: McGraw-Hill Book Co., 1987. This is a collection of quality-improvement stories from large corporations such as IBM, AT&T, and 3M.

Isikawa, Kaoru. *What Is Total Quality Control? The Japanese Way.* Englewood Cliffs, NJ: Prentice-Hall, 1985. A how-to book focused on customer satisfaction and the Japanese approach to quality.

The Management of Quality

Deming, W. Edwards. *Out of the Crisis.* Cambridge, MA: Massachusetts
 Institute of Technology, 1986. This book presents a criticism of American
 management techniques and what is needed to improve productivity.

Garvin, David A. *Managing Quality: The Strategic and Competitive Edge.*
 New York: Free Press, 1987. This is a more advanced reading of the
 quality management function. This book includes empirical studies of
 the effect of quality improvement.

Juran, J.M. *Managerial Breakthrough.* New York: McGraw-Hill Book Co.,
 1964. This book describes a continual process of breaking through to
 new levels of managerial performance.

Schrock, Edward M., and Henry L. Lefevre. *The Good and the Bad News
 About Quality.* Milwaukee: ASQC Quality Press, 1988. This is a good
 introduction to quality assurance and the management function.

Statistical Techniques in Quality Assurance

Besterfield, Dale H. *Quality Control.* 2nd ed. Englewood Cliffs, NJ: Prentice-
 Hall, 1986. This is a clearly written, easy-to-read guide to using statistics
 for sampling, SPC, and other quality functions.

Ishikawa, Kaoru. *Guide to Quality Control.* Tokyo: Asian Productivity
 Organization, 1976. This book is an excellent guide to using simple
 statistical techniques for problem solving. It includes a review of SPC.

Juran, J.M., and Frank M. Gryna. Jr. *Quality Planning and Analysis.* 2nd
 ed. New York: McGraw-Hill Book Co., 1980. This is an excellent book
 for learning the basics of analysis and quality assurance. Many of the
 questions for the certified quality engineer exam come from this text.

Continuous Improvement

Imai, Masaaki. *Kaizen: The Key to Japan's Competitive Success.* New York:
 McGraw-Hill Book Co., 1988. This is a well-written book on the process
 of never-ending improvement in the manufacturing environment.

Design of Experiments

Barker, Thomas B. *Quality by Experimental Design.* New York: Marcel Dekker, 1985. This is a fairly easy-to-read explanation of experimental methods that combines both classic and Taguchi methods.

Box, George E.P., William G. Hunter, and J. Stuart Hunter. *Statistics for Experimenters.* New York: John Wiley & Sons, 1978. This is a book for people experienced with statistics and familiar with experimentation. It is a hard read, but contains every vital topic related to experimentation. This book is considered a master work in the field.

Quality Costs

ASQC Quality Costs Committee. *Guide to Reducing Quality Costs.* Milwaukee: ASQC Quality Press, 1987. This guide contains techniques used to identify and reduce quality costs.

Reliability

O'Connor, Patrick D.T. *Practical Reliability Engineering.* 2nd ed. New York: John Wiley & Sons, 1985. This is an advanced book to read, but a good overview of the topic. You should read Juran and Gryna's *Quality Planning and Analysis* before tackling this book.

Auditing

Sayle, Allan J. *Management Audits: The Assessment of Quality Management Systems.* Hampshire, England: Allan J. Sayle Ltd., 1988. This is an excellent test for learning the details of auditing a quality system.

Index